Practical Proverbs

for

Your Problems

by

David Hocking

Promise Publishing Co.
Orange, CA 92667

Practical Proverbs for Your Problems
Copyright 1991 by Promise Publishing
Orange CA 92667

Edited by M.B. Steele

Printed in the United States of America

Library of Congress Cataloging-in-PublicationDate

Hocking, David
          Practical Proverbs for Your Problems

ISBN 0-939497-24-7

About the Author

David Hocking was raised in Southern California in a family where God was honored. His father was in the oil business during the exciting days of discovery and development of that industry in Southern California.

His formal education includes his graduation (magna cum laude) from Bob Jones University, and degrees from Grace Theological Seminary and Graduate School, the California Graduate School of Theology and an honorary degree from Biola University.

He and Carole, his wife, were married in 1962 and their home was blessed with three children, two of whom are now married and residing in Southern California.

David pastored Grace Brethren Church of Long Beach, California, for many years and has been pastor of Calvary Church in Santa Ana, California since 1982. He heads a large staff there which has an outreach to several thousand people.

His interest in radio dates back to 1974 when he was the speaker on "Sounds of Grace", the radio outreach of Grace Brethren Church. In 1982, he became the speaker on the Biola Hour where his acceptance as a radio speaker soared to a national level. He often represented Biola at rallies held in many cities all across the country.

In 1991, he stepped into his own radio mainistry called "Solid Rock Radio" headquartered in Orange, California, basing it on the hymn, "On Christ the Solid Rock I Stand". This is in keeping with his unswerving dedication to the Bible and to the gospel of Jesus Christ as it is taught in the Word.

Because

the Preacher

was wise,

he

set in order

many

proverbs.

Ecclesiastes 12:9

Table of Contents

CHAPTER 1

THE PROBLEM OF WISDOM

It has been a practice of my life to study the Book of Proverbs. For many years, our family read one chapter a day—thirty-one chapters, thirty-one days in the month. I analyzed Proverbs by subject for my own personal benefit.

I don't know what you think about this book, but I believe that the practical wisdom of Proverbs can change your life. If you would follow what this book says, your life would be radically changed for the Lord Jesus Christ. Your family would be different.

The book is filled with problems of life and discovering the solution. Many people believe the proverbs were written by Solomon as it tells us in Proverbs 1:1. In the last chapter, there is a reference to King Lemuel in verses 1 and 4. Some believe that is another man who wrote a portion of the book. Others believe that it is another name for Solomon, himself. Chapter one leaves no room for doubt—it says, *"Solomon the son of David, king of Israel."*

It's interesting to see how Jewish people look at the writings of Solomon. They see, for instance, the Song of Solomon, which was written when he was a young man writing about the love of his heart. They see the Book of Ecclesiastes, written when he was an old man, as he looked back at life concluding that all of life was "soap bubbles"—nothing in life giving him satisfaction. Ecclesiastes is a tremendous testimony to the futility of life lived without God. There is a lot of wisdom in Ecclesiastes. Jewish people teach that the Book of Proverbs was written when Solomon was middle-aged. I'm middle-aged and it's time for me to look at Proverbs!

The good point is that Proverbs is looked at from the standpoint of maturity-not of age, but of wisdom. It's an excellent study for all of us. It was my own father and mother that got me started studying and memorizing Proverbs, and I'm indebted to them for that. I urge you to study it and memorize the verses that stick out in your mind. You'll be amazed at the effect on your life and your thinking patterns.

Proverbs 1:1-7

The proverbs of Solomon the son of David, king of Israel: To know wisdom and instruction, To perceive the words of understanding, To receive the instruction of wisdom, Justice, judgment, and equity; To give prudence to the simple, To the young man knowledge and discretion-A wise man will hear and increase learning, And a man of understanding will attain wise counsel, To understand a proverb and an enigma, The words of the wise and their riddles. The fear of the Lord is the beginning of knowledge, But fools despise wisdom and instruction.

Right off the bat, we need to explain the translations of Proverbs. Let me warn you about trusting any one English translation because you can make enormous mistakes of application depending on which version you use. One example is in Proverbs 29:18. The Old King James version says, *"Where there is no vision, the people perish."* That statement appears in political an economical circles and in teaching seminars on leadership in the secular world. It carries a certain thought—we need visionary people so that their followers won't die on the vine. That has nothing to do with this proverb. The word *"vision"* is dealing with God's revelation, the Word of God, and the literal translation is, *"Where there is no revelation, the people cast off restraint; But happy is he who keeps the law."* We need the Word of God, otherwise there is no standard to live by and people turn society into anarchy, doing whatever they want to do-that's different from the King James' statement.

Proverbs is organized in such a way that we don't have rhyme in this poetic language, but contrast. We first have a statement made about the wise and then another one made about the fool. It is sometimes hard to discern what the connection is, but there is ALWAYS a connection. That's Jewish poetry. Sometimes there are two statements—one heavenly and one earthly—to emphasize one point. Sometimes there are two statements saying exactly the same thing, but stated differently to emphasize the real point. It's not always easy to discern what Proverbs is driving at. We'll try to be careful in handling it.

One thing is for sure, there is the way of the wise and the way of the fool. There is the way of the righteous and the way of the wicked. There is the way of the Lord and the way of the world. You will never find such stark contrast in your mind (how you think) and your emotions (how you feel) as you will when you study the Book of Proverbs. You will begin to see that it is black and white with God. You don't put one foot in the world and one foot with God and try to walk that line. It's "either/or" in Proverbs. It tells us that we need to have God's wisdom and we need to be very careful about being a fool.

WHAT IS WISDOM?

There are three statements in Proverbs which define wisdom for us. The first is that WISDOM IS THE ATTRIBUTE OF GOD BY WHICH HE CREATES, SUSTAINS, AND CONTROLS ALL THINGS.

The Lord by wisdom founded the earth; By understanding He established the heavens; By His knowledge the depths were broken up, And clouds drop down the dew (Prov. 3:19-20).

In the Book of Job, the point is strongly made that everything that happens in nature is under the direct control of God. He not only created everything, He sustains and controls it all. When we observe the laws of the universe, we see a reflection of the attributes and character of God, Himself. That is what we call wisdom.

The Lord possessed me [wisdom] *at the beginning of His way, Before His works of old. I have been established from everlasting, From the beginning, before there was ever an earth. When there were no depths I* [wisdom] *was brought forth, When there were no fountains abounding with water. Before the mountains were settled, Before the hills, I was brought forth; While as yet He had not made the earth or the fields, Or the primeval dust of the world. When He prepared the heavens, I was there, When He drew a circle on the face of the deep, When He established the clouds above, When He strengthened the fountains of the deep, When He assigned to the sea its limit, So that the waters would not transgress His command, When He marked out the foundations of the earth, Then I [wisdom] was beside Him, as a master craftsman; And I was daily His delight, Rejoicing always before Him, Rejoicing in His inhabited world, And my [wisdom's] delight was with the sons of men* (Prov. 8:22-31).

I, wisdom, dwell with prudence, And find out knowledge and discretion (Prov. 8:12).

The point that it is wisdom speaking here is very well established. The *"I ... me ... my"* of the text is wisdom. **Wisdom is the attribute of God by which He creates and sustains, and controls all things.**

That means that everything that happens in your life and mine is literally being controlled by wisdom. I have found that many things that happen in my life do not appear to be wise to me. Even when I suffer the consequences of my own foolish actions, I observe quickly that God was wise in letting me suffer. Did you see what I just said? GOD IS WISE EVEN WHEN HE LETS ME SUFFER. There are many things in life that are foolish, and some of us take years to learn a simple thing that a child could receive because of our own rebellion and sinful ways. We can easily be fools. Wisdom is God controlling our foolish actions so that we experience an adequate consequence that shows us that we need His wisdom. How fascinating is the wisdom of God!

WISDOM IS THE ASSET WHICH IS FAR MORE VALUABLE THAN ALL OTHER PURSUITS. Do we really regard it that way? If we did, we'd study it more. Let's see if wisdom really is that valuable. Maybe just a good education, a college degree or grad school is better. Solomon said that all the education of the world doesn't contribute to the wisdom of God. He learned that wisdom comes with grief, sorrow, and pain, misunderstanding and misapplication. Getting educated in what the world says is right or wrong is not necessarily being wise. I believe in getting all the education you can because it is better than being uneducated. You ought to know all that you can, but I've discovered that the more you know, the less you understand. The more "book learning" I have, the more my heart demands the wisdom of God.

Sometimes, what we know about things stands in the way of the wisdom of God! An old time evangelist made this classic statement, "I'd rather have a man say, 'I seen it,' if he

saw something than to say, 'I saw it,' if he didn't see anything!" That's wisdom! You may be educated beyond your
intelligence, not really understanding how to apply what you
know. Are you pursuing wisdom?

*Happy is the man who finds wisdom, And the man
who gains understanding; For her proceeds are better than the profits of silver, And her gain than fine
gold. She is more precious than rubies, And all the
things you may desire cannot compare with her.
Length of days is in her right hand, In her left hand
riches and honor. Her ways are ways of pleasant-
ness, And all her paths are peace. She is a tree of life
to those who take hold of her, And happy are all who
retain her* (Prov. 3:13-18).

*"Get wisdom! Get understanding! Do not forget,
nor turn away from the words of my mouth. Do not
forsake her, and she will preserve you; Love her, and
she will keep you. Wisdom is the principal thing;
Therefore get wisdom. And in all your getting, get understanding. Exalt her, and she will promote you; She
will bring you honor, when you embrace her. She will
place on your head an ornament of grace; A crown of
glory she will deliver to you"* (Prov. 4:5-9).

*Receive my instruction, and not silver, And
knowledge rather than choice gold; For wisdom is better than rubies, And all the things one may desire cannot be compared with her* (Prov. 8:10-11).

My fruit [says wisdom] *is better than gold, yes,
than fine gold, And my revenue than choice silver*
(Prov. 8:19).

*How much better it is to get wisdom than gold!
And to get understanding is to be chosen rather than
silver* (Prov. 16:16).

Later, when we study money, we will discover that
Proverbs is an incredible source of wisdom about money. If
you pursue money, you are going to be troubled by it. If you
pursue wisdom, you will understand how money works,
what it's for and what you should do about it. If you have a
"get rich quick" scheme, you are going to fall at some point.

Would you rather have wisdom or money? We say we want wisdom, then we go out and do everything we can to get money rather than wisdom. Think about it!

Wisdom is also THE APPLICATION OF GOD'S HOLINESS TO ALL WE SAY AND DO. That is a summary of the Book of Proverbs.

> Do not be wise in your own eyes; Fear the Lord and depart from evil (Prov. 3:7).

> I have taught you in the way of wisdom; I have led you in right paths. When you walk, your steps will not be hindered, And when you run, you will not stumble. Take firm hold of instruction, do not let go; Keep her, for she is your life. Do not enter the path of the wicked, And do not walk in the way of evil. Avoid it, do not travel on it; Turn away from it and pass on. For they do not sleep unless they have done evil; And their sleep is taken away unless they make someone fall. For they eat the bread of wickedness, And drink the wine of violence. But the path of the just is like the shining sun, That shines ever brighter unto the perfect day. The way of the wicked is like darkness; They do not know what makes them stumble (Prov. 4:11-19).

> For the commandment is a lamp, And the law is light; Reproofs of instruction are the way of life To keep you from the evil woman, From the flattering tongue of a seductress (Prov. 6:23-24).

> My son, keep my words, And treasure my commands within you. Keep my commands and live, And my law as the apple of your eye. Bind them on your fingers; Write them on the tablet of your heart. Say to wisdom, "You are my sister," And call understanding your nearest kin That they may keep you from the immoral woman, From the seductress who flatters with her words (Prov. 7:1-5).

Later on, we'll discuss seduction and show how God's wisdom gives us wisdom in this area, too.

> "The fear of the Lord is to hate evil; Pride and arrogance and the evil way And the perverse mouth I hate [says wisdom]" (Prov. 8:13).

A wise man fears and departs from evil, But a fool rages and is self-confident (Prov. 14:16).

There are many examples; I am only giving you a few of them. It is very clear in Proverbs that *"the way of the wise"* is the opposite of *"the way of evil"*. What is wisdom? It is the application of God's holiness to all we say and do. *"Fear the Lord and depart from evil"* is the simple, clear message.

WHERE DO WE GET IT?

For the Lord gives wisdom; From His mouth come knowledge and understanding (Prov. 2:6).

According to the Bible, wisdom comes from the Lord. It was there when the foundations of the earth were made. Wisdom was there, working and functioning before God created anything. Wisdom was there. The Bible says so. Wisdom is an attribute of God. *"From His mouth come knowledge and understanding."*

All Scripture is given by inspiration of God, and is profitable for doctrine, for reproof, for correction, for instruction in righteousness, that the man of God may be complete, thoroughly equipped for every good work (II Tim. 3:16-17).

The statement, *"all Scripture is given by inspiration of God,"* has only three words in Greek. It says, *"All," "Scripture"* [writing], and then a compound word, *"God breathed."* According to Proverbs, it is the *"mouth of the Lord that gives knowledge."* By the breath of God's mouth, we learn wisdom. All Scripture is the result of the creative breath of God. **There is no way that anybody gets wisdom apart from the Word of God we call the Bible.**

Look at this gracious remark by Peter about Paul. In it, he counts Paul as being wise with wisdom from God.

Account that the longsuffering of our Lord is salvation—as also our beloved brother Paul, according to the wisdom given to him, has written to you, as also in all his epistles, speaking in them of these things, in which are some things hard to understand, which those who are untaught and unstable twist to their own destruction, as they do also the rest of the Scriptures (II Peter 3:15-16).

He refers to Paul's writings as *"the wisdom that was given to him."* Wisdom comes from God and is the result of the breath of God. *"All Scripture is God-breathed."*

Wisdom comes from God and it is wisdom that is hard to understand. Because of this, there is an element we need to understand the wisdom that is in the Word of God.

If any [Since all] *of you lack(s) wisdom, let him ask of God, who gives to all liberally* [not just to a select few] *and without reproach, and it will be given to him. But let him ask in faith, with no doubting, for he who doubts* [comparing it with what you know from the world] *is like a wave of the sea driven and tossed by the wind. For let not that man suppose that he will receive anything from the Lord; he is a double-minded* [double-souled] *man, unstable in all his ways* (James 1:5-8).

God expects us to come to His Word, read it, and say, **"THAT is wisdom!"** People take a verse which is clear, and they say, "I'm not sure that applies to me." Christians mess up their lives because they don't follow the wisdom of God's Word. God is the only One who gives wisdom, and if we want His wisdom, we must come in faith. If you doubt the Book—think someone else has the answer, you're already in trouble! You'll never have wisdom or understand what God is saying. *"Ask in faith...with no doubting."*

I find the direct statements of God's Word hit me and I face a decision. Will I do what it says, or will I impose my view on it? We don't always understand the things in the Bible, some people say. I think that's a cop-out. Children accept it and it doesn't seem tough to them! It is tough to those of us who are adults.

It is not what we DON'T understand about the Bible that bothers us; it is what we DO understand! There's so much in this book that is absolutely clear! One of the reasons the devil, in his subtle deceits, keeps us from studying the Bible regularly is because it DOES confront us. In our lethargy, we let him divert us away from God's Word. It DOES tell us what's wrong and what's right! It's very clear. If we want wisdom, we have to get it from God.

WHY DON'T WE HAVE IT?

We are wise in our own eyes and it blocks us from seeking wisdom from God.

Do not be wise in your own eyes; Fear the Lord and depart from evil. It will be health to your flesh, And strength to your bones (Prov. 3:7).

When we think we're wise, we don't have any principle of God's Word to govern our actions, and we shut off the flow of God's wisdom. People don't have wisdom because they already think they know what's right and what's wrong. We make decisions based on our feelings. Be careful! Are you wise in your own eyes or is it truly the principles of God's Word that we are following.

Wisdom calls aloud outside [it's obviously for everyone to hear]; *She raises her voice in the open squares. She cries out in the chief concourses, At the openings of the gates in the city She speaks her words* [God's not trying to make it difficult]; *"How long, you simple ones* [naive, dumb, stupid, foolish], *will you love simplicity? For scorners delight in their scorning, And fools hate knowledge. Turn at my reproof; Surely I will pour out my spirit on you; I will make my words known to you. Because I have called and you refused, I have stretched out my hand and no one regarded, Because you disdained all my counsel, And would have none of my reproof, I also will laugh at your calamity; I will mock when your terror comes, When your terror comes like a storm, And your destruction comes like a whirlwind, When distress and anguish come upon you. Then they will call on me, but I will not answer; They will seek me diligently, but they will not find me. Because they hated knowledge And did not choose the fear of the Lord, They would have none of my counsel And despised all my reproof, Therefore they shall eat the fruit of their own way, And be filled to the full with their own fancies. For the turning away of the simple will slay them, And the complacency of fools will destroy them; But whoever listens to me will dwell safely, And will be secure, without fear of evil"* (Prov. 1:20-33).

Amen or no amen? Which is it? You see, **a lot of us don't have wisdom because we refuse it.** It shouts aloud at us many times through many circumstances—sometimes through a child. A child can say the truth and we know it; wisdom is shouting at us! A terrible circumstance in life can shout out the wisdom of God, but when we refuse and do not listen, we pay the price for it. There is a consequence and when we get in a jam and cry to wisdom, wisdom says, "No". Until we repent and get right with the Lord and deal with our reasons for spurning the wisdom of God, we never get straightened out.

One person I know of was in debt because they did not follow the wisdom of God. They violated everything in the Bible about money. The young man and his wife wanted to go into ministry. We began talking about it and when I read some of the verses in Proverbs, the antagonism was obvious. I offered to stop, but there was nothing to show them but what the Bible says. He said that everything I read to him was what they had done wrong. That was true! We kept going and I felt bad about pointing out that every decision they had made was wrong and they were in a terrible mess. At the end, he said, "Is there any way that God can show us right now what to do?" I told them to back up and correct each wrong step they had taken. "Can't we just go on from here?" he pled. He suggested bankruptcy as a way out and he didn't want to hear the verses I had to offer about that! He struggled with that for months, but he finally repented, went back, and straightened it out. Now, he is in the ministry and he knows what to say to people from the pulpit.

We have to deal with issues, and a lot of us don't. Then, we pay the price for it. That's what Proverbs is about! Wisdom cries out to us and says, "Stop! I can help you if you will listen to me! Please don't run away from my message. Don't listen to other people. Come and listen to me!" Wisdom is crying for your attention; calling out to you. Is anyone listening? That is the heart of Proverbs. It is a book for people who are hungry. It is for people who say, "I want to live my life the way God wants me to live!" If you're not interested, you'll be bored with this book. If you've got that hunger, you're going to love Proverbs.

There are only two ways in Proverbs—the way of the wise and the way of the foolish.

HOW DO WE KNOW WHEN WE HAVE IT?

There is a sense in which we don't really need to know
whether or not we have wisdom. If we do what God says, it
is wise whether we know it was wise or not. It is kind of the
Lord to tell us. Some of us need that encouragement.

**We are always wise when we sense deeply our account-
ability to God for everything we think, say and do.**

> *The fear of the Lord is the beginning of knowledge,*
> *But fools despise wisdom and instruction* (Prov. 1:7).

When we *"fear the Lord,"* we sense our accountability to
Him. That's the beginning.

> *The fear of the Lord is the beginning of wisdom,*
> *And the knowledge of the Holy One is understanding*
> (Prov. 9:10).

To know God is everything when you're talking wisdom.

> *The fear of the Lord is the instruction of wisdom,*
> *And before honor* [blessing] *is humility* (Prov. 15:33).

When we humbly bow before God and ask Him what He
wants us to do, we are wise. Whatever we think, say, or do,
we are accountable to God. That is *"the beginning of wisdom"*. If you don't start there, you get into a mess quickly.

**We know we are wise when we do not hate someone
who rebukes us.** Are you paying attention? Like you, I'm
not real thrilled about criticism. None of us ask God to send
people into our lives to attack and criticize us. Some people
think they have "the gift of criticism" and offer to exercise it
on us every day! There's a lot of nonsense in the body of
Christ. It's easy to get ticked when someone tells us something we don't want to hear.

> *Do not reprove a scoffer, lest he hate you; Rebuke*
> *a wise man, and he will love you* (Prov. 9:8).

> *The ear that hears the reproof of life Will abide*
> *among the wise* (Prov. 15:31).

There's a lot we could say about this but we'll only use
these two verses. Do we listen to criticism; do we listen to

reproof; do we hear rebuke? Many well-meaning people advise me not to say critical things. I continue to do so. Often people get really angry with me, but I believe the Lord has a purpose in that. It is His will that we listen to them. If, for nothing else, wisdom can teach us what not to be by the criticisms. Sometimes a rebuke can train you in how to answer wisely for the Lord. Sometimes you learn what not to do, as well as what to do. Wisdom listens!

My mother used to tell me (when I disagreed with something she said), "I'll share your opinion with your father when he comes home." It's amazing how much more responsive I became immediately. It's wisdom to listen to rebuke. Even if you disagree with it, listen to it! Understand that God is working in your life like a grain of sand works in an oyster. The friction develops the pearl. Sandpaper causes friction, but it also rounds off the rough edges.

If you reprove a scoffer, he will hate you. If you reprove a wise man, he will love you. He may not always agree with you, but he will accept your criticism.

You know you are wise when you get wiser by receiving more information. This is an interesting point in Proverbs. It points out that some people get worse when they learn more. They get all bent out of shape and don't want to hear any more facts because they already have their mind made up. A wise person always wants more information. When it comes and shows a wise person that he's wrong, he's grateful to have the facts! A fool sticks by what he has said even when there is evidence to show him wrong.

I don't always agree with myself! People accuse me of changing my view and ask me how I can do it. I can change my views because I now know that I was wrong before. It's good for people to believe they're right, even when they're wrong. Still, when they get more information and find that they were wrong, they ought to be able to change their view. A wise person will learn and grow. That is wisdom.

> Give instruction to a wise man, and he will be still wiser; Teach a just man, and he will increase in learning (Prov. 9:9).

> Listen to counsel and receive instruction, That you may be wise in your latter days (Prov. 19:20).

Could it be that some older people are not wise because they are not listening to "counsel"? Age does not produce

God's wisdom although the world has been telling us that.
It is not true! There are plenty of old people who are acting
"the fool" because they have not followed the way of the Lord.
I'm old enough to say that now; I couldn't say it so strongly
when I was younger. A lot of people have forsaken the way
of the Lord in old age and they have lost His wisdom. The
older we get, the wiser we should be! We should keep learning and never feel we have "arrived". God makes old people
beautiful when He fills them with His wonderful wisdom.

**We are wise when we plan ahead and prepare for dif-
ficult times**.

> *He who gathers in summer is a wise son, But he
> who sleeps in harvest is a son who causes shame*
> (Prov. 10:5).

There's a time to get organized and prepare for the future.
According to the Bible, when we prepare for expenses that
are coming and anticipate future hurdles, we are wise.
Prepare for difficult times when you are going to need more
money or time, or whatever crisis you can see ahead.
Prepare for it.

We are wise when we are submissive to authority.
Wise people are always submissive to authority.

> *The wise in heart will receive commands, But a
> prating fool will fall* (Prov. 10:8).

There is usually a difficult time when we are teenagers,
trying to find out who we are and to assert our independence.
That is the time to listen to Proverbs! If you are wise, you
will receive commands and submit to authority.

I have an axiom that I believe: The amount of
AUTHORITY a person exercises in his life is directly related
to the amount of SUBMISSION he has exercised in his life.
If you want to have authority and influence in your life, then
learn to be submissive. The more we are submissive to other
people and to authority, the greater will be our influence and
authority on others. That goes for parents, as well as for
kids. Sometimes we parents need to ask ourselves if we are
being submissive to authority. Our kids don't see our submission and, therefore, they don't feel the need to submit.

Everyone of us is accountable to God, no matter what
anybody else does—our parents, society, or anyone else
around us. If we are wise, we will submit to authority.

We are wise when we continue to learn.

Wise people store up knowlege, But the mouth of the foolish is near destruction (Prov. 10:14).

Are you really trying to learn? There is an elderly lady who blesses me because she tries to read an entire book every single week. She says it's hard for her, but she has a strong desire to learn. "There are so many wonderful things to learn about," she says. She's a wise person.

Have you stopped learning? Have you stopped growing? When we continue to learn, we are wise.

We are wise when we are controlled in the way we talk. This can be touchy! Are you wise?

In the multitude of words sin is not lacking, But he who restrains his lips is wise (Prov. 10:19).

The chance of saying something wrong increase with the volume of words—the verbage. We are wise when we restrain our words. That one is really convicting to a "motor mouth" like me!

He who is devoid of wisdom despises his neighbor, But a man of understanding holds his peace (Prov. 11:12).

You don't go to your neighbor and tell him why you don't like him. That's the kind of thing a man devoid of wisdom does. That is not wisdom. The wise man knows how to control what he says. He looks for the opportunity to encourage his neighbor and to deal with the problem without tearing him down.

Even a fool is counted wise when he holds his peace; When he shuts his lips, he is considered perceptive (Prov. 17:28).

These are just a few sample verses. There is quite a bit in Proverbs on this one point. Any fool can wax eloquent about something—just talk. I'm good at it; are you? God says that is not the way of wisdom. We need to be controlled and to think about what we're saying. We need to be sure that God's Word is controlling what we're saying.

How do we know when we have wisdom? According to the Bible **when we win souls, we are wise.**

> *The fruit of the righteous is a tree of life, And he who wins souls is wise* (Prov. 11:30).

This is a very misunderstood verse. Let's go back to verse 29.

> *He who troubles his own house will inherit the wind, And the fool will be servant to the wise of heart. The fruit of the righteous is a tree of life, And he who wins* [seizes] *souls is wise* (Prov. 11:29-30).

"Wins" means to take or to seize as spoil. Now a lot of people apply this to leading folks to Christ. That certainly is *"winning souls"* and that certainly is wise. However, I'm not sure that's the point of the proverb. The point here is that a person who doesn't deal with the inner spirit of people is making a big mistake. Righteous people who bless a lot of others, literally deal with the soul and with the heart of people. That's wisdom!

Have you ever been talking to someone and get the impression that what they're saying is not what they're really feeling? Perhaps they're saying something other than what they really think in their hearts. Wisdom goes after the HEART. Sometimes that's uncomfortable for the person you're talking to. It may sometimes be wisdom to back off, if you see embarrassment.

It's wisdom to deal with the heart. It's wisdom not simply to deal with the surface, not simply to come up to somebody and say, "How's it going?" They always say, "I'm fine" and they usually don't mean that. You tell them goodbye without ever getting an answer to your question. That's not wisdom.

If you knew something about that person, wisdom would say, "You look like you're hurting. Can I help in some way?" A simple question as to what is wrong and whether or not we can be of help is wisdom. Maybe it is something you said, but wisdom is not satisfied with the superficial, the veneer. Wisdom doesn't play games and just try to get by. It doesn't bury it's head in the sand and hope the problem goes away. Wisdom is after the hearts of people.

Ask yourself, do you go after people? Do you really want to have a "heart to heart" relationship with somebody? Or do you just want to play games?

People of other cultures say that Americans are one of the most gregarious societies in the world—but very superficial. We don't care about people's hearts. We just want to get by. We're outgoing and friendly, but we never get beneath the surface. We move on from one person to another without delving into anyone's heart.

Wisdom goes after the heart. Wisdom takes souls. Wisdom is not simply interested in the outside; it wants to know what's on the heart.

We are wise when we are prudent, discerning. Prudence is a very old word, and we don't use it much these days, but it is an excellent word.

> *The wise in heart will be called prudent* [discerning], *And sweetness of the lips increases learning* (Prov. 16:21).

The very way you talk shows your wisdom. We often say, "It's not so much what you say, as how you say it." That's what we're discussing. Someone can tell you something you know you need to hear, but if their spirit is wrong, it is very hard to receive it. The wise person understands that the way they say something is very important to the ability of the hearer to accept it.

Prudence is also translated as *"understanding"* in the Book of Proverbs and we find it all the way through. It's almost identical to wisdom! These are all the same Hebrew word. Knowledge comes easy to someone who's discerning.

> *Wisdom is found on the lips of him who has understanding* [discernment, prudence], *But a rod is for the back of him who is devoid of understanding* (Prov. 10:13).

When you speak, you care about how it is being received and applied—you care about how you're saying things.

> *A scoffer seeks wisdom and does not find it, But knowledge is easy to him who understands* [is discerning, has prudence] (Prov. 14:6).

> *Wisdom rests quietly in the heart of him who has understanding* [prudence, discernment], *But what is in the heart of fools is made known* (Prov. 14:33).

Wisdom doesn't need to parade itself because it is filled with understanding. It doesn't need to brag. Proverbs often tells us to let another man praise us and not our own words. Wisdom is very discerning about even when it shares itself. You don't share wisdom so that people will think you are wise. If that's what you think, you are already unwise. Wisdom doesn't want to make someone feel that you are wiser than they are. If you are a wise person, you know how to say things so that the listener knows you are aware that you need what you are saying as surely they do.

When you talk down to people, you're not wise—you're foolish! You're making a mistake if you try to make them feel that you're smarter than they are. It's not false humility we're talking about; it's discernment—caring about the people we talk to. We identify with them and try, by what we say, to get them to respond in a positive manner. That's wisdom!

The Bible is filled with wisdom! It is an attribute of God; an asset valuable above all else. We can only get it from the Lord.

CHAPTER 2

THE PROBLEM OF FOOLS

The New Testament quotes Proverbs over twenty times. Solomon wrote 3,000 proverbs. The style of poetry most frequently used is that of contrast; that is, statements that are antithetic to each other, but they have a central point. He compares things that are alike as well as comparing things that are not alike. In the Proverbs, there are many statements that illustrate either the way of the Lord or the way of the devil, the way of righteousness or the way of sin. Proverbs is a book about morality.

The Problem of Wisdom and The Problem Of Fools—these two serve as the foundation for understanding Proverbs. Solomon used eight words in Hebrew for "wisdom" and three words for "fool". If you want to know what wisdom is, it is learning how to walk with God and stay away from sin. That's what Proverbs is all about.

Interestingly, Proverbs is a book primarily for young people. It has escaped the attention of people as they read through Proverbs that its messages are addressed to young people. If there ever was a book that any student ought to study and master, with all of his or her heart, it's the book of Proverbs. It's what God has to say to people who have their whole lives in front of them.

There is also a sense in which there is a degree of sadness when you read Proverbs. If you have lived long and messed up your life by not walking with the Lord, Proverbs tells you why that has happened. There's also a sense of hope from a place of despair; there is a sense of faith when all seems like doubt, for in Proverbs, it gives us the clear impression that if we will only change, life will be different.

Proverbs never insinuates that just because you're old it's all over. Proverbs appeals to people of all ages. It's almost like God's protective covering to all who are young that says, "Here is the way of the Lord. If you want your life to be blessed mightily of God, then follow this way."

Luke 12 is a parable about a fool that will prepare us for the problem of fools in the Book of Proverbs.

> He [Jesus] *said to them, "Take heed and beware*
> *of covetousness, for one's life does not consist in the*
> *abundance of the things he possesses." Then he*
> *spoke a parable to them saying: "The ground of a cer-*
> *tain rich man yielded plentifully. And he thought*
> *within himself, saying 'What shall I do, since I have*
> *no room to store my crops?' So he said, 'I will do this:*
> *I will pull down my barns, and build greater, and there*
> *I will store all my crops and my goods. And I will say*
> *to my soul, "Soul, you have many goods laid up for*
> *many years; take your ease; eat, drink, and be*
> *merry."' But God said to him, 'You fool! This night*
> *your soul will be required of you; then whose will those*
> *things be which you have provided?' So is he who lays*
> *up treasure for himself, and is not rich toward God."*

According to Jesus, a fool is one who lays up treasure for himself. The fool is one who wants all the "goodies" of life to somehow sustain the dissatisfaction of his own heart. The fool is one who cannot see the purpose of God—it does not depend on what He does, nor on who He is. The fool is one who is not rich toward God.

THE PRACTICES WHICH IDENTIFY A FOOL

He Gets Into Arguments Easily

> *A fool's lips enter into contention, And his mouth*
> *calls for blows* (Prov. 18:6).

One of the first ways to identify a foolish person is how quickly they get into arguments. They're not trying to stop it; they're trying to start it.

> *It is honorable for man to stop striving, Since any*
> *fool can start a quarrel* (Prov. 20:3).

The next time you say, "We just love to argue," you had better think about it. The Bible says that's fool's talk.

He Treats Sin Lightly

> *To do evil is like sport to a fool, But a man of un-*
> *derstanding has wisdom* (Prov. 10:23).

> *A desire accomplished is sweet to the soul, But it
> is an abomination to fools to depart from evil* (Prov.
> 13:19).

They don't want to get away from evil. A foolish man
wants to be involved with it.

> *Fools mock at sin, But among the upright there is
> favor* (Prov. 14:9).

It is characteristic of a foolish person to mock at issues
of sin—to treat them lightly. In Ecclesiastes 5:1 (also written by Solomon), we read this statement,

> *Walk prudently when you go to the house of God;
> and draw near to hear rather than to give the sacrifice
> of fools, for they do not know that they do evil.*

Fools treat sin lightly, get involved in sin, and mock it and
don't think the issue is as severe as what the Bible teaches.
That's characteristic of a fool.

A Fool Responds to Seduction Easily and Quickly

> *With her enticing speech she caused him,* [this
> young man who's being counselled against this], *to
> yield, With her flattering lips she seduced him. Im-
> mediately he went after her, as an ox goes to the
> slaughter, Or as a fool to the correction of the stocks,
> Till an arrow struck his liver. As a bird hastens to the
> snare, He did not know it would take his life* (Prov.
> 7:21-23).

He Squanders Money

> *There is desirable treasure, And oil in the dwell-
> ing of the wise, But a foolish man squanders it* (Prov.
> 21:20).

That's a good admonition to us. It's not wrong to have
money. It depends on your attitude and how you use it. A
fool doesn't know the meaning of saving it. He can't see any
reason for keeping it—he squanders it. God calls him a fool.

He Develops Wrong Values

This comes from our passage in Luke 12. The product of
the farmer's harvest was really big that year, so he thought

it over and said, "What should I do? I'll just build bigger barns." The Bible says, *"You fool! This night your soul will be required of you; then whose will those things be?"*

A man who trusts in what he owns, who sees his self-worth and value in what he possesses, who believes that he's really something because he's acquired things in life, has a wrong value system. God calls him a fool. He lays up treasure for himself and not toward God.

He Harbors Anger and Resentment

> *A fool's wrath is known at once, But a prudent man covers shame* (Prov. 12:16).

> *He who is slow to wrath* [patient and long-suffering], *has great understanding, But he who is impulsive exalts folly* (Prov. 14:29).

> *A stone is heavy and sand is weighty, But a fool's wrath is heavier than both of them* (Prov. 27:3).

A fool is known for anger and resentment, and he often explodes at the most unexpected times.

> *Do not hasten in your spirit to be angry, For anger rests in the bosom of fools* (Eccl. 7:9).

There is also a passage in Ephesians, chapter 4 that tells us to *"be angry, and sin not."* There is a righteous anger which is always directed at what is wrong and sinful. Unrighteous anger is toward people, and for that, God says, *"Be slow to wrath."*

A fool is not slow to get angry. A fool is filled with anger and resentment. He's never solved the problem. He's bitterly angry and he's resentful at many things in life.

He Practices Deceit and Lying

> *The wisdom of the prudent is to understand his way, But the folly of fools is deceit* (Prov. 14:8).

There is no real effort here to bring clear understanding and accurate truth. There is an effort here to deceive.

> *The lips of the wise disperse knowledge, But the heart of the fool does not do so* (Prov. 15:7).

He doesn't want people to know the truth.

Excellent speech is not becoming to a fool, Much less lying lips to a prince (Prov. 17:7).

Fools are not known for speaking well and accurately; fools are known for lying and deceit. Now these are simply the practices of fools.

THE PRIDE WHICH CHARACTERIZES A FOOL

In the mouth of a fool is a rod of pride, But the lips of the wise will preserve them (Prov. 14:3).

The way of a fool is right in his own eyes, But he who heeds counsel is wise (Prov. 12:15).

He Believes He Is Right

One of my friends says, "I know I am right; otherwise, I'd change my view." There's something about that I like. I like people to say what they believe, and there IS a little humility in it, I believe, in spite of what sounds like arrogance. I believe there's humility here—an awareness that he could be wrong.

The fool always is right. The fool is right in matters that are not clear. Some things are clear. We know what is right on the basis, for instance, of what God says is right. Some issues in life are not like that. It's debatable; it could be discussed for hours and no one could come to a conclusion. The fool always knows he is right.

He Does Not Respond to Reproof

Reproof is more effective for a wise man Than a hundred blows on a fool (Prov. 17:10).

You just can't change him—no matter what! Have you ever said that you can't change anybody? That's not true. Many people are changed, even late in life. This reminds me of a letter I received. This lady had divorced her husband and wanted nothing to do with him. About four months before she became a Christian, her husband told her that he was still waiting for her, and was remaining celibate. Imagine that! He wouldn't involve himself with anybody else. He said, "I don 't care what you've done or how many men you've had, I'm still here and I'll forgive you. I want you back." She wanted nothing to do with him. She heard my message about a wife being submissive to her husband. God used that to speak to her heart, and in a few weeks, she came to receive Christ as Savior and Lord. She wrote and wanted me to know that she's remarrying her husband this September. She said that two of his friends who were also divorced heard what had happened, and she and her husband had the privilege of leading both of them to Christ. They also are going to get remarried to their former partners. That's what I call results from the Word of God!

I'll tell you how you can spot a fool: it doesn't matter how many times you confront him with the Word of God, or how many times you tell him that the Bible is directly against what he is doing, they do not respond to reproof or correction at all.

Do not speak in the hearing of a fool, For he will despise the wisdom of your words (Prov. 23:9).

Did you know that people who are wise have to even be careful about how they talk to a fool? He won't listen, so we have to back off from confronting that foolish person. We have to remember that God is the only One who can change the heart.

Though you grind a fool in a mortar with a pestle along with crushed grain, Yet his foolishness will not depart from him (Prov. 27:22).

I think some parents would like to shake their kids into wisdom; grab them and somehow, knock the foolishness out of them and get the wisdom of God into them. The Bible says, however, that even if you've ground him up with mortar, you are not going to get it out of him unless it comes out from the Lord. That's frustrating to a lot of parents.

Our only weapon now is prayer. Can you believe it's come to that?

He Trusts His Own Heart

The world has given a fool the message that he should trust his own feelings and trust his own heart. That's nonsense!

He who is of a proud heart stirs up strife, But he who trusts in the Lord will be prospered. He who trusts in his own heart is a fool, But whoever walks wisely will be delivered (Prov. 28:25-26).

The wise person trusts in the Lord. The fool trusts in his own heart. He thinks he knows! He thinks he can understand. He thinks his feelings are true. He thinks whatever he believes in his heart is correct, and that demonstrates how foolish he really is.

He Resists the Lord

A fool, in his pride, also resists the Lord.

A wise man fears and departs from evil, But a fool rages and is self-confident (Prov. 14:16).

The foolishness of a man twists his way, And his heart frets against the Lord (Prov. 19:3).

A fool wants nothing to do with the Lord. He resists the Lord on every hand in his life, and by it, he's demonstrating that he is a fool. He's self-confident, and he rages; he does not depart from evil; he does not fear the Lord. He doesn't sense his accountability to God; he thinks he knows what he's doing. He resists the Lord constantly.

He Hates Knowledge

"How long, simple ones [fools], will you love simplicity [folly]? For scorners delight in their scorning, And fools hate knowledge" (Prov. 1:22).

Fools don't want to know the truth. Fools don't want to hear the wisdom of God. Their pride keeps them from it. They believe they're right; they don't respond to correction; they trust in their own heart; they resist the Lord on every hand; and they hate truth. They hate the knowledge.

THE PATTERN OF SPEECH THAT IS OFTEN SEEN IN A FOOL

He Spreads Slander

You can tell a fool by the way he talks, and the Bible says he spreads slander. He delights in it.

*Whoever hides hatred has lying lips, And whoever
spreads slander is a fool* (Prov. 10:18).

He loves it. He thrives on it. Unfortunately, we see too
much of it in the Christian world. A number of years ago,
Tim LaHaye came to speak at our church. We were talking
with one man who said, "I want you to see this." Somebody
had written him a letter saying, "Isn't it tragic that Tim and
Beverly LaHaye got a divorce after all these years?" Tim
looked at it and said, "I didn't get divorced. I'm still married."

It was unbelievable, so we called the writer. You never
heard a more shocked person in all your life. "Hi, this is Tim
LaHaye. Just wanted you to know I'm still with Beverly. Why
did you write that letter?"

The gossip in the Christian world is terrifying. We need
to watch it! We're revealing what fools we really are. Fools
spread slander. The Bible says love protects and covers.
"Love covers a multitude of sins."

He Talks Too Much

*The words of a wise man's mouth are gracious,
But the lips of a fool shall swallow him up. The words
of his mouth begin with foolishness, And the end of
his talk is raving madness. A fool also multiplies
words. No man knows what is to be; Who can tell him
what will be after him?* (Eccl. 10:12-14).

When a fool talks, he doesn't even know what he's going
to say. And when he's done, no one's quite sure what he said.
That's a fool.

*For a dream comes through much activity, And a
fool's voice is known by his many words* (Eccl. 5:3).

The other day, I was talking to a lady who said that Jesus
Christ had come to visit her in the night. He sat on her bed
and had quite a conversation with her. I said, "No he didn't."
She said, "Yes, he did." I said, "No he didn't."

Finally, she said, "Well, I dreamed it! I know he was
there." I said, "You can dream! Maybe you ate too much
chili." She was offended, and said, "No, it was just as real
as though it happened." I said, "What was that again?" She
reverted to saying it really had happened but I asked if she

knew why it had happened. She didn't. I sympathized, "The Bible says you've been working too hard." Here it is! *"A dream comes through much activity."*

Don't trust what you dream about. Who knows why you're dreaming that? Have you ever noticed that things just don't make any sense in most dreams?

"A fool's voice is known by his many words." He talks too much. This is the same thing that we just read in Ecclesiastes 10:14, *"A fool also multiplies words. No man knows what is to be; Who can tell him what will be after him."*

He Relies on His Own Feelings

> *Wisdom rests quietly in the heart of him who has understanding, But what is in the heart of fools is made known* (Prov. 14:33).

It isn't really important what you think about something. What's important is whether it's true or not. A lot of us have never realized that. We need to be sensitive and caring, but I don't think it leads anywhere. It's not going anywhere. The Bible says this is a foolish way of dealing with things. What's in the heart of a fool is made known!

> *A fool has no delight in understanding, But in expressing his own heart* (Prov. 14:33).

People are tricky. For instance, if they know that you like to answer questions, they come up and ask you a question, when, in reality, they don't care what you're going to say. They have something else they want to communicate.

When you want to communicate, and you really know it's important to you, I've seen a lot of people look as if they're saying, "Why do you think that's important?"

Often we don't understand the other person, nor do we understand what God wants us to say or do. We're just trusting ourselves, and we get into big trouble.

You may believe in just "letting it all out". Well, the rest of us don't! You may think you just need to get it off your chest.

> *A fool vents all his feelings, But a wise man holds them back* (Prov. 29:11).

I've noticed that counsellors ask "feelings" questions, like, "How do you really feel about something?" Well, you can be thankful that I don't tell you how I feel about a lot of things. I'd be a wild man on this! I feel the funniest things sometimes.

I was at a Bible conference many years ago. There were numerous speakers, and a couple of my good friends who are also on the radio were there. One of them was going on and on and I didn't know what in the world he was talking about. I can pretty well follow things, but I listened to him. It wasn't my time to speak, but I heard him. Afterwards we had lunch. We were all sitting around the table and he said, "What do you think about what I said?" I said, "I'd rather not say." He said, "C'mon, David! Tell me how you feel!"

I said, "I feel you were really putting us on and you didn't know what you were talking about." He said, "I can't believe you said that!" Another guy at the table said, "Well that's exactly what I felt!" Finally, all of us just burst out laughing because it was true.

We need to be slow to express our feelings about things because our feelings may not be accurate. They may not be helpful. They may not be kind. They may not be building up anybody. You're not being deceitful because you hold it in. Our world has given us this psychological junk about how somehow we're really going to be honest and open with one another. Please don't, okay? I don't want to hear it. You may want to tell me how you feel. I don't want to know!

I'm don't mean to be insensitive. I read some of these things that are said about fools, just like you do, and if I point at others, the old thumb points right back at me and I feel it! There are aspects of all of these things that trouble all of us, but I'll tell you that this one is very common.

In review, to tell the pattern of speech in a fool, he spreads slander; it's a habit. He loves to tear people down. He's always critical of other people, and he's always talking too much with no content. The Indians said of a fool's talk: "High thunder, but no rain."

He Speaks Without Listening

He who answers a matter before he hears it, it is folly and shame to him (Prov. 18:13).

It's not always what you say, it's how you say it. That's for sure, but I want you to know it's more important to say the truth and to say it in the right way than to be deceitful and lie. It's more important to say what God says and leave the feeling matters to somebody else. Trust the Lord.

One of the great dangers in communication is speaking before you hear something. There are several reasons why we do that, and I'm as guilty as you are. First of all, you think you know what they're going to say, so you're saving time. It's like there's a little word or two that they bring up, or an event, or circumstance and right away you check into what it's all about. "Well, I know all about that, and here's the answer." The Bible says that we're fools for doing that.

"He who answers a matter before he hears it, it is folly and shame to him." Sometimes we're impatient, or maybe we've heard the story before, so we burst into the coversation and say, "Oh, I've heard that before!" Have you ever noticed how that blesses you? You're telling somebody something and you think it's a first and they say, "I've heard you say that before." Right away you check into your senility!

What we've looked at so far are the **practices** that identify a fool, the **pride** that characterizes a fool, and the **pattern of speech** that is found in a fool.

THE PAIN A FOOL CAUSES HIS OWN FAMILY

The proverbs of Solomon; a wise son makes a glad father, but a foolish son is the grief of his mother (Prov. 10:1).

Have you ever wondered why it doesn't say, "...the grief of his father"? I believe fathers grieve, but I believe there's a point to be made there that's very important. A son ought to be very careful how he treats his mother. A son, especially, needs to understand how his actions affect the emotional nature of his mother. A foolish son is a grief to his mother.

A fool despises his father's instruction, but he who receives reproof is prudent (Prov. 15:5)

One of the greatest blessings Carole and I have ever seen was at a Bible conference. We went out to a restaurant and had a bite to eat, and across the table was a son talking to his father. We were so close, we heard the whole conversation. We didn't talk because theirs was so much more interesting than what we were talking about. This guy at the table, a young man, was out with his father. He asked for the meeting to apologize to his father for being a foolish son. I'm telling you, I didn't know whether to cry or shout with joy or what! It was the most precious thing. Here was a Christian kid, and he had gone to Basic Youth Conflicts by Bill Gothard. His dad was obviously not a believer. The son even said, "I know you're not saved." Now that was direct. He said, "But I am and I know that I've done some very bad things. I have not respected you." I watched that son try to apologize to his father.

"We don't agree, we're different. We're so different! You like things I don't like. I've felt this all my life. I didn't really feel accepted by you, but I understand now more than ever before that I'm the problem. I want to ask for your forgiveness." His dad said, "Aw, don't even think about it." The young man said, "I'm sorry dad, I'm not going to let you get away w ith that. You may say it isn't important to you but I think that it is. It sure is important to me and I've got to tell you. It's up to you to decide what you want to do about it, but I've got to apologize to you for my attitudes. I didn't listen to anything you said because you are an unbeliever and I am a Christian, but I just learned that's wrong. I want to ask for your forgiveness."

I sat there so excited! I felt like saying, "Go for it; go for it! God bless you, amen!" I kept quiet because Carole kept patting my hand saying, "Easy, David."

A wise son makes his father glad, but a foolish man despises his mother (Prov. 15:20).

Kids say, "You don't know what my mom is like." It doesn't make any difference. She's your mother. You'd better be careful. There is terrible pain and grief which young people can cause their parents. You say, "They don't deserve any more; look at the way they treated me." It doesn't matter. God's holding you accountable for your attitudes toward them. "Well, what about them?" Don't worry, GOD will take care of them!

He who begets a scoffer does so to his sorrow, and the father of a fool has no joy (Prov. 17:21).

Why are some parents so unhappy? Because they've got a son or a daughter somewhere that never listens to them, never responds to their authority, and they don't like it. They don't have any happiness in their heart.

One of the greatest strengths in a parent's life is to have children that respond to them and their authority. The older you get, the more you know that half of what you said was wrong. The older you get the less authoritative you become. It is sweetness all the way to have a child who responds to your authority even when they think you're wrong. Nothing can rip the heart out of a parent more than a child that does not respect their authority and position.

A lot of us are still suffering because we have never gone to our parents and straightened it out. A young man in our church told me about his father and his grandfather. This father treated his grandfather terribly. He mocked him and everything. He grew up hating his grandfather. The grandson kind of liked his grandfather, but he grew up hating his father. This boy is a Christian, but he's not sure about his dad. He claims to be a Christian but this problem has existed all their life. It makes family occasions terrible. They don't like Thanksgiving or Christmas, or any occasion where the family comes together. They're getting old now.

The son told me about it, and I talked to that dad. He was ten or fifteen years older than I am. I was a young pastor and I felt very uncomfortable doing it, but God used my stumbling ways, and I saw a man who went to his father after many, many years and apologized to him. Two days later his father died, and I remember that man giving his testimony—sharing as tears flowed down his face. He said, "I almost ruined my life by two days."

He wasn't really happy about his attitudes towards his dad. There were a lot of things about his dad he didn't like. There were things that his dad said that he felt were wrong, but his attitude was wrong toward his dad. And now his son who happened to like the grandfather was deeply troubled over this conflict. It was hurting that boy's life. This father changed; I've rarely seen a man change so much in later life. That man all of a sudden came on fire for God. It was like that one thing, his attitude towards his dad, was holding him back from everything God wanted to do in his life.

There is more pain in the body of Christ over foolish children who have failed to respect their parents than perhaps any other matter. It's serious; we need to deal with it.

A foolish son is a grief to his father [the same thing that was said about the mother earlier], *and bitterness to her who bore him* (Prov. 17:25).

A foolish son is the ruin of his father, and the contentions and the arguments of the wife are a continual dripping (Prov. 19:13).

This is not our favorite verse, but it appears three times, and they're the same. It drags down, tears apart, ruins.

THE PROBLEM WE FACE IN TRYING TO CONFRONT A FOOL

Do not speak in the hearing of a fool, for he will despise the wisdom of your words (Prov. 23:9).

Do not answer a fool according to his folly, Lest you also be like him. Answer a fool according to his folly, Lest he be wise in his own eyes. He who sends a message by the hand of a fool Cuts off his own feet and drinks violence (Prov. 26:4-5).

If a wise man contends or argues with a foolish man whether the fool rages or laughs there is no peace (Prov. 29:9).

There's a terrible problem in trying to confront a fool.

THE PERILS WHICH A FOOL WILL EXPERIENCE IN HIS LIFE AND FUTURE

Fools die for lack of wisdom (Prov. 10:21).

You have, first of all, **THE DISPLEASURE OF GOD.**

When you make a vow to God do not delay to pay it for He has no pleasure in fools (Eccl. 5:4).

God is not pleased with foolish people. **THE DESTRUCTION OF HIS LIFE** is a terrible peril in addition to the displeasure of God.

The first reason a fool's life will be destroyed is **because of his conversation**—the way he talks.

Wise people store up knowlege, but the mouth of the foolish is near destruction (Prov. 10:14).

A fool's mouth is his destruction, and his lips are the snare [the trap] of his soul (Prov. 18:7).

Because of his conversation, he's going to have many perils in his life. A second reason would be **because of his companions**—who he hangs around with. His life will be destroyed.

He who walks with wise men will be wise, but the companions of fools will be destroyed (Prov. 13:20).

A third reason is **because of his complacency.**

The turning away of the simple will slay them, and the complacency of fools will destroy them (Prov. 1:32).

They're totally apathetic to what God says and to the fact that they're foolish. They're complacent and indifferent to the ways of the Lord. That's going to destroy them, that complacency.

A fool is also going to see the **DEATH OF HIS DESIRE FOR SUCCESS AND GREATNESS.** Our world constantly parades success and greatness. God says that is never going to happen in a fool's life.

The wise shall inherit glory, but shame shall be the legacy of fools (Prov. 3:35).

The wise at heart will receive commands, but a parading fool will fall. He who walks with integrity walks securely, but he who perverts his ways will become known. He who winks with the eye causes trouble, but a parading fool will fall (Prov. 10:8).

He who troubles his own house will inherit the wind, and the fool will be servant to the wise of heart (Prov. 11:29).

You think you've "arrived" when you have a foolish heart. You think you're in charge; you think you don't need to listen to anybody. I'll tell you what's going to happen to you.

You're going to be a servant to him who is wise. According to the Bible, if you trouble your own house, if you're a grief to your mother, a pain to your father, you're going to inherit the same thing. That's the point of that proverb (11:29).

> *As snow in summer and rain in harvest, so honor is not befitting a fool* (Prov. 26:1).

Forget honor; forget greatness; forget success. Forget being stable the rest of your life. You are headed for serious trouble because you're a fool.

THE PLEA TO FOOLS
FROM THE HEART OF GOD

If any of these matters have hit your heart or if they remind you of someone in your family, or your friend, or circle of friends, then here' s what you need to hear: The plea to fools from the heart of God.

> *Oh you simple ones! Understand prudence. And you fools, be of an understanding heart* (Prov. 8:5).

The first time I read that I felt a little touch of encouragement in a very depressing study time for this message. I heard God appeal to foolish people and say, "You can have a understanding heart." I realize that it's never too late as long as you have a breath to breathe. You can stop the pattern of foolishness and turn to the Lord. God appeals to us via an understanding heart, "Stop this!"

> *Forsake foolishness and live, and go in the way of understanding* (Prov. 9:60).

It is possible to forsake foolishness; it is possible to change. You're going in one direction, but you can turn around; go the other way. Instead of the way of foolishness, you can walk in the way of understanding.

One day after His resurrection, Jesus was walking on a road to a little city called Emmaus, and he joined two people as they walked along. He began to talk to them, and they were really excited with all he was telling them.

> *"... certain women of our company, who arrived at the tomb early, astonished us. When they did not find*

*His body, they came saying that they had also seen
a vision of angels who said He was alive. And certain
of those who were with us went to the tomb and found
it just as the women had said; but Him they did not
see"* (Luke 24:22-24).

They were reasoning about this. Now look at what Jesus
said to them.

*"O foolish ones, and slow of heart to believe in all
that the prophets have spoken! Ought not the Christ
to have suffered these things and to enter into His
glory?" And beginning at Moses and all the Prophets,
He expounded to them in all the Scriptures the things
concerning Himself* (Lk. 24:25-27).

They later said, *"Did not our heart burn within us
while ... He opened the Scriptures to us?"* (Lk.24:32)

I learned a point from this verse that was really encouraging. *"O foolish ones, and slow of heart to believe in all that the
prophets have spoken."* The answer to a foolish heart is to
turn to the Word of God. It's to turn to what God says and
to commit your life to follow it. Just stop going the way you
are going and turn to the way of the Lord.

The Bible says to parents, *"Train up a child in the way* [of
the Lord] *and when he is old he will not depart from it."* You
say, "No, it says, *'the way he should go'."* Once you study
Proverbs and that immediate context, you know exactly what
it means. It's not talking about the way YOU want him to
go. It's not even talking about the way their gifts and abilities
designed them to go. It's the talking about the way of the
Lord. We are, according to the Bible (especially fathers), to
bring up our children in the discipline and instruction of the
Lord. That's what it says. It's *"the way of the Lord"* that
people desperately need in their lives.

*"Trust in the Lord with all your heart And lean not
on your own understanding; In all your ways acknow-
lege Him, And He shall direct your paths"* (Prov. 3:5-
6).

Walk in the way of the Lord. We need to follow the Lord.
If I have described YOU or any circumstance of your life, and
you know that this characterizes you, I ask you, "What will
you do about it?" God appeals to all of us who have been

foolish and says, "Stop it! I love you. You don't need to let it go on. Go in the way of understanding. Get it straightened out. You can walk with the Lord. Don't keep going on."

The loving heart of God appeals to all the foolish ones to become wise in heart and follow what He says in His Word.

CHAPTER 3

THE PROBLEM OF TEMPTATION

The problem of temptation is indeed a contemporary problem, a deep serious problem in our society. It amazes the saints of God who study the Word of God, the volume of Scripture that is given to the matter of temptation, seduction, and immorality. It is the character of man and his depravity to take all that God does in extending His wonderful gifts to us and corrupt them and abuse them, and to use them in a way that He never designed.

Perhaps one reason for the volume of Scripture dealing with this subject is that one of the greatest blessings that God ever gave to man in terms of his physical life here on earth is the whole matter of sex and marriage. The devil, with his constant efforts to counterfeit and deceive us, and the depravity of our own hearts always bend away from God. We see a constant pressure, a constant struggle, a constant difficulty among those even who love the Lord and want to serve Him that is unbelievably strong.

God created us with sexual desire, yet there are two kinds of people—those who have it and those who don't. You say, "Are there really people who don't?" Well, then obviously you've got it. Some are saying, "So what is the problem?" And you obviously are one that doesn't have it. We all represent one side or the other.

I Corinthians 7 says it is a charismatic gift. It comes from the Holy Spirit of God. You either are gifted for marriage, you have strong sexual desire, or you in fact are not, and can choose that high and exalted position and state before God of celibacy to be a mighty servant of the Lord not encumbered by marriage and family responsiblity. Whichever side you are on, the warning of God is clear.

There are those among us that do not have intense sexual pressure, yet who in a moment of weakness and vulnerability and through the enticement and baits of the enemy, have fallen into sin. There are some who struggle with it constantly and say, "Is there any hope of ever having victory?" Isn't is interesting that the Book of Proverbs in its opening words

of instruction to sons and young people says in Chapter
1:10, *"My son, if sinners entice you, Do not consent"?*

*My son, pay attention to my wisdom; Lend your
ear to my understanding, That you may preserve discretion, And that your lips may keep knowlege. For
the lips of an immoral woman drip honey, and her
mouth is smoother than oil; But in the end she is bitter as wormwood, Sharp as a two-edged sword. Her
feet go down to death, Her steps lay hold of hell. Lest
you ponder her path of life—Her ways are unstable;
You do not know them. Therefore hear me now, my
children, And do not depart from the words of my
mouth. Remove your way far from her. And do not go
near the door of her house, Lest you give your honor
to others, And your years to the cruel one; Lest aliens
be filled with your wealth, And your labors go to the
house of a foreigner; And you mourn at last, When
your flesh and your body are consumed, And say:
"How I have hated instruction, And my heart
despised reproof! I have not obeyed the voice of my
teachers, Nor inclined my ear to those who instructed
me! I was on the verge of total ruin, In the midst of
the congregation and assembly."* [Now comes the advice.] *Drink water from your own cistern, And running
water from your own well. Should your fountains be
dispersed abroad, Streams of water in the streets?
Let them be only your own, And not for strangers with
you. Let your fountain be blessed, And rejoice with
the wife of your youth. As a loving deer and a grace-
ful doe, Let her breasts satisfy you at all times; And
always be enraptured with her love. For why should
you, my son, be enraptured by an immoral woman,
And be embraced in the arms of a seductress? For
the ways of man are before the eyes of the Lord, And
He ponders all his paths. His own iniquities entrap
the wicked man, And he is caught in the cords of his
sin. He shall die for lack of instruction, And in the
greatness of his folly he shall go astray* (Prov. 5:1-23).

No matter what the age of children, they should hear what
God has to say about temptation. It's better that they hear
what the Word of God has to say than to hear it off the streets
or from some kid at school. Worse yet, many children hear
about it from sex education that's without moral and tradi-
tional values.

When we look at the problem of temptation in society, I have a parade of articles from secular magazines (not Christian) that indicate the enormity of the problem in society. One discussion about sex in the workplace was so mind-boggling one wonders if the survey was accurate. Three out of every four people are involved according to this particular survey. It seems to be a game. A game to get ahead sometimes. A game that people play because there's nothing else to do, or as one person said, "It keeps work interesting."

We are living in a wicked society! According to reports of the American Family Association, our television programming in prime time is turned toward sexual stimulation. It seems like the great goal is to parade every kind of sexual sin known to man in front of our prime time audiences—supposedly designed for children. Sexual jokes and sexual remarks now dominate almost every television program.

It's astounding to discover that one study showed a continual infiltration of sensuality and sexual remarks in news broadcasting. What have we come to when advertising of any item be it clothes, cosmetics or cars insists upon sexual provocation?

In spite of efforts by parents, churches, and organizations to do something about it, the onslaught of the enemy's attack in this area has increased; it has not weakened. It's so bad now that some Christians are giving up. It's so thorough in society that we've decided to change what we stand for and just work on the "biggies". It's such a problem that pornographic matters (which Christians have tried to attack) now have become issues of dealing only with hard core or child abuse and to simply skip the other issues. Seemingly there's no hope or help. It's time again to look at the Word of God.

THE CHARACTERISTICS OF SEDUCTION

According to the Bible, all of God's people (and especially young people) are to take careful notice of how seduction works. What are the characteristics? I'll give you six of them from the Book of Proverbs.

Verbal Compliments

It ought to be characteristic of the speech and mouth of a Christian that he regularly and frequently compliments people around him. That's much better than tearing folks down. We ought to encourage and we ought to compliment people—to show appreciation. However, we must be aware that there are verbal compliments that have a wrong motive.

To deliver you from the immoral woman, from the seductress who flatters with her words (Prov. 2:16).

For the lips of an immoral woman drip honey and her mouth is smoother than oil (Prov. 5:3).

To keep you from the evil woman, from the flattering tongue of the seductress (Prov. 6:24).

That they may keep you from the immoral woman, From the seductress who flatters with her words. With her enticing speech she caused him to yield, With her flattering lips she seduced him (Prov. 7:5, 21).

It is very evident in the Bible that seduction begins with verbal compliments—compliments that are not rooted in an effort to encourage somebody who may be discouraged of heart, but compliments that are rooted in the desire to seduce, to entice, and to deceive.

Sensual Conversations

The immoral woman says to an unsuspecting young man,

I have spread my bed with tapestry, Colored coverings of Egyptian linen. I have perfumed my bed With myrrh, aloes, and cinnamon. Come, let us take our fill of love until morning; Let us delight ourselves with love [literally, lovemaking] (Prov. 7:16-18).

Here we're not simply giving verbal compliments and flattery we're now speaking very boldly about sensuality and becoming involved in immoral activity. Sensual conversation is being stimulated by marketing and advertising in our culture today. Some of what we just read in verses 16-18 appear in billboards and magazine articles that are selling items they want us to buy. It's almost as though the purpose behind the selling of these items is to get us all to sin against God—to get us all to compromise our convictions and our moral values for the pleasures of sin for a season.

It's absolutely frightening when children are being used in this way, but we should've known a long time ago that all of these ads that picture people in sensual clothes and inviting settings (usually involving somebody's bed) are not intended to do anything but sell us down the path of immorality and sin. Wake up to the fact that people who are in that marketing business and distribution of that kind of advertising are no friend to God. In fact, in a recent study of marketing people who are marketing products in our culture today it was found that 92% of them have no moral values whatsoever as it relates to sex and marriage. They couldn't care less. All they want to do is sell their product.

Verbal compliments, then sensual conversations, are invitations to sexual sin. A single man in our church told me that out of fifteen women he dated over a five-year period of time (during which he tried to live for the Lord) all but one of them invited him or encouraged him to have sexual involvement on the first or second date. It's easy to go along with the world isn't it? Even in the name of love and Christian ministry we sometimes say it's OK. Well, it's not OK! Verbal compliments and sensual conversations are setups.

Weak Commitments

Lest you ponder her path of life—Her ways are unstable; You do not know them (Prov. 5:6).

She may look good, but the fact that she's enticing you and seducing you is saying a great deal about her. Her ways are unstable.

She was loud and rebellious, Her feet would not stay at home (Prov. 7:11).

She doesn't hesitate to speak boldly about these matters. This woman is married, by the way, so your idea of prostitution has to be a little bit changed when you read the story of Proverbs. This is a married woman who, with her husband gone, is unfaithful. Verse 12 says, *"At times she was outside, at times in the open square, Lurking at every corner."* She has a weak commitment to her husband.

My husband is not at home; He is gone on a long journey; He has taken a bag of money with him, And will come home on the apppointed day (Prov. 7:19-20).

Change the word "money" into credit cards and you get the idea. He's gone. Obviously to do some business and he won't be back. He told her when he was coming back and it

would be a while. They had the opportunity. Weak commit-
ments lead to serious temptation and seduction.

Spiritual Confusion

It is very important that the people of God understand
this and not run away from it, or (like the proverbial ostrich)
put our head in the sand and hope it goes away. It's not
going to go away! What we often find among Christians that
there is justification of sexual sin. A spiritual confusion
comes out.

> *I have peace offerings with me; Today I have paid
> my vows* (Prov. 7:14).

She is saying, "You don't need to worry about my relationship with God. Everything is fine."

> *So I came out to meet you, Diligently to seek your
> face* (Prov. 7:15).

"I've dealt with my commitment to God and I'm strong
there. I want you to know that everything is okay between
me and God." Let's make it clear, no matter what your walk
with the Lord, no matter what your stand is for the word of
God and for what is right, we're all susceptible to sin. It
doesn't make it right because you claim to be "on the ball"
for the Lord. Spiritual confusion is often among the people
of God. We don't take a stand. We don't even want to deal
with it.

When I spoke on this subject of sexual sin some time ago,
a certain radio station wrote asking that (due to the blunt-
ness of my talk) we remove it from the series. They felt that
Christian people might be offended by the blunt talk. It's
about time we start talking straight to each other on the
basis of the Word of God and quit messing around.

Immodest Clothing

That's a subject that hardly any church in America today
will even say a word about.

> *And there a woman met him, With the attire of the
> harlot, and a crafty heart* (Prov. 7:10).

She is not a prostitute; she is a married woman. She's
involved in sexual immorality. How does she dress on this
occasion when her husband is not at home? *"With the attire
of a harlot,"* the Bible says, *"and a crafty heart."*

I believe that men need to be careful about the way they dress (as well as women), especially in our society, but as you know, the Word of God primarily deals with women. I have no desire to put an unnecessary burden or guilt trip on any woman, but I want to say a hearty thank you to every woman who desires to be modest in her wearing apparel. I want to honor every woman who goes to public meetings or shopping having a desire to honor the Lord and not to appeal to any man in a sensual way. It's important to be balanced.

There are some among us who are looking for husbands. I understand that you want to be attractive and sometimes there is a real thin line between your desire to attract and being modest. I understand the problem. I'm not sure what to do with that, but it seems to me, that you'll always win by leaning to modesty.

You may not agree with this but this is the Word of God. You may want to think the problem is in my interpretation, and it's not the the Word of God, so I'll try to be as careful and cautious as I can and you do the same.

> In like manner also, that the women adorn themselves in modest apparel, with propriety and moderation, not with braided hair or gold or pearls or costly clothing, but, which is proper for women professing godliness, with good works (I Tim. 2:9-10).

Now stop right there before you go on. To "adorn themselves" is talking about beauty. God isn't into ugliness, in case you haven't figured that out. You say, "He must be. Look at my husband!" Hang on there! God sees beauty in everything, and God wants us to be careful about the ugly role.

In this passage, there is a very interesting analysis that I think needs to be given. The word "modest" is from a Greek word referring to the cosmos—the arrangement of things in the universe. That's the word from which we get the word cosmetics. Cosmetics refers to the orderly arrangement of the face and hopefully you've got yours on straight. God said that women are to adorn themselves in apparel that is orderly and neatly arranged. What you have in the opening statement is a condemnation of sloppiness which is a form of rebellion to eliminate male and female distinction. It was existing in that day; it is existing in our day. The word "modest" is not talking about the sexual overtones as much as it is condemning sloppiness. Women should dress in a well-arranged manner—that which is conducive to emphasizing your femininity and your beauty.

The following statements are very definitely related to sex. There are two words used, *"propriety"* and *"moderation"*. The emphasis is not to be on the external (e.g., how you arrange your hair), or the wearing of jewelry or extravagant clothes. When it says *"propriety and moderation,"* it's talking about two sides of one coin. The one deals with what a woman feels in herself. Some women, feeling very sensuous, will dress in a certain way. The second side deals with how it affects men. I've heard many women speakers who seem to imply that man is at fault for having a problem in this area. Speaking as a man, I want you to know that we are very interested in how you look. If that's a surprise to you, you really need counsel! We are very interested in how you look and we look at you. As a matter of fact, our problem is how long and how often we look. I'm sure you appreciate that, especially those of you who are looking for a husband.

The Greek is very obvious, and I think it is obvious in English, too. There is a danger in the way women dress as to what they cause in a man, as surely as there is a problem in their own hearts. Let me explain that to you. It is very possible that a Christian woman has no desire to entice or seduce any man by what she wears. That is very possible and very common among Christian women. What we often forget is that a woman may not be guilty of the one but still be guilty of the other because (by what she wears) she may be enticing a man even though that isn't her own desire.

If she is married, which this context deals with, I suggest it becomes the husband's responsibility to be careful about his wife, how she appears, how she looks, knowing that he is a man—knowing how men think and how they look at women. He is responsible God. The woman can only be responsible for what she herself feels in her own heart, but sometimes we need to face very squarely the fact that God created men with sexual desire. They like to look at women. God frequently mentions that, and women have to be aware of why they are looking and how long they are looking and what men want to achieve by looking. The Lord Jesus dealt with that in the Sermon on the Mount.

Physical Contact

This is a troublesome area. In the New Testament, God's people obviously had a great deal of physical contact. There is frequent mention of embracing and hugging. There is also frequent mention of kissing even so strong that it says to *"greet all the brothers with a holy kiss."* Exactly how are we to interpret that?

To eliminate all affection from God's people is certainly an immature attitude. God had no reason for putting the word *"holy"* in front of the word *"kiss"* if there had not been a problem. God assumes that there will be physical affection (a hug, an embrace, or a kiss on the cheek) to say, "I love you," in times of crisis and hurting. Those are appropriate.

However, all of us realize that the problem of physical contact becomes very severe when the motive in the heart is messed up.

> *Why should you, my son, be enraptured by an immoral woman, And be embraced in the arms of a seductress?* (Prov. 5:20).

The motive here is to cause the person to sin. The motive here is not to stand for the Word of God or encourage marital fidelity. The motive here is to fall into sin.

> *So she caught him and kissed him; With an impudent* [shameless] *face she said to him: "I have peace offerings with me; Today I have paid my vows* [the time is right to make love] (Prov. 7:13).

She went after him. She was not greeting a Christian brother with a holy kiss. The purpose was immorality and sin. Physical contact is going to occur. God's people must be aware of something. The subtleties of our old sin nature, the characteristics of love before God is such a delicate nature that sometimes we can cross the line. We can go from a spirit-filled attitude and heart to a carnal action without even realizing the steps that led us there. In one moment, our hearts can be centered on the Lord, desiring to do whatever is pleasing to Him. Then, without even knowing what's happening, we suddenly move into carnality and sin.

There is a sense in which I believe God has left us with that problem so that we can learn to trust the Lord. The Bible says to watch and pray so that we will not enter into temptation for the *"spirit is willing, but the flesh is weak"*. God leaves us with weak flesh because it is through that avenue that we learn to trust God. We learn to say, "No" to what our hearts may desire to do. That builds our integrity and the character of our hearts.

It is silly, immature and foolish to say that it's not your problem. If you're trying to put up a false front of legalistic attitudes as though this is not a problem for you, then you have misread the entire Word of God. It is better that we all say that we would all do the same, but for the grace of God. Let's learn to depend on the Lord and to see our strength coming from Him. Let's not feel that "we can handle it". More young people fall into sexual sin because they think they can handle it, than for any other single reason. They are warned, but they believe they can handle it. They don't believe it's a problem. We can't handle it. The Bible warns us that we need to trust the Lord concerning this.

THE CONSEQUENCES OF SEXUAL SIN

One of the quickest ways to be **defeated spiritually** is to be involved in sexual sin. You can fool people around you, but when your glands are not under control, it is hurting your walk with the Lord.

> For the ways of man are before the eyes of the Lord, And He ponders all his paths. His own iniquities entrap the wicked man, And he is caught in the cords of his sin. He shall die for lack of instruction, And in the greatness of his folly he shall go astray (Prov. 5:21-23).

Emotional distress is a second consequence and it can be terrible. This can tear you up inside.

> Whoever commits adultery with a woman lacks understanding; He who does so destroys his own soul. Wounds and dishonor he will get, And his reproach will not be wiped away (Prov. 6:32-33).

If you sense deep wounds in your soul, and deep turmoil, perhaps it's evident that you're a believer. It can also be one of the consequences of sexual sin.

> Beloved, I beg you as sojourners and pilgrims, abstain from fleshly lusts which war against the soul (I Peter 2:11).

The emotional conflict of sexual sin in conflict with your soul will be enormous.

We also have an interesting insight into the life of Lot given by Peter.

> ... and delivered righteous Lot, who was oppressed with the filthy conduct of the wicked (for that righteous man, dwelling among them, tormented his righteous soul from day to day by seeing and hearing their lawless deeds) (II Peter 2:7-8).

In a series on pornography that was done on television, I was asked to participate to give a religious point of view. On that program, the moderator asked me whether or not there was any proof in the Bible that God would not approve of nor allow pornography. He seemed to think I would have to search for it. I turned to this passage and pointed out that Lot (who was righteous) was tormented simply by seeing and hearing lawless deeds. Sexual immorality, as viewed on TV or movies, is going to affect those that walk with God. When we see it, we had better deal with it right now! We'd better say to our children that it is wrong; it is sin! Then, explain what God's holy and righteous standards really are.

A lot of us let this go on without realizing that we are tormenting our righteous souls. There is emotional distress.

The third consequence of sexual sin is **family devastation.** Nothing ruins a marriage or a family faster than this.

> Can a man take fire to his bosom, And his clothes not be burned? Can one walk on hot coals, And his feet not be seared? So is he who goes in to his neighbor's wife; Whoever touches her shall not be innocent. People do not despise a thief If he steals to satisfy himself when he is starving. Yet when he is found, he must restore sevenfold; He may have to give up all the substance of his house. Whoever commits adultery with a woman lacks understanding; He who does so destroys his own soul. Wounds and dishonor he will get, And his reproach will not be wiped away. For jealousy is a husband's fury [also a wife's fury]; Therefore he will not spare in the day of vengeance. He will accept no recompense, Nor will he be appeased though you give many gifts (Prov. 6:27-35).

Family devastation is a consequence of sexual sin.

My son, give me your heart, And let your eyes observe my ways. For a harlot is a deep pit, And a seductress is a narrow well. She also lies in wait as for a victim, And increases the unfaithful among men (Prov. 23:26-28).

Spiritual defeat, emotional distress, family devastation—all follow sexual sin, and so does **physical disease.** Solomon said that there is nothing new under the sun. It doesn't matter if you are talking about AIDS, syphilis, gonorrhea, any kind of venereal disease, the whole world knows that having sex outside of marriage is a serious risk to our physical well-being. Physical disease is running rampant.

The Center of Disease Control in Atlanta, Georgia, says that it is at epidemic proportions. They have warned Americans that the attention given to AIDS is covering the rise in other sexual diseases. They are at epidemic levels and they see no help in sight. The whole program is designed to find acceptable solutions which allow people to keep their sexual immorality. Isn't it fascinating that they are trying to develop medicines to solve these problems so that people can continue to sin against God?

One of the officials at the Center said that the epidemics could be controlled in one generation without any trouble at all, if people would return to having sexual intercourse within marriage alone. We'd better wake up!

You mourn at last, When your flesh and your body are consumed, And say: "How I have hated instruction, And my heart despised reproof! I have not obeyed the voice of my teachers, Nor inclined my ear to those who instructed me! I was on the verge of total ruin, In the midst of the congregation and assembly" (Prov. 5:11-14).

God gave them up to vile passions. For even their women exchanged the natural use [it's a God-given right to have a desire for a man] *for what is against nature. Likewise also the men, leaving the natural use of the woman* [God gives a natural desire for women], *burned in their lust for one another, men with men committing what is shameful, and receiving in themselves the penalty of their error which was due* (Rom. 1:27).

I'm thoroughly convinced that the devil would do anything to keep us from reading these passages in the Bible. The natural desire of a man for a woman, or a woman for a man, must be controlled within the bonds of marriage; however, it is God who has planted that natural desire in our hearts. It is unnatural, against God's laws, for a man to desire a man, or a woman to desire a woman.

> *Do you now know that he who is joined to a harlot is one body with her? For "The two," He says, "shall become one flesh." But he who is joined to the Lord is one spirit with Him. Flee sexual immorality. Every sin that a man does is outside the body, but he who commits sexual immorality sins against his own body* (I Cor. 6:16-18).

You tell me what that means! Bible teachers are convinced that there are two possibilities—either physical disease or diminishing of sexual desire because of immorality.

One of the characteristics among young people today is to redefine the issues of sexual sin. They will point out that many times, God is speaking about adultery. Some Bible teachers even attempt to reduce the term "sexual immorality" to matters of adultery. Everything we learn from Greek literature, as well as the use of Greek in the Bible, points to the fact that word *"pornea"* refers to adultery, homosexuality, incest, rape, beastiality (sex with animals), and pre-marital sex.

Is it OK for two people to have sex if nobody gets hurt? What an argument! It is NEVER all right to have sex outside the bonds of marriage. The only safe sex that there is, is between a husband and a wife. The sad fact about our world is that sexual disease is now being discussed in terms of how we can cure the problem without stopping the sin. My message is that no matter what cures are discovered, you will never escape the judgment of God for immorality.

The moment you discover a cure for one, there will be another disease. God's Word stands. It is a sin against your own physical body to commit immorality. All others are in the realm of the heart, the mind, the soul, but one is against the body—that is sexual immorality.

Congregational disapproval is another consequence for believers who sin in sexual immorality. Something needs to be said that is very pointed in this matter. Many Christian leaders do not know what is going on in private. It's also obvious that we don't want to go on a witch-hunt into everybody's personal life.

Any Christian who CONTINUES in sexual sin, without repentance, after they have been confronted on the matter, according to the Bible is to be put out of the church. The purpose is not to avoid contact with such a person, although the Bible tells us to do that. The purpose is not to heap greater burdens on such a person or to say that the church does not care about such a one. The purpose of all church discipline is to see that the wayward one gets right with the Lord. When we Christians continue to tolerate sexual sin among our friends and say and do nothing, we are compromising and there is guilt at our doorstep.

> *I wrote to you in my epistle not to keep company with sexually immoral people. Yet I certainly did not mean with the sexually immoral people of this world, or with the covetous, or extortioners, or idolaters, since then you would need to go out of the world. But now I have written to you not to keep company with anyone named a brother, who is a fornicator, or covetous, or an idolater, or a reviler, or a drunkard, or an extortioner—not even to eat with such a person. For what have I to do with judging those also who are outside? Do you not judge those who are inside? But those who are outside God judges. Therefore "put away from yourselves that wicked person" (I Cor. 5:9-13).*

I don't see how it could be any clearer.

THE CHALLENGE TO SANCTIFICATION

Paul wrote to a new church which was in a society filled with sexual immorality and the matter needed to be straightened out.

> *Finally then, brethren, we urge and exhort in the Lord Jesus that you should abound more and more, just as you received from us how you ought to walk and to please God; for you know what commandments we gave you through the Lord Jesus. For this is the will of God, your sanctification: that you should abstain from sexual immorality; that each of you should know how to possess his own vessel in sanctification and honor, not in passion of lust, like*

the Gentiles who do not know God; that no one should take advantage of and defraud his brother in this matter, because the Lord is the avenger of all such, as we also forewarned you and testified. For God did not call us to uncleanness, but in holiness.

Therefore he who rejects this does not reject man, but God, who has also given us His Holy Spirit (I Thess. 4:1-8).

Stay away from those who are immoral. Sometimes our kids get involved in serious sin because they hang around the wrong people *"Evil companions corrupt good morals,"* the Bible says. We need to be careful.

If sinners entice you, do not consent (Prov. 1;10).

Do not walk in the way with them, Keep your foot from their path (Prov. 1:15).

Remove your way far from her, And do not go near the door of her house (Prov. 5:8).

At the window of my house I looked through my lattice, And saw among the simple, I perceived among the youths, A young man devoid of understanding, Passing along the street near her corner; And he took the path to her house In the twilight, in the evening, In the black and dark night (Prov. 7:6-9).

Do not let your heart turn aside to her ways, Do not stray into her paths (Prov. 7:25).

Stay away from people who are immoral! It's almost a game which I've observed for a long time: Christian people see how close they can get to the rotten people of this world. Kids hang around the wrong crowd on the school campus and then are rebellious toward their parents.

Stop disobeying the Word of God! There is only one reason to hang around with evil people and that's to win them to Jesus Christ. When you lose your ability to boldly confront people with the gospel of Christ, get out of there! Don't compromise under any circumstances.

Stop lusting with the purpose of sexual sin. This is a private thing that happens in your heart.

> *Do not lust after her beauty in your heart, Nor let her allure you with her eyelids* (Prov. 6:25).

> *Flee youthful lusts* (II Tim. 2:22).

Just to say, "Stop lusting" will not help a lot of people. We do have sexual desires. God is not saying to stop sexual desires. Jesus had something to say about this.

> *"You have heard that it was said to those of old, 'You shall not commit adultery.' But I say to you that whoever looks at a woman to lust for her has already committed adultery with her in his heart"* (Matt. 5:27-28).

One guy told me that he was leaving the church because one of his favorite pastimes was looking at women. We talked about it and I shared with him that the word *"looks"* is a present tense and is not referring to the fact that men enjoy the beauty of women. That is not what Jesus is talking about. It is a continual habit; a constant looking.

Notice carefully, also, that the word *"woman"* is in the singular, not the plural. God is talking about constantly looking at a particular woman. Every man knows what I'm talking about. If God said it is wrong to look at women in general, we'd all have a problem. Whoever looks at a particular woman over a period of time is what is being discussed.

The next statement is *"to lust for her"* and tells us clearly that the purpose of the look was not to admire her beauty and attractiveness. The purpose of the looking is to commit adultery. We cannot run away from the fact that when we look at a particular woman [or a woman looks at a man] in order to commit sexual sin with that woman (no matter whether we have actually done it or not), God says we have already done it in our hearts. That's what God says. We need to bring every thought into captivity to Jesus Christ.

There's a line here. People have sexual desires, especially since we have been programmed for marriage, to be used for the happiness of our partners. However, when we decide to set our focus to have sexual intercourse with a person other than our spouse and we continue to carry that in our minds and hearts, we have committed adultery in our hearts whether we have actually done it or not.

That's why pornography is so dangerous. Stop lusting with the motive of committing immorality. You may think you can't stop, but that's not true. Every believer has the Holy Spirit within him and He wars against our flesh and we are given the ability to obey Him by God. We can obey Him and He can control our habits. We can keep saying, "No" to sexual immorality. Our old sin nature wants to say, "Yes," but we don't have to give in. We want to obey God and honor Him. We can stop lusting—desiring to commit immorality. All of us designed for marriage have strong sexual desires, but when we decide to fulfill that outside of marriage, we are setting ourselves up to sin.

The third part of my challenge is to **seek satisfaction from your marital spouse or remain celibate.** If you're not married, remain celibate.

> *Rejoice with the wife of your youth. Let her breasts satisfy you at all times; And always be enraptured with her love* (Prov. 5:18-19)

It's interesting that God tells us that *"He shall die for lack of instruction"* (Prov. 5:23).

> *For the commandment is a lamp, And the law is light; Reproofs of instruction are the way of life, To keep you from the evil woman, From the flattering tongue of a seductress* (Prov. 6:23-24).

I see the *"reproofs of instruction"* as the main point of this chapter. How sad that Christians would think that we can make it on our own without the instructions of the Lord. We need to **submit to the Word of God.** If you're having a problem in this area, I challenge you to pour your heart and mind full of the Word of God. Take key verses like *"Walk in the Spirit, and you shall not fulfill the lusts of the flesh"* (Gal. 5:16) and memorize them. Put them on cards and on the dash of your car if you're struggling with sexual sin. Feed your mind and your heart with the Word of God. Of course, we are always to **seek the Lord's help** in the area of our trials. NEVER think that you can handle it yourself!

> *"Watch and pray, lest you enter into temptation. The spirit indeed is willing, but the flesh is weak"* (Matt. 26:41).

CHAPTER 4

THE PROBLEM OF MONEY

A major subject in the Book of Proverbs is finances. Proverbs cuts across the grain of a lot of our practices concerning money. It attacks some things and encourages us in others. It shows us what's wrong as well as what's right. It is a book of contrasts.

The Bible is filled with instruction about money including a passage from Paul to Timothy to instruct churches about matters of church life—including money.

> *Godliness with contentment is great gain. For we brought nothing into this world, and it is certain we can carry nothing out. And having food and clothing, with these we shall be content.*

> *But those who desire to be rich fall into temptation and a snare, and into many foolish and harmful lusts which drown men in destruction and perdition. For the love of money is a root of all kinds of evil, for which some have strayed from the faith in their greediness and pierced themselves through with many sorrows.*

> *Command those who are rich in this present age not to be haughty, nor to trust in uncertain riches but in the living God, who gives us richly all things to enjoy. Let them do good, that they be rich in good works, ready to give, willing to share, storing up for themselves a good foundation for the time to come, that they may lay hold on eternal life* (I Tim. 6:6-10, 17-19).

There are three basic problems concerning money in the Book of Proverbs. There are three practical questions that Solomon put together for us. He was one of the wealthiest men of ancient times, so he had some experience in this area.

WHY DO YOU WANT IT?

Obviously, this is a question of motive. I want to deal with four areas.

It Is a Question of Values

There is one who makes himself rich, yet has nothing; And one who makes himself poor, yet has great riches (Prov. 13:7).

In this proverb, we see that he is dealing with more than material things. He is saying that material gain is not necessarily the real riches of a person's life. One who "makes himself rich" materially, but has nothing spiritually is poor. However, the person who gives away their material wealth can be wealthy spiritually.

That's true in terms of values according to the Lord's teaching, too. He told us to *"lose our lives"* for His sake. We're not to try to keep and protect them.

Better is a little with the fear of the Lord, Than great treasure with trouble. Better is a dinner of herbs [vegetables] *where love is, Than a fatted calf with hatred* (Prov. 15:16-17).

This means a great deal to me. First of all, one of our family members has decided to be a vegetarian, for the time being. I believe that a person can eat anything, but on his birthday, we eat vegetables in his honor. I like vegetables, but I also like other things. Nevertheless, a dinner of vegetables where love is, is better than prime rib! This is simple to understand.

Since money is a problem of values, we will see the word "better" used a number of times by Solomon to get us to see value.

Better is a little with righteousness, Than vast revenues without justice (Prov. 16:8).

A man who does right and is poor, is better off than a rich man who has compromised.

Better is a dry morsel with quietness, Than a house full of feasting with strife (Prov. 17:1).

> *Better is the poor who walks in his integrity Than one who is perverse in his lips, and is a fool* (Prov. 19:1).

It's always better to be poor and have integrity, than it is to have lots of money and lose your integrity and your walk with God.

> *He who loves pleasure will be a poor man; He who loves wine and oil will not be rich* (Prov. 21:17).

We're not talking about the oil that makes gasoline for our cars, we're talking about the luxurious aspects of a person's lifestyle. When you look at this, it is very interesting in terms of what is going on in today's society. *"He who loves pleasure will be a poor man."* Society has already taught us that.

In the modern workplace, pleasure is a main deal. It really is! It's a "bum trip" to go to work on Monday morning. It's great to check out on Friday, and all that you've earned between those days is supposed to bring you pleasure. It is supposed to give you the money to do the things you want to do to enjoy yourself. It is always tough to face the weekend without a lot of money to spend. That's today's philosophy!

I don't know where these ideas came from but they are a wrong concept. It doesn't represent America and its economic principles. It has grown in today's thinking, but the Bible says, *"He who loves pleasure will be a poor man."*

We ought to work just for the sheer joy of working. There are people who love work. That four-letter word is a good one! The Bible says that if you work, you will sleep well. "The sleep of a laboring man is sweet whether he eats little or much," I like to say.

> *A good name is to be chosen rather than great riches* (Prov. 22:1).

Again, we see values here. We are to value a good name more than we value wealth.

> *By humility and the fear of the Lord Are riches and honor and life* (Prov. 22:4).

The Bible tells us how to have a rich life—*"by humility and the fear of the Lord."*

> *Better is the poor who walks in his integrity Than one perverse [twisted] in his ways, though he be rich* (Prov. 28:6).

Some people give you the idea that the epitome of American life is to be rich. They tell you how many people became millionaires last year. They have little charts in the newspaper and they write about the median income in different sections of the country. It is amazing to read of the wealth that is flowing into people's hands. You may be reading this and wondering who they are. Those who desire to be rich fall into a trap as surely as do the rich; be careful!

Why do we want to be rich? What is important to us? It is a question of values—always a question of values.

> *Two things I request of You (Deprive me not before I die): Remove falsehood and lies far from me; Give me neither poverty nor riches—Feed me with the food You prescribe for me; Lest I be full and deny You, And say, "Who is the Lord?" Or lest I be poor and steal, And profane the name of my God* (Prov. 30:7-9).

That is a fascinating analysis of values as it relates to money. We don't want to be so rich that we think we don't need the Lord. The rich often think it was their own ingenuity and their own talent that gave them their riches. God can take them away at any time! *"What do you have that you did not receive?"* asks I Corinthians 4:7. The obvious answer is, "Nothing!" *"Every good gift and every perfect gift is from above,"* James tells us (1:17).

The more money we get, the more we have a tendency to think, "I worked hard for this money. I did it!" Really! God could change the circumstances in our economy and show us that, in fact, no matter how hard you work, you may wind up being poor anyway.

Solomon also asked that he not be poor. He didn't want to be tempted to steal just in order to have something to eat. He's asking God to give him contentment. The issue of why we want money, is an issue of values.

It is a Question of Priorities

Here's where it gets tough. We hear people saying that money isn't everything ... but it's way ahead of whatever is second. That is not really funny, when we come to the Bible. When you decide how much you are going to give to the

Lord's work, it is definitely a matter of priorities—what's first?

> "Do not lay up for ourselves treaures on earth, where moth and rust destroy and where thieves break in and steal; but lay up for yourselves treasures in heaven, where neither moth nor rust destroys and where thieves do not break in and steal. For where your treasure is, there your heart will be also. The lamp of the body is the eye. If therefore your eye is good [healthy], your whole body will be full of light. But if your eye is bad, your whole body will be full of darkness. If therefore the light that is in you is darkness, how great is that darkness! No man can serve two masters; for either he will hate the one and love the other, or else he will be loyal to the one and despise the other. You cannot serve God and mammon [money]" (Matt. 6:19-24).

You cannot serve them both. When we talk about money, we have to ask why we want it. It is a question of values and it is also a question of priorities.

> The blessing of the Lord makes one rich, And He adds no sorrow with it (Prov. 10:22).

It is not talking about money here. Some people read it that way. In the "health/wealth" gospel of today, many people use this verse to prove their point. That's not talking about money at all! In fact, if you read other of Solomon's writings, he says that money brings a lot of sorrow with it. There are many problems in the whole issue of money. When you try to pay your bills and juggle the income with the bills on hand, you realize that it is the blessing of the Lord that makes us rich. We're wealthy, no matter how much money is in our bank accounts. It has nothing to do with how much we spend. *"The blessing of the Lord makes one rich, And He adds no sorrow with it."* We need this reminder as we work at managing our money. The blessing is what makes us rich. It is a question of priorities.

> Riches do not profit in the day of wrath, But righteousness delivers from death (Prov. 11:4).

This priority relates to eternal destiny. No matter how much money you have, you'll not buy your way out of God's judgment and His righteousness is the only thing that will deliver in that day of judgment. What a tremendous reminder to all of us! It is better to know where we're going to spend eternity than to know where we'll earn our next dollar.

It Is a Question of Security

Do you feel more secure with money in your pocket? When we ask why we want to have money, we must acknowledge that it is a matter of security. Sometimes, we just forget to bring our money with us. This is an embarrassment! We can feel very insecure, if we don't have any money on us.

There is the problem of our checkbook. Perhaps we have a negative balance and have mailed a check when we know the money isn't there to cover it. We just hope we'll get it to the bank before they charge us a fee. There's a feeling of insecurity in that!

If you have a nice fat saving account, you may get the feeling that everything's OK. Really? The elderly put away money to take care of themselves in their old age. Then, they find out that Medicare will only help you when you have $1800 dollars left. If you have any money, anywhere, they will take it. Money goes real fast when you're in a nursing home. Suddenly, you realize that it costs about $36,000 a year, if you have to stay there. If you have $80,000 saved, it will last about three years—that's all. Only then will Medicare help. This comes as a shock to most people.

With the "graying of America", we have a massive problem in our society. I've seen people who saved money to enjoy their retirement find out that bad health stripped them of everything. This is reality.

Security is in the Lord. It is not in what you have! No matter how much money you've stored up, no matter what your investments or savings are, they can be stripped from you in a moment of time. Circumstances change. We need to know that our security is in the Lord Himself. He alone knows the sparrow that falls from the tree and He's promised to take care of us.

One lady lost all her money in a five-year period. She was left dependent on Medicare. I was talking to her about it and she said, "I'm happier than I have ever been in my life! I haven't got a dime! When they come around with the cart, I don't even have the money to buy a candy bar, and I don't want any. It is so exciting to see how God provides for me!"

Be honest with yourself about money. Why do you want it? It's a question of security.

> *He who trusts in his riches will fall, But the righteous will flourish like foliage* (Prov. 11:28).

> *Command those who are rich in this present age not to be haughty, nor to trust in uncertain riches but in the living God* (I Tim. 6:17).

We must never think that wealth gives us security. No! the Lord gives us security.

It Is a Question of Greed

If you asked the average person if they are greedy, they would say, "No." They would talk about someone else who they think is greedy. Greed is prevalent in all the marketplace, but it is not easy to face. It is evident in business deals. Some people like to "wheel and deal". Making business deals is a hard thing to do. A moment of greed can creep in at one tiny moment. It can happen to any of us.

> *So are the ways of everyone who is greedy for gain; It takes away the life of its owners* (Prov. 1:19).

When greed gets in your heart, it will strip you of the life God wants you to have. I Timothy says it will cause many problems, it will destroy your soul! That's what it says. *"The love of money is the root of all kinds of evil which some have coveted after,"* says I Timothy 6. They are greedy.

> *He who is greedy for gain troubles his own house, But he who hates bribes will live* (Prov. 15:27).

Greed leads to bribery. The man who hates them, will live and his household will be blessed. If you get greedy, your whole family will suffer. You may say that you're only doing it for your family. Really!

We ought to go to work, just for the enjoyment of it! Some time we should tell our employer that we don't want to get paid that week, we just want to work. He might have a heart attack, and we could get his job! People don't believe that can happen!

> *Do not overwork to be rich; Because of your own understanding, cease! Will you set your eyes on that*

which is not? For riches certainly make themselves
wings; They fly away like an eagle toward heaven
(Prov. 23:4-5).

Don't spend your energy trying to get rich. If God wants
you to be rich, He will work it out for you. Enjoy your work
and never exert another ounce of energy trying to get rich.
Those who desire that, plunge themselves into many hurtful things. It is a question of greed.

A faithful man will abound with blessings, But he
who hastens to be rich will not go unpunished (Prov.
28:20).

A man with an evil eye hastens after riches, And
does not consider that poverty will come upon him
(Prov. 28:22).

Such a man thinks money will solve everything. The improper use of money leads to money troubles. Sometimes
then people are dominated by their apparent need for money.
That isn't the solution. It's sad but true, that when money
problems dominate a Christian's heart, it is very hard to concentrate on spiritual riches. It takes over your mind every
day and you think that the solution is to have more money.
That's not the solution. We need to learn to be content when
we don't have anything and to be content when we have a
lot (see Phil 4:11-13).

It is a question of **values, priorities, security and greed**
—that's why we want money.

WHAT DID YOU DO TO GET IT?

Proverbs asks a series of questions on this subject. Let's
ask ourselves these questions, too.

Did You Inherit It?

Houses and riches are an inheritance from fathers
(Prov. 19:14).

If you leave something for your family, do you wonder if
they will remember that they got it from you. I've heard
enough family squabbles over inheritances to make me want
to throw up. It's a dangerous thing. It's a very difficult thing.

I've read a lot about it, but it seems to me that when we inherit something that we didn't work for, it damages us in
some way. You may disagree with me and you may be a good
steward of an inheritance. However, after what I've seen, I
think I'd rather see everything I've accumulated go to the
Lord's work after basic needs are met. I believe my children
would be hurt by receiving an inheritance.

I came to this conclusion one day when I sat down to
receive the inheritance of my own parents. I decided that I
didn't want to take it. I didn't want anything to do with it.
It's interesting that the government has decided to take it
anyway! "The Lord giveth and the government taketh away!"
Medical bills have taken all my parents had. Then, you realize that you need to "parent" your parents.

It is sad that many people do not understand that role.
Your parents took care of you all during your days of growing up and one day you may have to return the favor in a
way you never dreamed possible.

When you receive an inheritance, you didn't do anything
to get it! To show us how important this is, the next line says,
"A prudent wife is from the Lord." The *"prudent wife"* knows
that it is better to have the Lord's riches than to have earthly riches. That kind of a woman truly comes from the Lord!
It is a lot better to have a discerning wife than to have any
inheritance you could get.

> *An inheritance gained hastily at the beginning Will
> not be blessed at the end* (Prov. 20:21).

Here the Bible exposes us for going after an inheritance.
It reverts to the question of motive again. What did you do
to get your money? Did you inherit it?

Did You Take a Bribe?

We call them "deals" now, but they are bribes!

> *He who is greedy for gain troubles his own house,
> But he who hates bribes will live* (Prov. 15:27).

This is a tough one! People bribe me all the time. "Please
come and speak, and the honorarium is ...." Hold it! I don't
want to know. Over thirty years, I've never asked how much
the honorarium was. I've seen scores of Christian workers
that continually talk about what they will receive before they

come and minister. They've got to live! I know that. I believe in treating God's ministers well. It bothers me, none-the-less, when ministers ask about honorariums. We'd better clean up our act! God's in charge of blessings!

It's the same as taking a bribe when you require a certain amount before you'll accept an engagement. I don't have a fee. I've never had one and I don't intend to get one. I don't want to think that way. Everyone has to decide what they're going to do about this. Even in the Christian world we find this all the time.

I walked into a store, a Christian bookstore, and the owner offered me a ten percent discount because I am a minister. I suggested he charge me ten percent more to make up for it. I told him that a lot of laymen need the discount more than preachers do. I'm not real popular in some places!

> A wicked man accepts a bribe behind the back [under cover] To pervert the ways of justice (Prov. 17:23).

Is it a gift or a bribe? Is it offered because someone loves you?

> A gift in secret pacifies anger, And a bribe behind the back, strong wrath (Prov. 21:14).

There's quite a bit of difference between a bribe and an actual gift. If you give it, you aren't expecting anything in return. If you're bribing someone, there's something you want—that's why you gave it.

Did You Borrow it?

> The rich rules over the poor, And the borrower is servant to the lender (Prov. 22:7).

Some people think you should never get a loan at all, even if you can make the payments. I don't see it that way myself, but I do believe that if you borrow, you should be able to pay. I also think it's dangerous to borrow if your liabilities are greater than your assets. That to me, is debt.

This verse in Proverbs tells us what we face when we borrow. In a sense, we are servant to the one who loans us money. God wants us to be free to confront, and witness and speak openly without problems that arise when we borrow money.

One pastor I met got into terrible problems because he borrowed money. He had to move! Even his church loaned him money, time after time, and he couldn't repay it. He was in serious trouble. He was ruined. No matter who you are, the borrower is servant to the lender—no matter what!

Did You Steal It?

There is tremendous stealing going on in the business world. Workers take things home that belong to the company. It's an enormous problem in society.

> *Wealth gained by dishonesty will be diminished,*
> *But he who gathers by labor will increase* (Prov. 13:11).

Kids are stealing money from their parents' purses and wallets. This is a terrible problem!

> *Whoever robs his father or his mother, And says, "It is no transgression," The same is companion to a destroyer* (Prov. 28:24).

God has no sympathy for this whatsoever. Ephesians 4:28 says, *"Let him who stole steal no longer, but rather let him labor, working with his hands what is good, that he may have something to give him who has need."*

Did You Take Advantage of Someone?

> *He who oppresses the poor reproaches his Maker, But he who honors Him has mercy on the needy* (Prov. 14:31).

Did you oppress the poor? I called up a religious organization one day that made it their practice to visit widows to get money from them for their organization. They nailed my mother, so I called them. I gave them a day to get it straightened out. They gave her money back. In the process, they realized that what they were doing was not right and I've been able to teach them on this subject. God has terrible things to say to those who take advantage of folks—especially the elderly.

> *Bread gained by deceit is sweet to a man, But afterward his mouth will be filled with gravel* (Prov. 20:17).

Getting treasures by a lying tongue Is the fleeting fantasy of those who seek death (Prov. 21:6).

He who oppresses the poor to increase his riches, And he who gives to the rich, will surely come to poverty (Prov. 22:16).

Do not rob the poor because he is poor, Nor oppress the afflicted at the gate for the Lord will plead their cause, And plunder the soul of those who plunder them (Prov. 22:22-23).

A poor man who oppresses the poor Is like a driving rain which leaves no food (Prov. 28:3).

One who increases his possessions by usury and extortion Gathers it for him who will pity the poor (Prov. 28:8).

Did You Work For It?

He who deals with a slack hand becomes poor, But the hand of the diligent makes one rich (Prov. 10:4).

God blesses diligence! God blesses work! Employers tell me that one of the big problems in business is getting employees who will work. Everybody is trying to get out of work. That should never be said of Christians.

He who tills his land will be satisfied with bread, But he who follows frivolity is devoid of understanding (Prov. 12:11).

If a Christian and a non-believer are working side by side, at the same salary, the Christian should excel every time!

The hand of the diligent will rule, But the slothful will be put to forced labor (Prov. 12:24).

The slothful man does not roast what he took in hunting, but diligence is man's precious possession (Prov. 12:27).

> *The soul of the sluggard desires, and has nothing; But the soul of the diligent shall be made rich* (Prov. 13:4).

> *The desire of the slothful kills him, For his hands refuse to labor. He covets greedily all day long, But the righteous gives and does not spare* (Prov. 21:25-26).

The righteous labors so he has busy hands and he is in a position to give.

> *He who tills his land will have plenty of bread, But he who follows frivolity will have poverty enough!* (Prov. 29:19).

There are many verses on this subject. Those are only a few. We need to have diligence in our work.

HOW DO YOU INTEND TO USE IT?

To Provide For Your Family

I Timothy 5:8 says that if a man does not provide for his family, he is denying the faith and is worse than an infidel.

I Timothy 6:6-8 says to be content if we have food and clothing.

> *Be diligent to know the state of your flocks, And attend to your herds; For riches are not forever, Nor does a crown endure to all generations. When the hay is removed, and the tender grass shows itself, and the herbs of the mountains are gathered in, The lambs will provide your clothing, And the goats the price of a field; You shall have enough goats' milk for your food, For the food of your household, And the nourishment of your maidservants* (Prov. 27:23-27).

To Pay Your Debts

> *Do not withhold good from those to whom it is due, When it is in the power of your hand to do so. Do not say to your neighbor, "Go, and come back, And tomorrow I will give it," When you have it with you* (Prov. 3:27-28).

The goal of believers should be to get out of debt. Very clearly, we are to pay those to whom we are in debt. Because of this, I think there is an order to paying your bills. The first check is to be the "firstfruits" offering to the Lord. The next check is to pay your debts instead of postponing payment. There will be a freedom in what you have left.

Credit cards have given us the opportunity to buy a lot of things we want even when we couldn't afford them. We carry those charges over every month. Make it a goal in your life and in your family to pay those off every month. If you don't pay it and there is a finance charge, pay it and understand you are in debt at that point.

In terms of liquid cash and what you make, you are unable to pay what you owe. Companies want you to be in debt. They make money off the finance charges. When you pay it off, they will offer you more and more credit cards.

We may not want to deal with this, but when we pay our debts, it gives us great freedom to function. Don't let things ride and do other things you want to do.

Pay your debts!

To Acquire Friends

Some of you are going to say that we can't buy friends. But we can! We keep fighting this, but the Lord blesses us for giving a gift in secret, and we'll acquire a friend! I think you know what I mean, but let's take a look at Scripture.

> *The poor man is hated even by his own neighbor, But the rich has many friends* (Prov. 14:20).

That may seem negative in your mind, but it is stated as a simple fact in Scripture. The rich man will surely think about why people want to be his friend.

> *Wealth makes many friends, But the poor is separated from his friend* (Prov. 19:4).

> *Many entreat the favor of the nobility, And every man is a friend to one who gives gifts. All the brothers of the poor hate him; How much more do his friends go far from him! He may pursue them with words, yet they abandon him* (Prov. 19:6-7).

The Bible isn't encouraging this; it is stating facts. The admonition to do this *"as unto the Lord"* isn't there!

And I say to you, make friends for yourselves by unrighteous [no spiritual quality to it] *mammon, that when you fail* [or it fails], *they may receive you into everlasting habitations* (Lk. 16:9).

In the vernacular, this says that people will be glad to see you in heaven if you have used your money to make friends. There will be a tie between friends, even in heaven, because of a gift given when a person needed it. Jesus taught that!

To Help People Who Are in Need

Every Christian should be sensitive to people who are in need. Of course, there are those who will rip you off. Of course, there are people who won't work. We're not to support them! Care for the homeless needs to be carefully analyzed because some want that role since they don't want to work. If they won't work, they should not eat, that's what the Bible says. It's hard for Christians to think that way. This is a serious problem. Nevertheless, we are to help those who are really in need.

He who oppresses the poor reproaches his Maker, But he who honors Him has mercy on the needy (Prov. 14:31).

If you honor the Lord in your life, then you are going to have mercy and compassion on people who are in need.

He who mocks the poor reproaches his Maker; He who is glad at calamity will not go unpunished (Prov. 17:5).

He who has pity on the poor lends to the Lord, And He will pay back what he has given (Prov. 19:17).

Whoever shuts his ears to the cry of the poor Will also cry himself and not be heard (Prov. 21:13).

The rich and the poor have this in common, The Lord is the maker of them all (Prov. 22:2).

He who has a bountiful eye will be blessed, For he gives of his bread to the poor (Prov. 22:9)

He who gives to the poor will not lack, But he who hides his eyes will have many curses (Prov. 28:27).

The righteous considers the cause of the poor, But the wicked does not understand such knowledge (Prov. 29:7).

The Bible teaches in Old and New Testament that we are to work to have money, and to give to those who have need.

To Honor the Lord

Honor the Lord with your possessions [everything you own], *And with the firstfruits of all your increase; So your barns will be filled with plenty, And your vats will overflow with new wine* (Prov. 3:9-10).

Here is the principle: You cannot outgive the Lord. It cannot be done. It is fun to watch how money passes from hand to hand as we give it. The moment you stop the process and start loading up for yourself, everything changes. You cannot outgive the Lord.

There are people who are giving money that they need to live on. You may know someone who does that, but it's rare. They need to take care of their basic needs. They ought to feed and clothe their children. I'll tell them that. That isn't our major problem, however.

We need to learn to honor the Lord by the way we give. A lot of us are having financial difficulties because we are not honoring the Lord with the firstfruits of our substance. We tend to think the church is on a crusade to get money. That's not what the Bible says! The church always needs money; that's obvious! The **motivation for us to give** to the Lord, however, is far from that! We aren't to give because of the **need**; we're to **give with joyful hearts**, as unto the Lord! We're to **give in order to honor the Lord!**

We're going to stand before Him one day and we will answer to Him. God promises to bless us when we give. He says, "Give, and it will be given to you" in abundance. I'd like to challenge you to outgive the Lord!

Is there joy in your heart? Give to the Lord!

CHAPTER 5

THE PROBLEM OF FRIENDS

There have been many descriptions of friends and many books have been written on the subject. One book said, "A friend is one who knows all about you and still will be seen in public with you." I like that. "A friend is someone who doesn't mind that you didn't call before you dropped by their house."

The words, *"friend," "companion,"* and *"neighbor"* are translated from six different Hebrew words. A friend can be someone you love, depend upon, associate with, work with, or simply be someone who lives near you. The most common Hebrew word is used 42 times in the Old Testament as *"friend"* but 104 times as *"neighbor".* The same thing happens in the Proverbs where the same Hebrew word is sometimes translated *"friend",* sometimes *"neighbor".* In Proverbs the word, *"friend,"* appears 13 times; the word, *"neighbor,"* appears 19 times.

What you see is that Proverbs talks a lot about friends. Abraham was called *"the friend of God"* (James 2:23). Being a friend to the world is condemned strongly in James 4:4. You can't be a friend to God and a friend to the world.

Thank God! Jesus is the friend of sinners! He was criticized for that. If you befriend sinners, maybe you will be criticized for it, too.

> *Two are better than one, Because they have a good reward for their labor. For if they fall, one will lift up his companion* [friend]. *But woe to him who is alone when he falls, For he has no one to help him up. Again, if two lie down together, they will keep warm; But how can one be warm alone? Though one may be overpowered by another, two can withstand him. And a threefold cord is not quickly broken* (Eccl. 4:9-12).

Some people think this last phrase refers to a person having two friends, but that's not it. It means that when you have a friend, you are as strong as a three-fold cord.

We could probably analyze friendship as many books do and see it as being close to someone, or intimate. However, I decided we'd go straight into the Word of God and ask ourselves what **insights, instructions** and **ingredients** of true friendship the Bible teaches.

INSIGHTS ABOUT FRIENDSHIP

There are four things I want us to see. Ecclesiastes (in the verses above) tells us the same thing that Proverbs tells us.

We All Need Friends

A lot of people think they don't need friends; however, God says that we all need friends. It doesn't matter whether you think you need them or not, God says you do.

People are Friends Because of Money and Gifts

You may think that's awful. You may react negatively or positively to this statement. However, no matter how you react to it, this is a fact of life. Proverbs reports it,

> *The poor man is hated even by his own neighbor,*
> *But the rich has many friends* (Prov. 14:20).

If you feel you're poor, you won't like this. Proverbs simply reports on a fact of human nature. We become friends quickly when money or gifts are shared.

> *Wealth makes many friends, But the poor is*
> *separated from his friend* (Prov. 19:4).

When wealth has been given to someone, that person becomes a friend. Then, even when wealth runs out, they often give back to the person who gave to them. So the history of friendship tells us that it is not contingent on the wealth. The attitude that wealth does not make "real" friends, is not true.

Don't just think of the homeless. This proverb may mean the *"poor"* as someone who is not intending to give a gift. Perhaps the fact that a person is not willing to share, and will not give gifts, is the reason he doesn't have friends. That is very definitely a possibility here.

> *Many entreat the favor of the nobility, And every*
> *man is a friend to one who gives gifts. All the brothers*
> *of the poor hate him; How much more do his friends*

*go far from him! He may pursue them with words, yet
they abandon him* (Prov. 19:6- 7).

The idea is that someone needs financial help and this
person is only willing to give them words.

*Whoever has this world's goods, and sees his
brother in need, and shuts up his heart from him, How
does the love of God abide in him?* (I Jn. 3:17).

*If a brother or sister is naked and destitute of daily
food, and one of you says to them, "Depart in peace,
be warmed and filled," but you do not give them the
things which are needed for the body, what does it
profit?* (James 2:15-16).

If we can back off the attitude that people "buy" friends,
we can recognize that it is just the normal human behavior
to be friends with someone who gives to you, who is generous
to you, who doesn't hesitate to help you in time of need.

Brothers and sisters in the Lord need to be more generous
with each other. If you have a need right now, you will agree
with this! Most of us are uptight about making ends meet
in our own homes; we have more month than money. But
Proverbs says that the generous man is going to be blessed
mightily of the Lord. If we are willing to give of what we have,
God is going to bless us.

*He [Jesus] said, "Make friends for yourselves by
unrighteous mammon, that when you fail, they may
receive you into everlasting habitations* (Lk. 16:9).

Money (*"mammon"*) is not sinful; it has no moral character. *"When you fail"* refers to when the money runs out.
"They" means those that knew your generosity. To put it into
the vernacular, "Be generous so that people will be happy to
see you in heaven because they remember what you did on
earth to help them."

Whether this is bad or good, it is an insight into
friendship. You build bridges into people's lives when you
are generous with them. Don't knock it—just understand
that it is crucial to friendship.

Too Many Friends Can Be a Problem

Some people are namedroppers, and sometimes this can
get amusing. People are hungry for friendship and they will

do deceitful things because of it. They will claim to be friends with people even when they hardly know them.

But too many friends can be a problem, too. The extremes are both found in Proverbs 18.

> *A man who isolates himself seeks his own desire*
> (verse 1).

> *A man who has friends must himself be friendly*
> *But there is a friend who sticks closer than a brother*
> (verse 24).

That last verse is the most troublesome verse in the Hebrew language because the first phrase has only three words; it says, *"Many friends ruin."* It's amazing that out of those three words, they got, *"A man who has friends must himself be friendly."* What most people believe is that the translators couldn't believe that a man could have too many friends, so they came up with this translation. It's good advice—if you want to have friends, be friendly. But that's not what the verse says!

It says that many friends are an emotional drain on your life and can ruin it, but there is a friend (singular) who sticks closer than a brother. That's good wisdom. If you want a real close friend, be careful about trying to have too many "real close friends". Too many of this kind of friends, drain you and you can't apply that kind of friendship in time of need, when you want to.

You can have many social acquaintances. Sociologists tell us that you will be well acquainted with a maximum of approximately two hundred people, but some people can have over a thousand acquaintances. You can know that many people, know their names and addresses and recall something about them. That's a possibility, especially for some who are people oriented in business. To be well acquainted, we can only handle about two hundred people or it will drive us crazy. For intimate, close friends, we need to have less than ten—some people say only two or three people, max.

Some of us aren't willing to spend the time with one person to build a close friendship. We scatter our shots to the point that we have many associations which we call "friends". In a time of crisis, that doesn't meet our need.

People Want to Be Friends With Those Who Are Sincere and Kind

He who loves purity of heart And has grace on his lips, The king will be his friend (Prov. 22:11).

People want to be friends with those who are sincere and who speak kindly. It goes so far as to use hyperbole and say that *"even a king"* would want to be friends with that kind of person. Such a person doesn't have a hidden agenda.

There is a problem here with those who are salespeople. I understand the problem, in that they want to be your friend; however, when you know what they want, suddenly, you're not all that thrilled about being their friend. I like it when a person is "up front" about this.

One man said he wanted to be my friend, but he was in the business of selling items that are needed in the ministry. He told me that he didn't even want to consider the things he sells in order for us to be friends. Later he said, "Of course, if you have any needs...." We smile about this, but it's true that when people have another agenda, it makes friendship difficult.

A person who comes into your life with *"purity of heart"*— no agenda at all—is the one who is desirable as a friend. And if he *"has grace on his lips"* and speaks kindly and tenderly, you want to be with him! This is a very simple insight into friendship.

INSTRUCTION ABOUT FRIENDSHIP

God has given us instruction about friends. Some of it is kind of simple and some of it is heavy duty.

Love Your Friends

It is interesting that we are told over and over, in both the Old Testament and the New, to love our friends. *"Love your neighbor as yourself"* uses the same word, "friend". What is wrong with us, when we want to have friends, and do nothing to show it? *"Love your friends,"* the Bible repeats over and over again. Everything God says about loving people is to be applied here. In Matthew, we have a discussion of God's law. A young man came to Jesus and asked how to have eternal life. In the middle of it, Jesus quoted the Ten Commandments:

> *"'Honor your father and your mother,' and 'You*
> *shall love your [friend] as yourself"* (Matt. 19:19).

Exactly how much should we love our friends? *"Just like you love yourself,"* the Bible says. Ephesians 5:29 says, *"No one ever hated his own flesh, but nourishes and cherishes it, just as the Lord does the church."* You don't hate yourself; you love yourself and take care of yourself! "Do the same for your friends," the Bible tells us.

A lawyer came to Jesus and asked what the greatest commandment of the Law is. Jesus answer was,

> *"'You shall love the Lord your God with all your*
> *heart, with all your soul, and with all your mind.' This*
> *is the first and great commandment. And the second*
> *is like it: 'You shall love your neighbor as yourself.'*
> *On these two commandments hang all the Law and*
> *the Prophets"* (Matt. 22:37-39).

So, the first instruction from God about our friends is that we are to love them.

Don't Forsake Them When There is a Need

About the best way to lose a friend is to fail to be there when there is a time of need.

> *Do not forsake your own friend or your father's*
> *friend, Nor go to your brother's house in the day of*
> *your calamity; For better is a neighbor* [a friend] *near-*
> *by than a brother far away* (Prov. 27:10).

I don't know about you, but I happen to have some friends who I believe are better friends to me than my blood relatives. It is wonderful to have a blood relative who is also a close friend; however, most of us do not experience that.

My brother is a missionary in Africa and, because we both understand the problems of the distance, we joke about how little good we are to each other. We both know that a friend nearby, in a time of need, is more helpful than a faraway relative.

Choose Them Carefully

This third instruction about friends is very important because this is where we get into trouble.

*The righteous should choose his friends carefully,
For the way of the wicked leads them astray* (Prov.
12:26).

No matter how strong you are in the Lord, if you have
wicked friends, they are going to lead you astray. The Bible
is very clear about this. Young people who hit the campus
need to remember this—choose your friends carefully! Don't
just desire to be in the "in" crowd. Be careful who you choose
for your friends.

*He who walks with wise men will be wise, But the
companion* [the friend] *of fools will be destroyed* (Prov.
13:20).

Learn to walk with people who are wise and don't hang
around with people who are given to foolishness and wickedness.

*A perverse man sows strife, And a whisperer
separates the best of friends. A violent* [angry] *man
entices his neighbor, And leads him in a way that is
not good* (Prov. 16:28-29).

Once again, choose your friends carefuly. If you're
whispering about that friend, you're destroying that
friendship.

The soul of the wicked desires evil; His neighbor
[friend] *finds no favor in his eyes* (Prov. 21:10).

Kids get involved with friends they don't really want to be
around. Then, someone in the group does something evil,
and if they're caught, they discover there is no friendship
there at all. If a person wants to lead you into wickedness,
they are not a real friend. Don't hang around them.

*Make no friendship with an angry man, And with
a furious man do not go, Lest you learn his ways And
set a snare* [a trap] *for your soul* (Prov. 22:24).

Choose your friends carefully!

*Do not be deceived: "Evil company corrupts good
morals"* (I Cor. 15:33).

All of us need to recognize that there are people who only
want to do wickedness—they are setting a trap for us. Their
ways will lead us into sinful actions, if we stick with them.

Don't Look Down on Them

The moment you start looking down on your friend, you
have hurt your friendship.

> *The poor man is hated even by his own neighbor*
> [friend], *But the rich has many friends. He who
> despises* [looks down on] *his neighbor sins; But he
> who has mercy on the poor, happy is he* (Prov. 14:20-
> 21).

What a good balance! Any attitude of condescension is a
sin and it hurts the friendship you have with those people.

Don't Betray Their Confidence

> *He who covers a transgression seeks love, But he
> who repeats a matter separates the best of friends*
> (Prov. 17:9).

Those of us who have close friends often know something
about that friend that might hurt them. We know when they
failed. We know about the times they've blown it. *"He who
covers a transgression seeks love."* When you decide to tell
the whole world about their fault, you've decided against
being their friend.

When you repeat something that has been told you in
confidence, you are going to lose that friend no matter how
good a friendship you have had. That doesn't mean that we
sweep sin under the rug, but it does mean that we try to help
and we don't share a friend's secret with others.

Don't Accuse Them Without Cause

> *Do not be a witness against your* [friend] *without
> cause, For would you deceive with your lips? Do not
> say, "I will do to him just as he has done to me; I will
> render to the man according to his work"* (Prov. 24:28-
> 29).

That's not friendship! Don't do it!

> *Do not go hastily to court; For what will you do in
> the end, When your [friend] has put you to shame?
> Debate your case with your [friend] himself, And do*

not disclose the secret to another; Lest he who hears it expose your shame, And your reputation be ruined (Prov. 25:8-10).

A man who bears false witness against his [friend] Is like a club, a sword, and a sharp arrow (Prov. 25:18).

You're not blessing him; you're beating him over the head! Be careful! Don't accuse your friends without cause. You're going to lose your friendship the moment you do that. Sometimes we make an accusation in ordinary conversation and it becomes an attack on somebody. That hurts friendship.

Don't Overstay Your Welcome

Seldom set foot in your [friend's] house, Lest he become weary of you and hate you (Prov. 25:17).

Dropping in too often can end a good friendship.

Don't Guarantee Their Debts

My son, if you become surety [a guarantee] for your friend, If you have shaken hands in pledge for a stranger, You are snared by the words of your own mouth; You are taken by the words of your mouth, So do this, my son, and deliver yourself; For you have come into the hand of your friend: Go and humble yourself; Plead with your friend. Give no sleep to your eyes, Nor slumber to your eyelids. Deliver yourself like a gazelle from the hand of the hunter, And like a bird from the hand of the fowler (Prov. 6:1-5).

It is possible to give illustration after illustration of the point of these verses. It is not rare among Christians. These are things commonly found in churches and among other Christian friends. We'd better pay attention to these instructions about friendship found in the Word of God.

I don't know how many people have borrowed money from a friend and lived to regret it. Sometimes they can't pay it back or something else happens and they are sorry they ever got into that situation. Aren't friends supposed to care? Yes! But don't guarantee their debts; give them money to pay them off. Many of us get into situations that destroy our friendships with each other.

In the Old Testament, Jews could not charge each other interest and I think that's a good principle to apply to Christians. If you loan someone money, don't charge interest. That's what I believe. Don't make money off your Christian friends by charging them interest. The Bible warns against that. A lot of us don't see the danger and get trapped by it.

Don't loan money for interest and if you already have done it, get out of it! This is a very difficult situation if you want to keep your friendship going. The Bible says whoever borrows becomes a servant to the lender. It hinders close friendship whether you can see it or not.

Should we ever borrow money from a friend? It is a good idea never to do this. If you have loaned money to a friend, don't charge interest. If we loan money to a Christian friend in time of need, we should not expect to get it back.

If you have borrowed money, be sure you pay it back or the Lord is going to judge you deeply. You're going to pay a terrible price for not paying your debts. You are to pay your debts. "Owe no man anything" except to love one another. It's two-fold: Don't expect to get it back but pay it back, if you are the borrower.

Just the faithfulness of someone paying on a debt has caused many Christians I know to say, "I cancel your debt." Some people don't understand this about Christians. Many who loan people money to help them aren't interested in getting the money back, but they are interested that borrower's character be demonstrated by paying it back.

A man devoid of understanding shakes hands in a pledge, And becomes [guarantee] *for his friend* (Prov. 17:18).

Some Bible teachers don't believe in co-signing. We have a debt-oriented society. We are so used to debt that it's very hard for us to see the principles in Proverbs. We should work like crazy to get out of debt. Your assets may be much greater than your liabilities and so you just owe a lot, but you are not in debt unless something goes wrong.

The Bible speaks about the *"uncertainty of riches"*. If there is a crisis, we don't know what will happen to our ability to pay. We don't really know if a friend will pay back his debt or not, but there is the subtle tendency in all of our hearts to get out of our problems—not pay off our debts. Pay your debts! Try to get out of debt! That's a principle.

If you have the Lord's means and you decide to help some- one, don't tie it up—give it! If it's a loan, don't worry about its being paid back. All you want to do is to encourage the borrower's integrity to pay it back. If you need to have the money back, don't loan it in the first place. Some of us are confused because we don't know how to straighten out the things we've already done.

I've spent a lot of years, shoveling money back and forth, between myself and many friends, and I am convinced that it's always better to give it than to loan it. If a brother is in need, don't offer a loan; give him what he needs. "Give, and it shall be given to you."

Be careful about debt, borrowing, loans, co-signing, etc. Don't do it! Just give what you can.

Show Concern About How You Are Perceived and Received

> He who blesses his friend with a loud voice, rising early in the morning, It will be counted a curse to him (Prov. 27:14).

If you call early with a bright greeting, don't expect to be appreciated! A lot of us are not sensitive about these things. We're like a bull in a china shop. Our attitudes are wrong. We do the wrong thing. We need to show concern about how our friends receive what we offer. If we're doing something that's irritating to them, it can be changed.

Be humble in your attitude towards your friends.

INGREDIENTS OF TRUE FRIENDSHIP

There are five words that will cause you to be a true friend to others. It is better to be a friend than to have one.

Friendship Includes Counsel

Friendship is not just hanging around together. True friendship is composed of counsel.

> Ointment and perfume delight the heart, And the sweetness of a man's friend does so by hearty coun- sel (Prov. 27:9).

"Hearty counsel" means "counsel of the heart." Not just counsel that is a walking information booth, but someone who has a heart for you. This kind of counsel says, "I love you and this will help you to be more effective for the Lord." This is not judgmental, but encouraging counsel.

> As iron sharpens iron, So a man sharpens the countenance of his friend (Prov. 27:17).

This is the same message. If you really are a person's friend, you are going to do what you can to help them to be more effective in their life for the Lord.

Friendship Includes Confrontation

This is not done out of anger or grabbing your friend by the collar. Sometimes the most difficult way to express your love to someone is to confront them.

> The first one to plead his cause seems right, Until his friend comes and examines him (Prov. 18:17).

> Open rebuke is better than love carefully concealed. Faithful are the wounds of a friend, But the kisses of an enemy are deceitful (Prov. 27:5-6).

We ought to memorize these verses. Sometimes, a real friend has to be confronted. We don't want to hurt them, but we have to confront them. When we say "Give counsel", we usually mean to encourage them. However, when we say "confront", we obviously mean that something is wrong.

It could be a small thing—like a crooked tie or a button that isn't buttoned. Friends will tell you things that no one else will tell you. Friends will offer you a breath mint!

Friendship Includes Closeness

I love that word! A friendship includes closeness.

> [Too many friends bring ruin], But there is a friend that sticks closer than a brother (Prov. 18:24).

Many people have applied that to Jesus and it is certainly true, but that is really LESS than what Jesus is. It is talking about a human being who is really special.

Closeness means that you can share whatever you want to share and know that your friend will receive it in the right spirit and do what he can to help you. It means that you aren't hiding from your friend. You have transparency, openness, honesty between you. A lot of people who are married aren't best friends. There is little counsel or confrontation that happens between spouses sometimes. If it does, things break out in open hostility and war. There is very little closeness in some marriages today.

Friendship Includes Compassion

Jesus told a story about a man who went down from Jerusalem to Jericho and he fell among thieves.

> "A certain man went down from Jerusalem to Jericho, and fell among thieves, who stripped him of his clothing, wounded him, and departed, leaving him half dead. Now by chance a certain priest came down that road. And when he saw him, he passed by on the other side. Likewise a Levite, when he arrived at the place, came and looked, and passed by on the other side. But a certain Samaritan, as he journeyed, came where he was. And when he saw him, he had compassion on him, and went to him and bandaged his wounds, pouring on oil and wine; and he set him on his own animal, brought him to an inn, and took care of him. On the next day, when he departed, he took out two denarii, gave them to the innkeeper, and said to him, 'Take care of him; and whatever more you spend, when I come again, I will repay you.' So which of these three do you think was friend to him who fell among the thieves?"
>
> And he said, "He who showed mercy on him." Then Jesus said to him, "Go and do likewise." (Luke 10:25-37).

Do you want to be a friend? Good! You'll need compassion. When you friend has a need, do something about it.

Friendship Includes Consistency

Friends are never short-term.

> A friend loves at all times, And a brother is born for adversity (Prov. 17:17).

It doesn't build your friendship if you're uncaring when your friend's dog dies. "Call somebody else!" you tell him. "But you're my friend," he'll say. "I don't like dogs. Call somebody who cares about dogs. I've got things to do," you might say. I'm exaggerating this, but I think it happens too frequently. We lose our friendship and we don't understand what happened.

You're in trouble when a friend comes to you and you don't do anything about his adversity. *"A brother is born for [the moment of] adversity."* That's what friendship is all about. That's why we need friends—to help us in our hour of crisis and need.

Sometimes our friends are "up" and so much fun to be with, but sometimes they are "down" and it's tough to hang around them. *"A friend loves at all times."* Sometimes your friend is laughing; sometimes he's crying; sometimes he's mad. Sometimes your friend may have his act together. Other times, he may not be able to get his act together and all he has is problems. That may be all he can talk about. *"A friend loves at all times."*

The interesting thing to me is that our Lord Jesus Christ is the best friend of all. Everything that is true friendship—He is! He is a constant, consistent, true friend. He counsels and confronts us when we need it, and He is closer to us than anyone else can be. *"He is in us and we are in Him"* and we can enjoy a close, intimate relationship with Him.

CHAPTER 6

THE PROBLEM OF MARRIAGE

Proverbs 31:10-31

Who can find a virtuous wife? For her worth is far above rubies. The heart of her husband safely trusts her; So he will have no lack of gain. She does him good and not evil All the days of her life. She seeks wool and flax, And willingly works with her hands. She is like the merchant ships, She brings her food from afar. She also rises while it is yet night, And provides food for her household, And a portion for her maidservants. She considers a field and buys it; From her profits she plants a vineyard. She girds herself with strength, And strengthens her arms. She perceives that her merchandise is good, And her lamp does not go out by night. She stretches out her hands to the distaff, And her hand holds the spindle. She extends her hand to the poor, Yes, she reaches out her hands to the needy. She is not afraid of snow for her household, For all her household is clothed with scarlet. She makes tapestry for herself; Her clothing is fine linen and purple. Her husband is known in the gates, When he sits among the elders of the land. She makes linen garments and sells them, And supplies sashes for the merchants. Strength and honor are her clothing; She shall rejoice in time to come. She opens her mouth with wisdom, And on her tongue is the law of kindness. She watches over the ways of her household, And does not eat the bread of idleness. Her children rise up and call her blessed; Her husband also, and he praises her: "Many daughters have done well, But you excel them all." Charm is deceitful and beauty is vain, But a woman who fears the Lord, she shall be praised. Give her of the fruit of her hands, And let her own works praise her in the gates.

How in the world do you find the right woman? Solomon was greatly influenced about this question. God had told him that if he wanted to be a successful king, he should watch three areas of his life—horses (armaments), money, and wives. These three were areas of warning. Too many armaments would cause Solomon to trust in his military power. Too much money would corrupt the hearts of the people and make them forget to rely on the Lord. Wives were a danger since they have such a great influence on a man.

> But King Solomon loved many foreign women, as well as the daughter of Pharaoh: women of the Moabites, Ammonites, Edomites, Sidonians, and Hittites- from the nations of whom the Lord had said to the children of Israel, "You shall not intermarry with them, nor they with you. For surely they will turn away your hearts after their gods." Solomon clung to these in love. And he had seven hundred wives, princesses, and three hundred concubines; and his wives turned away his heart. For it was so, when Solomon was old, that his wives turned his heart after other gods; and his heart was not loyal to the Lord his God, as was the heart of his father David. For Solomon went after Ashtoreth the goddess of the Sidonians, and after Milcom the abomination of the Ammonites. Solomon did evil in the sight of the Lord, and did not fully follow the Lord, as did his father David. Then Solomon built a high place for Chemosh the abomination of Moab, on the hill that is east of Jerusalem, and for Molech the abomination of the people of Ammon. And he did likewise for all his foreign wives, who burned incense and sacrificed to their gods (I Kings 11:1-8).

> And I find more bitter than death The woman whose heart is snares and nets, Whose hands are fetters [chains]. He who pleases God shall escape from her, But the sinner shall be taken by her. "Here is what I have found," says the Preacher, "Adding one thing to the other to find out the reason, Which my soul still seeks But I cannot find: One man among a thousand I have found, But a woman among all these I have not found. Truly, this only I have found: That God made man upright, But they have sought out many schemes" (Eccl. 7:26-29).

Obviously, this is not any woman's favorite passage and it doesn't bless them to say that God made man *"upright"* but women seek out *"many schemes"* which take man away from the Lord. Yet, there is a lesson to be learned. There is a problem in marriage. Many people's hearts and lives have been hurt by choosing the wrong person.

Sometimes, people wait too long to marry and they become desperate. Then, in a moment, they make a rash decision without giving place to the biblical principles. Once married, we are under a bondage, according to the Bible, that only death can sever. It is very important to consider who we are going to marry beforehand.

When Solomon was younger, he knew who his "one and only" was. It was Abishag who is mentioned in II Kings, chapters one and two. This poem in Proverbs 31 describes her. The opening question found in Proverbs 31 points out the problem of finding a partner who really loves the Lord.

The word *"virtuous"* might be confusing. It is a Hebrew word that refers to honor or integrity. It is used of men of valor who are trustworthy in battle. Integrity is probably the best translation. *"Who can find a woman of integrity?"* It refers to character—what she is inside, not what she looks like on the outside.

The same word is used of Ruth in Ruth 3:11 as Boaz discerned that Ruth was a woman of integrity—virtuous. She was virtuous because she didn't go after younger men. There is nothing wrong with going after men of your own age but Ruth chose to go after a man who was in a special place, with a special ministry which would involve them both in the future. So, Ruth ignored the opportunity to be with men of her own age and chose rather to go to Boaz who was a lot older than she was; however, he was in the Messianic line.

She had made a commitment, being a Moabitess, that she would follow the Lord God and Boaz saw that she didn't go after the handsome young men, but rather wanted to be a part of the Messianic hope. He concluded she was a *"virtuous woman"*. She had character—commitment to the Lord.

In Proverbs 31, we have a **romantic poem**, written to a woman who is a woman of integrity. A romantic poem doesn't rhyme in Hebrew, but it is an acrostic. There are twenty-two verses (vss. 10-31) and there are twenty-two letters in the Hebrew alphabet. The first letter is *"aleph"*—like our letter "a". In verse 10, the first word in the Hebrew language is a word that begins with the letter *"aleph"*. In verse 11, the first letter begins with *"beth"*, like "b" in English. It goes all the way down in the perfect order of the Hebrew alphabet.

What is the purpose of an acrostic? It helps us understand the problem of marriage and why it is so important for believers to comprehend the principle of spiritual integrity in their lives.

In Hebrew poetry, an acrostic has three purposes; one is **artistic.** It certainly is a beautiful thing. It is also found in Psalm 119 and in Lamentations. More than that, an acrostic poem describes the beauty of what is said. In Psalm 119, the beauty of God's Word is seen in an acrostic poem. In Proverbs, the inner beauty of a woman in marriage is seen by this acrostic poem.

An acrostic is also valuable as an **aid to memorize.** Jewish people love to have these aids for memorizing. Some of us do that, too. We play word games, and do picture associations to help us memorize. The Jews use an acrostic to remember which word comes in the order. It aids the memory. This acrostic in Proverbs 31, is designed to tell us, "Don't forget!"

The third thing about an acrostic is that the whole **alphabet is used.** It carries the idea of being comprehensive. We say the same thing, "... from A to Z." It includes everything. What is shown here is the marvelous completeness of what is described.

You have "superwoman" here. What a woman! She does everything right! She works night and day and always looks great, and her family looks great, too. Now before you revolt, just understand that an acrostic poem is comprehensive. God is looking at the total picture of what beauty is really all about.

Here are some other verses that use this word *"virtuous,"* *"excellent,"* or a *"woman of integrity."*

> An excellent [virtuous] *wife is the crown of her husband, But she who causes shame is like rottenness in his bones* (Prov. 12:4).

God commends this woman and says that a man's real reward in life, is a good woman. We may talk about all that we achieve, but the real prize of a man's life, is his wife. If you look at his wife, you will see that she is the *"crown of his life"*.

He who finds a wife finds a good thing, And obtains favor from the Lord (Prov. 18:22).

The question in Proverbs 31 was, *"Who can FIND a virtuous woman?"* Here Solomon uses the same word ... *"finds a wife...."* There is a connection in his mind.

Solomon was not against marriage—that's for sure! He didn't say, *"He who finds an excellent wife ...!"* He said that in Proverbs 31, but here he just says *"... a wife".* So, just to get married is a good thing, not bad. But we must think deeper than that. He's saying that when you obtain favor from the Lord by finding a wife, you are realizing that a woman of integrity is the Lord's tool to bring blessing into a man's life. Every woman does not do that, but the point is still strong.

Then, it takes it a step further and says, *"You will also obtain favor from the Lord."* You may not see yourself in Proverbs 31, but chapter 18 tells us that it can be you. There's not a woman of God anywhere in the world who cannot be the woman of Proverbs 31. Sometimes, we look at that and say, "I could never do all of that!" But the emphasis here is not on what she could do, but on her INWARD BEAUTY and INTEGRITY. Every woman who loves the Lord can be that. God can bless a man abundantly through the wife that he chooses. It is a very interesting principle.

Houses and riches are an inheritance from fathers, But a prudent wife is from the Lord (Prov. 19:14).

In order for a woman to be what is described in Proverbs, it must come from the Lord. No woman, no matter how wonderful, has the natural tendency to be all that God has in mind. Men don't either; we all need the Lord to be all that He meant for us to be. The point of this verse is powerful.

Houses and riches come to men without working—they come from their fathers. A good wife doesn't come because of anything a man can do, either. She comes from the Lord. The point is that, if you wind up with a woman like this, she came from the Lord. Understand that! The ingredient that makes her what God wants her to be is truly the Lord working in her life. That in turn, becomes a great blessing to the husband. What a blessing that can be.

THE VIRTUOUS WOMAN IS CONTRASTED
WITH THREE OTHERS

One way to learn what something is, is to show what it is not. The order of the Book of Proverbs is important. He places the poem at the end, but he sets you up for it all through the book. He keeps telling you about women who are not women of integrity so that you will understand what such a woman is all about. He contrasts this excellent woman with three others.

The Immoral Woman

He calls her *"immoral," "evil,"* and *"foolish"* in Proverbs. The issue here is moral integrity. He concentrates on a woman who really loves the Lord. What is true of the woman here, is also true of men. Most of us have trouble because we are looking at the outward appearance (see I Samuel 16:7). People can fool us by appearing kind and spiritual and yet, inside, they can be rotten.

Many of us who are married, have gotten far away from the Lord and are sloppy about caring for this part of our lives. We are not *"crowns"* to our spouses and are literally tearing them down ... along with ourselves. These admonitions are good for all of us.

> To deliver you from the immoral woman, From the seductress who flatters with her words, Who forsakes the companion of her youth, And forgets the covenant of her God (Prov. 2:16-17).

Moral integrity is rooted in commitment to the Lord. Look at that last phrase. The moment your commitment to the Lord gets weak, your commitment to your spouse starts slipping.

> For the lips of an immoral woman drip honey, And her mouth is smoother than oil; But in the end she is bitter as wormwood. Why should you, my son, be enraptured by an immoral woman, And be embraced in the arms of a seductress? (Prov. 5:3,20).

> The commandment [of God] is To keep you from the evil woman, From the flattering tongue of a

> *seductress. Do not lust after her beauty in your heart,
> Nor let her allure you with her eyelids* (Prov. 6:23-25).

> *... That they may keep you from the immoral
> woman, From the seductress who flatters with her
> words* (Prov. 7;5).

> *There a woman met him, With the attire of a har-
> lot, and a crafty heart. She was loud and rebellious,
> Her feet would not stay at home* (Prov. 7:10-11).

> *The mouth of an immoral woman is a deep pit; He
> who is abhorred* [forsaken or despised] *of the Lord will
> fall there* (Prov. 22:14).

Solomon knew! Among his hundreds of wives, there were
many immoral women.

> *This is the way of an adulterous woman: She eats*
> [referring to her sexual escapades] *and wipes her
> mouth, And says, "I have done no wickedness"* (Prov.
> 30:20).

There is no conviction of sin. There's no broken heart.
There's no repentant attitude. She says, "I haven't done anything." Then, she goes right out and does it again.

He has called her *"immoral," "evil"* and *"adulterous"*. One
other word, Solomon uses for this kind of woman who lacks
moral integrity is *"foolish"*.

> *A foolish woman is clamorous* [she talks a lot]; *She
> is simple, and knows nothing* (Prov. 9:13).

She thinks she knows a lot, and can get her own way but
she doesn't know what's good or bad. She's foolish. She
doesn't understand moral truth. Solomon keeps contrast-
ing this godly woman he can't seem to find with all the other
women he's known who are immoral and evil. That also
means that Solomon was also immoral and evil. The Bible
is very clear about it.

What's the answer? Jesus said that out of the heart come
all kinds of depravity. The best of us, under the right
provocations, will fall into sin. What is the solution?

Most people today will **not** describe themselves as immoral even when they admit to committing adultery! Sexual

involvement is now tolerated even among some believers. How **many** times you have sexual intercourse outside of marriage is not important. The Bible say even **one time** is sin. It makes you an adulterer, immoral and evil. Potentially it can come out of any of our hearts. Age is not a factor, either. It can happen to our senior citizens—I've seen it!

> *Then the scribes and Pharisees brought to Him a woman caught in adultery. And when they had set her in the midst, they said to Him, "Teacher, this woman was caught in adultery, in the very act. Now Moses, in the law, commanded us that such should be stoned. But what do You say?" This they said, testing Him, that they might have something of which to accuse Him. But Jesus stooped down and wrote on the ground with His finger, as though he did not hear. So when they continued asking Him, He raised Himself up and said to them, "He who is without sin among you, let him throw a stone at her first." And again he stooped down and wrote on the ground. Then those who heard it, being convicted by their conscience, went out one by one, beginning with the oldest even to the last. And Jesus was left alone, and the woman standing in the midst. When Jesus had raised Himself up and saw no one but the woman, He said to her, "Woman, where are those accusers of yours? Has no one condemned you?" She said, "No one, Lord." And Jesus said to her, "Neither do I condemn you; go and sin no more"* (John 8:3-11).

> *Such were some of you. But you were washed, but you were sanctified, but you were justified in the name of the Lord Jesus and by the Spirit of our God* (I Cor. 6:11).

Aren't you glad there's hope? What sweet words of forgiveness and cleansing Jesus spoke to her!

The Contentious Woman

This one may be more troublesome, so we must look into it. The issue here is emotional—emotional irritation.

> *A foolish son is the ruin of his father, And the contentions of a wife are continual dripping* (Prov. 19:13).

Your husband would be wise not to refer to these verses too often. If he puts it on a plaque and hangs it on the wall, you know you're in big trouble! At some point, we must look at the Word of God. This word refers to being argumentative, to dissension, and conflict, but it's most common usage refers to nagging.

It is better to dwell in a corner of a housetop, Than in a house shared with a contentious woman (Prov. 21:9).

If your husband is scarce around the house, there may be a reason!

It is better to dwell in the wilderness, Than with a contentious and angry woman (Prov. 21:19).

This is not easy to teach! I'm trying to bring you only what the Word of God teaches. Yes, husbands sometimes nag, too!

It is better to dwell in a corner of a housetop, Than in a house shared with a contentious woman (Prov. 25:24).

Ask yourself why he repeated what he had just said!

A continual dripping on a very rainy day And a contentious woman are alike (Prov. 27:15).

Let me show you why this is bad.

A brother offended is harder to win than a strong city, And contentions are like the bars of a castle (Prov. 18:19).

Contentions do not draw spouses together. It drives you apart. Arguments, dissensions, conflicts, constant nagging, and emotional irritation all put up barriers.

The Lovely Woman Without Discretion

A ring of gold in a pig's snout, So is a lovely woman who lacks discretion (Prov. 11:22).

This verse has bemused Bible students for a long time. What is he talking about? First of all, Solomon was never against beautiful women. He like them. Neither is the Bible against beautiful women. It speaks pointedly about their beauty—both in form and in appearance. God's not against physical beauty; He made us! Some of us don't see ourselves as beautiful as compared to someone else. Our young people feel unwanted if they aren't considered to be one of the "beautiful people". We Christians should be at the forefront of society teaching what true beauty is all about.

"Beauty is only skin deep," is one of our proverbs, but God puts it in a way that you can hardly run away from it. The *"ring in a pig's snout"* uses a word that can refer to the ear or the nose. In many cultures, a ring in the nose is considered a mark of great beauty. This ring of gold (beautiful) looks like it doesn't belong when you put it on a pig! That's the point. The Bible uses enormous contrast so no one can miss the point.

On a pig! God says, "I'm glad you don't like that because that's the way beautiful women are who lack discretion and integrity." Discretion is used to mean insight in the Bible and also for *"taste"*. When they tried the manna in the wilderness, they said, *"This tastes like corriander seed."* That's the same word—*"taste"*. Job 6:6 says, *"Is there any taste in the white of an egg?"* The same word is translated *"discretion"* here in Proverbs 11.

In the first case, we had a problem of **moral integrity;** in the second, a problem of **emotional irritation.** In the third case, we have a problem of **spiritual insight.**

One of King David's wives is an example of a woman who had *"discretion"*, spiritual insight. The same Hebrew word is used of her. David was a military conqueror and God was using him in a mighty way, but he was having a hard time. He was tired out from all his battles.

> *The name of the man was Nabal, and the name of his wife Abigail. And she was a woman of good understanding and beautiful appearance* (I Sam. 25:3).

Here was a woman who had it all. The problem was that Nabal treats David poorly and Abigail runs out to bribe them not to ruin Nabal's life in retaliation. She was married to him and yet she admitted that he was worthless and deserved to die. She begged David not to punish him. "People will never know why you took vengeance and they will think you were unjust."

> *Then David said to Abigail: "Blessed be the Lord
> God of Israel, who sent you this day to meet me! And
> blessed is your advice [discretion, insight] and
> blessed are you, because you have kept me this day
> from coming to bloodshed and from avenging myself
> with my own hand. For indeed, as the Lord God of Is-
> rael lives, who has kept me back from hurting you, un-
> less you had hastened and come to meet me, surely
> by morning light no males would have been left to
> Nabal." So David received from her hand what she
> had brought him, and said to her, "Go up in peace to
> your house. See, I have heeded your voice and
> respected your person" (I Sam. 25:32).*

What do you think David did when he heard her husband
was dead? She became David's wife.

There are three kinds of women who make the problem
of marriage difficult; **THE IMMORAL WOMAN, THE EMO-
TIONAL WOMAN** who brings constant contentions, and
THE WOMAN WHO LACKS SPIRITUAL INSIGHT.

In contrast to that we have the excellent woman of
Proverbs 31.

THE VIRTUOUS WOMAN

I want to just list seven of her excellent qualities. What
makes the woman so good, such a blessing?

Faithfulness to Her Husband

> *The heart of her husband safely trusts her; So he
> will have no lack of gain. She does him good and not
> evil All the days of her life* (vss. 11-12).

Her faithfulness is not simply staying away from sexual
sin, but faithfulness in doing him good. She is a woman who
encourages him.

Diligence in the Way She Works

God never blesses idleness or laziness. You may feel lazy
at times, but a lifetime of idleness is despicable in the eyes
of God. God wants us to be faithful in the way we work.

Idleness is the opposite of diligence. Verses 13 to 19 tell
you about her diligence. Verse 24 says,

She makes linen garments and sells them, and supplies sashes for the merchants.

She watches over the ways of her household, And does not eat the bread of idleness (vs. 27).

Compassion Toward Those in Need

The excellent woman, who is a blessing of the Lord to her husband, is compassionate toward those in need.

She extends her hands to the poor, Yes, she reaches out her hands to the needy (vs. 20).

A gracious woman retains honor, But ruthless men retain riches (Prov. 11:16).

The word *"gracious"* refers to compassion. A woman who really cares and has sensitivity to the needs of others, retains honor, the Bible says. Do you want honor from your husband and from others? Then, your compassionate heart will bring honor to your life.

Kindness in the Way She Talks

As I read this list, I believe that all men should do the same things.

She opens her mouth with wisdom, And on her tongue is the law of kindness (Prov. 31;26).

This is a beautiful description. She's controlled by a law, every time she speaks to anyone—the law of kindness. That is extremely attractive to men. It's the opposite of the woman who is irritating, whose contentions and arguments are like the dripping of the rain. This woman is kind in her words.

Often there is a great deal of pressure on a woman to be **unkind** in response to a **lack of kindness** in her husband. We all need to be especially kind at a time like that. When we run into that which is unlovely and unkind, we need to be all the more kind and loving. We overcome evil with good, according to the Scripture.

Discernment in How She Handles Things

It is very common for men to be judgmental about the way their wives handle things. Perhaps it is a part of what is wrong with men. Men want to think they can take care of things. That's a part of being a man even though it's stupid.

She considers a field and buys it (vs. 16). *She perceives that her merchandise is good* (vs. 18). *She is not afraid* (vs. 21). *Strength and honor are her clothing; She shall rejoice in time to come* (vs. 25).

We're not talking about losing the car keys. We're talking about a woman who thinks about things. She understands things. That is a blessing from the Lord.

Carefulness About Her Appearance

God puts no premium on being sloppy. Not at all!

She makes tapestry for herself; Her clothing is fine linen and purple. Her husband is known in the gates, When he sits among the elders of the land (vss. 22-23).

We're taking top of the line here. She looks good. One of my friends was going to college and he and his wife were very poor. He was working hard in a janitorial service. I noticed that he had one white shirt and a pair of dark blue pants. Every day he came to school with that shirt pressed. His pants were pressed. His wife had only a couple of dresses but every time you saw her, she looked sharp. She kept their clothes pressed and clean. They were some of the poorest people I've ever met, but they believed in looking good.

Then a lot of us have almost anything you can imagine from a closet filled with clothes. We act like we're dedicated to looking bad! The Lord Jesus said that if you've been fasting and praying all night, you should wash your face and comb your hair so they won't be able to tell what you've done. There is something about integrity that causes us to do the best we can with what we have. It doesn't come from pride, but because we honor what the Lord Himself has done.

God has made it very clear that He condemns sloppiness. It's an uncaring attitude of the heart. We don't want to say that righteousness is in the way we look. However, this Proverbs woman was careful about the way she looked and God honored her for it.

Dedication to the Lord

Charm is deceitful and beauty is vain, But a woman who fears the Lord, she shall be praised (Prov. 31:30).

Dedication to the Lord is what makes a woman excellent—a crown to her husband, a blessing to him.

THE VIRTUOUS WOMAN IS COMPLIMENTED BY OTHERS

Her children...call her blessed; Her husband... praises her (vs. 28). *...she shall be praised* (vs.30). *Let her works praise her in the gates* [publicly] (vs. 31).

A prudent wife is from the Lord (Prov. 19;14).

The most outstanding compliment to be given to any woman of God is given by the Lord Himself in I Peter, chapter 3. He tells the wives to be submissive to their husbands.

Do not let your beauty be that outward adorning of arranging the hair, of wearing gold, or of putting on fine apparel; but let it be the hidden person of the heart, with the incorruptible ornament of a gentle and quiet spirit, which is very precious in the sight of God (I Peter 3:3-4).

It is a woman's spirit that is attractive to others, but most of all it is attractive to our blessed Lord.

Everything I've said, could also be said of men. Who can find an excellent spouse? The qualities are the same for men as they are for women. The problem in marriage is: Where are the people who want to live for the Lord? The single most hurtful thing in a marriage is one partner, or both, who are not dedicated to the Lord. You can have more than a good marriage, you can have a great marriage, if both partners are dedicated to the Lord and understand that real beauty lies in the heart. It comes from the Lord.

CHAPTER 7

THE PROBLEM OF PRIDE

*These six things the Lord hates, Yes, seven are an
abomination to Him: A proud look, A lying tongue,
Hands that shed innocent blood, A heart that devises
wicked plans, Feet that are swift in running to evil, A
false witness who speaks lies, And one who sows dis-
cord among brethren* (Prov. 6:16-19).

We are all aware that OTHER PEOPLE have the problem
of pride! God has spoken many times in His Word about
humility and our right relationship with Him, so in order to
understand the problem, I want to give you seven statements
about it. We need to take a little time with the first one.

When we ask ourselves where pride comes from, we find
a very clear answer in the Bible.

IT IS THE PROBLEM THAT LED TO THE
DEVIL'S CONDEMNATION

In the Bible, the devil is the source of pride and he has
infected the entire human race. In the qualifications for
leaders of the church, we read some interesting words.

... not a novice [a new convert], *lest being puffed
up with pride he fall into the same condemnation as
the devil. Moreover he must have a good testimony
among those who are outside, lest he fall into reproach
and the snare* [the trap] *of the devil* (I Tim. 3:6-7).

*And a servant of the Lord must be ... patient, in
humility correcting those who are in opposition, if God
perhaps will grant them repentance, so that they may
know the truth, and that they may come to their senses and escape the snare of the devil* [pride], *having
been taken captive by him to do his will* (II Tim. 3:24-
26).

There are two passages often used to tell the story of the devil's pride. Whether or not they refer to the devil in actuality, is a matter of interesting Bible study. People believe that they are referring to the devil and his problem of pride. In order to understand our pride problem, we have to clearly see what his problem was. We got our problem from him.

> "How are you fallen from heaven, O Lucifer, son of the morning! How you are cut down to the ground, You who weakened the nations! For you have said in your heart: 'I will ascend into heaven, I will exalt my throne above the stars of God; I will also sit on the mount of the congregation On the farthest sides of the north; I will ascend above the heights of the clouds, I will be like the Most High.' Yet you shall be brought down to Sheol [the grave], To the lowest depths of the Pit (Isa. 14:12-15).

The problem here is found in Isa. 14:4 where we see that these words are not addressed to the devil, but to the King of Babylon, "... take up this proverb against the king of Babylon ...." The king of Babylon is called, "one who is fallen from heaven." Did that apply to the king of Babylon? The king of Babylon is called "Lucifer, son of the morning." Does that really describe him? The king of Babylon is the one who "weakened the nations"—plural. That probably fits him.

The king of Babylon supposedly said, "I will ascend into heaven." Does that fit him? The king of Babylon supposedly said, "I will exalt my throne above the stars of God." That could easily fit him since it is well know that they were star gazers and thought about their position and throne to be higher than the stars of God.

The point I bring out is that we are not really sure whether or not it refers to Satan. We are very sure that it does refer to the king of Babylon. Most Bible teachers say that the king of Babylon is simply manifesting the devil's problem.

So then, in this passage in Isaiah 14, it switches from the king of Babylon, predicting his downfall after he has destroyed the Jewish people in 586 B.C., and becomes a "type" of the downfall of Satan himself.

In terms of the figure, "how you are fallen from heaven," it is probably expressing the problem of Nebuchadezzar when he went berserk and became like a madman. He lost his sanity and he was literally out of his head (see the Book of Daniel). He went from being the top man in the world to

a maniac roaming the fields.   According to the Bible,
Nebuchadnezzar came to his senses and turned to the Lord
at the end of his life.   The destruction of Nebuchadnezzar is
what is being pictured in Isaiah 14.   From that we get some
knowledge about the devil's pride, but it really doesn't say
that it is the devil there.

Sometimes I find it hard to be careful and accurate with
the Scriptures when there are so many prevalent views of
Christians that have been roaming around for years.   People
sometimes think you are attacking a well-known Bible
doctrine when, in fact, you are simply carefully explaining
the Word.   What we just looked at in Isaiah is one example.
As long as anyone can remember, Christians have said that
is a prophecy about the devil.   It really doesn't say that.

We have the same problem in Ezekiel 28 which is the
other passage used to teach the pride of the devil.

> *The word of the Lord came to me again, saying,*
> *"Son of man, say to the prince of Tyre, 'Thus says the*
> *Lord God ... (Ezek.28:1).*

Tyre is in what is Lebanon today.   It is a little island city
off the coast of Lebanon in the Mediterranean.   It became a
great fortress and almost seemed unconquerable.   It was
Alexander the Great who fulfilled this prophecy in Ezekiel
28 and literally destroyed the city of Tyre.   He was used by
God, with thousands of slaves who built a ramp out to the
island, to destroy the city.   Many slaves died in the process,
but he took the city before he was thirty-three years old.   He
took almost all the major cities of the world but Tyre was one
that he especially turned his wrath against.   It fulfilled this
Bible prophecy which was written several hundred years
before the time of Alexander the Great.

> *"Because your heart is lifted up, And you say, 'I*
> *am a god, I sit in the seat of gods, In the midst of the*
> *seas,' Yet you are a man, and not a god, Though you*
> *set your heart as the heart of a god (Behold, you are*
> *wiser than Daniel! There is no secret that can be hid-*
> *den from you! With your wisdom and your under-*
> *standing You have gained riches for yourself, And*
> *gathered gold and silver into your treasuries; By your*
> *great wisdom in trade you have increased your riches,*
> *And your heart is lifted up because of your riches),"*
> *'Therefore thus says the Lord God: "Because you*
> *have set your heart as the heart of a god, Behold,*

therefore, I will bring strangers against you, The most terrible of the nations; And they shall draw their swords against the beauty of your wisdom, And defile your splendor. They shall throw you down into the Pit, And you shall die the death of the slain In the midst of the seas" (Ezek. 28:1-8).

Moreover the word of the Lord came to me, saying, "Son of man, take up a lamentation for the king of Tyre, and say to him, 'Thus says the Lord God: "You were the seal of perfection, Full of wisdom and perfect in beauty. You were in Eden, the garden of God; Every precious stone was your covering: The sardius, topaz, and diamond, Beryl, onyx, and jasper, Sapphire, turquoise, and emerald with gold. The workmanship of your timbrels and pipes Was prepared for you on the day you were created. You were the anointed cherub who covers [we believe this refers to Satan]; *I established you; You were on the holy mountain of God; You walked back and forth in the midst of fiery stones. You were perfect in your ways from the day you were created, Till iniquity was found in you* (Ezek. 28:11-15).

We have to ask ourselves if the king of Tyre was in the Garden of Eden, and the answer is, "No". Whatever the king of Tyre is in his pride, he is representing the devil who was in the Garden of Eden. It was as if the king of Tyre was being possessed by the devil himself.

Was the king of Tyre *"perfect"*? No, every man has been born in sin. But that statement **is true** of the devil. He was perfect when God created him, an angel, an anointed cherub.

Here's what I believe about these two passages: I believe they are primarily prophecies against the king of Babylon and the king of Tyre. These prophecies were fulfilled in history. I also believe that there is the inference that what led to their pride was the devil's involvement.

I think we need to understand that when Paul wrote to Timothy about not generating pride in new converts, it is the same condemnation as the devil. We can see that the pride of the kings of Tyre and Babylon is the same as the problem the devil had. There is warning to Timothy about pride and the connection with Satan's involvement.

This is important for all believers. From the day that Adam and Eve fell into sin, we have been born with sinful natures. We don't become sinners because we sin; we sin because we're sinners. We have a depraved nature and in that depravity, we are dominated by pride. The devil's problem is pride, so the devil will directly and personally involve himself and his demons in our lives in order to lead us into the same trap and condemnation he fell into. He wants us to be destroyed (he's called, the Destroyer); he wants to ruin your life and mine and he does it best with pride. The thing that destroyed him is the same thing that will destroy us.

There is nothing more sickening than to see someone with a lot of potential for God who has a lot of pride, they are not only not used, they are destroyed. Their whole testimony and life and effectiveness is ruined by this one thing: Pride. Pride is a problem that grips us all and Satan knows it!

IT IS THE PRACTICE WHICH THE LORD HATES

I don't think you really get hold of the problem of pride in your life until you understand God's attitude. God is not sweeping it under the rug. He does not *"wink"* at our problem. God hates pride! Pride is a terrible thing and we all have the problem, it just comes out in many different forms.

A lot of people program themselves to appear to be humble. This can be one of the worst kinds of pride imaginable. Pride affects us all. It is not always the obvious kind of conceit that stands in front mirror, admiring itself. That's unfortunate, but pride is usually more subtle than that. It is a practice which the Lord hates!

These six things the Lord hates,, Yes, seven are an abomination to Him: A proud look ... (Prov. 6:16-17).

The fear of the Lord is to hate evil; Pride and arrogance and the evil way And the perverse mouth I hate (Prov. 8:13).

Is it proper to hate evil? Yes? Then I'll give you something to hate—hate your own pride. The Lord hates pride.

It is an abomination to Him. He has no sympathy with it whatsoever.

> *Surely He scorns the scornful, But gives grace to the humble* (Prov. 3:34).

Don't let the word *"scornful"* throw you off track. Pride often manifests itself in scorn. This verse is repeated in the New Testament, in James—*"God resists the proud."* Putting people down, making a remark to cut someone a little is pride and God hates it. He resists it. *"He scorns the scornful."* Pride is the first on the list of things God despises.

> *Everyone who is proud in heart is an abomination to the Lord* (Prov. 16:5).

We often look for pride in some outward manifestation, but God looks on the heart (see I Sam. 16:7). Sometimes people who appear to be proud aren't as proud as the one who is proud in his heart. I've found that some people with bad self esteem, who really don't understand their relationship with God, can manifest very prideful ways when, in fact, they are not very proud at all. They may be scared to death, and insecure. The thing to understand is that pride grips the heart even though it may not be manifest outwardly. That pride, in our hearts, is an abomination to God.

> *Everyone who is proud in heart is an abomination to the Lord; Though they join forces, none will go unpunished* (Prov.16:5).

You may think you can hang around with others who have this attitude and get away with it, but you will not. God is going to punish proud people. Do you hate what the Lord hates? Then, you are going to hate pride in yourself.

Some people try to say that they hate themselves, but these are expressions of pride. Ephesians 5:29 says that *"no one ever hated his own flesh"*. It is a severe and serious form of pride to say that you hate yourself. You are so proud that you want to bore the rest of us by saying that you hate yourself. Don't do that! The truth is that you love yourself and, if I were you, I would try to love God with all my heart and love *"your neighbor as* [much as you love] *yourself"*. Pour your interest into other people and not into yourself since this stirs up the pride problem.

IT IS THE PERSECTIVE OF ONE WHO WILL
NOT SUBMIT TO ANOTHER'S AUTHORITY

We were in Oklahoma City, having a marriage seminar, and we met a cute little girl. We were talking, and I said, "You want to obey your Daddy, don't you?" "Absolutely not!" she replied. That's characteristic of a lot of us. When we have pride in our hearts, we don't want to submit to anyone's authority. It's pride that keeps us from doing that.

For instance, a wife is to submit to her husband's authority. Children are to submit to their parents' authority. Husbands are to submit to their wives, not in authority, but in love and caring for their needs. It's interesting that a lot of us don't want to submit to authority in our lives. We dislike someone in political office, so we don't want to submit to their authority. We don't like the character of our boss, so we don't want to submit to his authority.

And we justify it all the time! We defend our lack of submission because they don't "deserve" it, or that we have a right to rebel. This is simply a manifestation of the pride of our own hearts.

The wise in heart will receive commands, But a prating fool will fall (Prov. 10:8).

This issue of pride and submission is a fundamental one. I get a paper of what is going on in the public schools and one report told of the lack of submission among young people today. It was an interesting study because rebellion against authority is everywhere. Some said that the lack of discipline in the home has led to a generation of people who don't want to submit to anyone's authority. There's a lot of truth to that.

The article also pointed out that the character of people in authority has undermined people's confidence in them until they don't want to submit. There's something there, also. When people in authority don't walk with God, it presents a scenario that generates rebellion because of the pride of our hearts. We look at them and see the way they live, and we don't want to accept their authority.

An interesting point was also presented in that article about consequences. People don't submit to authority because there are no consequences to be faced. This starts in the home, and is carried out in society. We tolerate sinful actions and disobedience to the point that there is never any consequence to pay. So, the child grows up believing that he can get away with anything. Why submit to authority?

One thing that was not in the article which should have been is that the depravity of our own hearts makes us resist authority. If it were not for the intervention of God, all of us would be in a state of rebellion and we would have a state of anarchy. This problem is widespread. We can see it among Christians who ought to know better.

We also see the abuse of authority. Pride can cause people who are in authority not to have a servant attitude and to abuse their authority. That's for sure!

IT IS THE PERSUASION OF ONE WHO
BELIEVES HE IS ALWAYS RIGHT

Pride has ruined more Christians who wanted to serve the Lord than perhaps anything else. It will cut off the blessing of God.

A lot of us are so dogmatic, that we believe that others will, in time, come to believe what we believe. That's pride. We like to say that others will see that we're right when we get to heaven. It is not necessarily bad to want to be right. Thank God, there are still some people who care about being right, but there is something awful about believing that you can never be wrong.

Do not be wise in your own eyes; Fear the Lord and depart from evil (Prov. 3:7).

The problem with pride is that you are *"wise in your own eyes"*. You say something and like it so well that you can't wait to say it again to show people how wise you are! There's something about pastors that intrigues me. Pastors have to be right and they believe that they should be right. They believe that it's dangerous to be wrong, but sometimes it causes people to fight over something that isn't that important. I thank God for pastors who are concerned about being right. However, if it becomes clear that they are wrong, it becomes very difficult to back up.

I have that problem because my sermons are on tape and sometimes people bring me a tape from ten years ago on

which I said something different from what I just said. They
want to know what I really believe. I tell them that I'm growing and learning all the time. We may have to wait until we
get to heaven to know which one is right.

God makes very clear what's wrong when you think you're
right in your own eyes.

The way of a fool is right in his own eyes, But he
who heeds counsel is wise (Prov. 12:15).

I like people who think they're right about something, but
I sure hope they have the courage to say they were wrong if
they find out differently. According to the Bible, the one who
believes he is right in his own eyes, is one who will not listen to anyone else's counsel. If you want to deal with the
pride problem about always being right, then listen to the
viewpoints of other people. Listen to counsel! That will soft-
en your heart. You will still have convictions about what you
believe but listen to the counsel of others so you may control the problem of pride. Don't fall into the devil's trap.

Every way of a man is right in his own eyes, But
the Lord weighs the hearts (Prov. 21:2).

It's interesting that we think what we have done is right.
Sometimes, we even know the Bible says something against
it, but even then, we struggle to do what we want to do. We
try to explain it, or justify it, or defend it. What we do is right
in our own eyes, but God knows what's going on inside. We
need to sense our accountability to God and the possibility
that we are, in fact, wrong instead of being right.

Pride makes us see ourselves as always being right and
it keeps us from seeing it any other way. It keeps us from
listening to anybody's counsel and it makes us closeminded
to everything around us.

IT IS THE PROMINENCE THAT A PERSON
BELIEVES HE DESERVES

When you think you deserve prominence, that is pride.
It's like walking into a restaurant, expecting to get a nice
table because of who you are. We see it many times. We
never see anyone asking for a table next to the kitchen where
they pass the food right over your head. Probably, if anyone

did that, it would be in order to have them insist you take a better place! Pride is subtle.

We want people to respond to us according to what we deserve. That shows how messed up we are in our thinking because, if we got what we deserve, we would get hell! It shows that we actually believe that because of something we've done in life, we deserve something better than the lowly person beside us. We set ourselves above others because of what we've accomplished or done.

A lot of people grow up thinking that people don't treat them as good as they deserve to be treated. We should be thrilled that people don't treat us like we deserve to be treated! *"It is of the Lord's mercies that we are not consumed because His compassions fail not."*

> *In the mouth of a fool is a rod of pride, But the lips*
> *of the wise will preserve them* (Prov. 14:3).

The way a proud man talks is like a *"rod"*, hitting people over the head. Some people blister others by the way they talk. They put you down.

> *Do not exalt yourself in the presence of the king,*
> *And do not stand in the place of great men; For it is*
> *better that he say to you, "Come up here," Than that*
> *you should be put lower in the presence of the prince,*
> *Whom your eyes have seen* (Prov. 25:6-7).

One year, I went to a convention which was like the world's largest Christian zoo; it was an unbelievable assortment of "wackos" from all over the world. It was like a "who's who" of Christian people-ten thousand of them. More people came just to get signatures and to be next to someone they think is important.

In the elevator, we were with Jerry Falwell, Oral Roberts, Pat Robertson, Jim Bakker, and James Kennedy. I wrote it down so I would remember. They were on the elevator when Carole and I got on. I said, "Hi," to the ones of them I knew. We didn't talk much.

An elderly man got on the elevator on the third floor and you could tell he thought he had died and gone to heaven! He looked at us and just gasped and had everyone sign his Bible.

When he got to Carole and me, he said, "Who are you?" I told him and he said, "I never heard of you!" I told him I'd never heard of him, either! Everyone laughed and I realized that Carole and I had a problem of recognition!

We've seen it with politicians and sports figures. It is a sickness! People are just waiting to touch these sports guys and get them to sign something. It's a curse.

Have you ever run into someone who is a namedropper? They just have to mention everyone famous they know. This is pride and we seem to think these things give us a claim on prominence.

There is a generation—oh, how lofty are their eyes!
And their eyelids are lifted up (Prov. 30:13).

If that isn't a picture of arrogance, I don't know what is! A whole generation is like that! They think they are really important.

Do you know what God says about us? He says we're nothing but a clod of dirt, but he loves us anyway! We're nothing but a weed that dies in a day. We're nothing but a flower whose beauty is soon gone. He loves us anyway! Praise the Lord!

IT IS THE POSITION OF ONE WHO SCOFFS AT OTHER OPINIONS AND CAUSES STRIFE

You can always tell a person dominated by pride. They scoff at other people's opinions.

By pride comes only contention, But with the well-advised is wisdom (Prov. 13:10).

Why do arguments get started? The Bible says to stop quarrels before they get started. Once people's pride enters into a discussion, you can only have arguments.

A proud and haughty man—"Scoffer" is his name;
He acts with arrogant pride (Prov. 21:24).

Cast out the scoffer, and contention will leave; Yes,
strife and reproach will cease (Prov. 22:10).

To get rid of arguments, you have to get to the core of the matter—it's pride! A scoffer is proud.

He who is of a proud heart stirs up strife, But he who trusts in the Lord will be prospered (Prov.28:25).

If you have been foolish in exalting yourself, Or if you have devised evil, put your hand on your mouth. For as the churning of milk produces butter, And as wringing the nose produces blood, So the forcing of wrath produces strife (Prov. 30:32-33).

IT IS THE PERIL THAT LEADS TO A
PERSON'S DOWNFALL

The Lord will destroy the house of the proud, But He will establish the boundary of the widow (Prov. 15:25).

You may blame your downfall on a number of things, but pride is the thing that leads to a person's downfall. The Bible repeats this many times.

Pride goes before destruction, And a haughty spirit before a fall (Prov. 16:18).

Before destruction the heart of a man is haughty, And before honor is humility (Prov. 18:12).

A man's pride will bring him low, But the humble in spirit will retain honor (Prov. 29:23).

In the little Book of Obadiah, we read of the people of Petra. I have been there. You have to fly to Amman, Jordan and from there, you take a day-long ride. After you get off the bus, you get on a horse or a donkey and you ride through the crevices into the mountains. You can understand why it was such an incredible fortress and was impossible to conquer, when you see it. It is literally built into the rocks. It is majestic and you wonder how they ever built it. Obadiah was the prophet who prophesied to these people. They were the people of Edom who came from Esau.

They were the ones who would not let the Children of Israel pass through their land and they spent years wandering through the desert. God never forgot it.

> *"The pride of your heart has deceived you, You
> who dwell in the clefts of the rock, Whose habitation
> is high; You who say in your heart, 'Who will bring me
> down to the ground?' Though you exalt yourself as
> high as the eagle, And though you set your nest among
> the stars, From there I will bring you down," says the
> Lord* (Obad. 3-4).

Nobody has ever achieved a position, no matter how exalted, who will not be brought down by the Lord.   God
brought down the greatest rulers in history when they were
filled with pride from Nebuchadnezzar down through history.

God will bring down any servant of the Lord who lets pride
dominate his life, instead of the Lord. Pride is a terrible sin
and evil and it destroys our Christian testimony and witness
and effectiveness.

James 4 is a heavy duty discussion of pride. Notice what
James says:

> *Where do wars and fights come from among you?
> Do they not come from your desires for pleasure that
> war in your members? You lust and do not have. You
> murder and covet and cannot obtain. You fight and
> war. Yet you do not have because you do not ask.
> You ask and do not receive, because you ask amiss,
> that you may spend it on your pleasures. Adulterers
> and adulteresses! Do you not know that friendship
> with the world is enmity with God? Whoever there-
> fore wants to be a friend of the world makes himself
> an enemy of God. Or do you think that the Scripture
> says in vain, "The Spirit who dwells in us yearns
> jealously"? But He gives more grace. Therefore He
> says: "God resists the proud, But gives grace to the
> humble."*

> *Therefore submit to God. Resist the devil and he
> will flee from you. Draw near to God and He will draw
> near to you. Cleanse your hands, you sinners; and
> purify your hearts, you double-minded. Lament and
> mourn and weep! Let your laughter be turned to
> mourning and your joy to gloom. Humble yourselves
> in the sight of the Lord, and He will lift you up* (James
> 4:1-10).

Our world is dominated by pride. We see it everywhere we turn. We see politicians who are filled with pride. We see sports figures filled with pride. We see men in finance and business filled with pride. We see it in the movies. We see it in the field of music. We see it in the pulpit. We see it in the Sunday School classrooms and in our homes and families. We see it in children who refuse to submit to parents. We see it in parents who have never submitted to the Lord and are not examples to their kids. We are filled with pride as a nation.

God has called us to humble ourselves and call upon His name. Let's draw near to God and humble ourselves in His sight. Instead of expecting honor and position for what we have done, let's confess our sin and humble ourselves in the sight of God.

CHAPTER 8

THE PROBLEM OF ANGER

The opposite of peace is anger. One man asked that I pray for him so that he could control his anger. He described throwing things and getting mad over little things and scaring his family. A young couple I met had trouble in the early years of their marriage because of the husband getting mad and blowing off steam. He couldn't control his anger.

When are we justified in getting angry? When is it right before God? When is it wrong? All of us are troubled at some time over the problem of anger. We all have it even though we express it in different ways.

WHY DO WE GET ANGRY?

This I say then: Walk in the Spirit, and you shall not fulfill the lust of the flesh. For the flesh lusts against the Spirit, and the Spirit against the flesh; and these are contrary to one another, so that you do not do the things that you wish. But if you are led by the Spirit, you are not under the law. Now the works of the flesh are evident, which are: adultery, fornication, uncleanness, licentiousness, idolatry, sorcery [the word for drugs], hatred, strife [arguments], jealousy, [outbursts of] wrath, factions [selfish ambitions], seditions, heresies, Envyings, murders, drunkenness, revelings, and the like; of which I tell you beforehand, just as I also told you in time past, that those who practice such things will not inherit the kingdom of God. But the fruit of the Spirit is love, joy, peace, longsuffering [slow to anger], kindness, goodness, faithfulness, gentleness, self-control. Against such there is no law. And they that are Christ's have crucified the flesh with the affections and lusts [with its passions and desires]. If we live in the Spirit, let us also walk in the Spirit. Let us not be conceited, provoking one another, enying one another. Brethren, if any man be overtaken in a [trespass], you who

spiritual restore such a one in the spirit of meekness
[the opposite of anger], *considering yourself lest you
also be tempted. Bear one another's burdens, and so
fulfill the law of Christ* (Gal. 5:16-26, 6:1-5 KJV).

It Is Our Natural Tendency

If I asked if you ever get mad, you might get mad at me
for asking. People get mad in different ways. Some throw
things, some blow up; in fact, a lot of people think the only
way to get rid of your anger is to blow off steam. People like
to say that it is a good thing. They'll say, "That's the way I
am! Just take me or leave me!" We often would rather leave
them. The Bible does not teach that we should blow up like
that.

A lot of us are mad and we don't know whether it's right
or wrong. If you're a Christian, you may be carrying a lot of
guilt in your heart because of anger. Sometimes it's hard to
face that.

The Bible says *"outbursts of anger"* are wrong, but some
of the most serious kinds of anger are the ones that people
hold inside and will never talk about them. They bear deep-
rooted bitterness and resentment.

You will never get victory until you admit what God says
about you. All of these things flow out of the human heart.

*Where do wars and fights come from among you?
Do they not come from your desires for pleasure that
war in your members?* (James 4:1).

The problem is inside of us. Even though we are quick
to blame our environment or some treatment we have
received in the past, the problem of anger comes from within.
It is our natural tendency.

It Is Encouraged by Demonic Forces

We need to recognize that Satan and demons are at work
in our lives to make us angry and to blow up. I'm not sure
how this works, but I can imagine a demon whispering in
our ear, telling us that we shouldn't let people treat us the
way they do. There are lots of powerful suggestions that
the enemy can place within our mental framework. It is encouraged by demonic forces.

*We wrestle not against flesh and blood, but
against principalities, against powers, against the*

rulers of the darkness of this age, against spiritual hosts of wickedness in the heavenly places (Eph. 6:12).

But if you have bitter envy and self-seeking in your hearts, do not boast and lie against the truth. This wisdom does not descend from above, but is earthly, sensual, demonic. For where envy and self-seeking exist, confusion and every evil thing will be there (James 3:14-16).

We need to understand that the demonic world is working hard to appeal to our old sin nature.

Let no man say when he is tempted, "I am tempted by God"; for God cannot be tempted by evil, nor does He Himself tempt anyone. But each one is tempted when he is drawn away by his own desires and enticed (James 1:13-14).

We are also enticed, baited by the enemy. These two things go together.

We Lack God's Wisdom and Are Self-confident

If we think we can handle things, it's easy to get angry.

He who is devoid of wisdom despises his neighbor, But a man of understanding holds his peace (Prov. 11:12).

It is a tendency of those who don't have the understanding of God, to despise their friends. That's what it says!

A wise man fears and departs from evil, But a fool rages and is self-confident (Prov. 14:16).

Anger is the opposite of the wisdom of God and God calls us fools when we rage and blow our tops.

He who is slow to wrath [longsuffering] *has great understanding, But he who is impulsive exalts folly* (Prov. 14:29).

Somebody who has "a short fuse" and gets mad at the slightest provocation is "exalting folly", and they lack wisdom. The don't have understanding. If they had that, they would be slow to fly off the handle.

We Can't Rule Our Own Spirit

*He who is slow to anger is better than the mighty,
And he who rules his spirit than he who takes a city*
(Prov. 16:32).

In parallelism, in Jewish poetry, sometimes things are being compared, and sometimes they are being contrasted. Here we have a comparison that leads to contrast. If you don't control your anger, you don't control your spirit.

Whoever has no rule over his own spirit Is like a city broken down, without walls (Prov. 25:28).

I often feel like taking a survey to find out how many of us get out of control and do crazy things when we get mad. Most of us normally do things when we are angry that we wouldn't do otherwise. This is typical of people who do not have rule over their own spirits.

"Like a city broken down, without walls" describes the fact that when we are angry, we have no protection whatsoever. When we lose our tempers, we give the devil a base of operations from which he can lead us into all other kinds of sin.

We Are Slandered or Criticized by Someone Without Our Knowing About It

When you hear that someone has criticized or slandered you and they don't even know the situation, it doesn't endear them to your heart. They think you won't find out what they said. That is one of the most difficult things to hear that someone has talked behind your back, especially when they don't know what they're talking about.

The north wind brings forth rain, And a backbiting tongue an angry countenance (Prov. 25:23).

Accountability rests on both sides, according to this verse: the person who got mad is wrong, and so is the person who did the backbiting. God is accusing both of them of wrongdoing. Understand that a "backbiting tongue", slandering or criticizing someone behind their back, brings an angry countenance—that's what God says.

Whoever secretly slanders his neighbor, Him I will destroy; The one who has a haughty look and a proud heart, Him I will not endure (Ps. 101:5).

God has no kind words for people who slander and criticize other people. It inevitably leads to the stimulation of anger. The person shouldn't get angry because of that, but the person who caused it is also held accountable by God.

We Are Jealous

Wrath is cruel and anger a torrent, But who is able to stand before jealousy? (Prov. 27:4).

God is a *"jealous"* God and there is a certain sense in which jealousy is right. That which belongs to you, you are to be jealous for it and you have a certain responsibility for it. However, jealousy is often evil and is listed in many of the lists of sins in the Bible.

Jealousy can mean that you are disappointed that you don't have the same advantages as others, or perhaps you feel bad when someone is honored and you are not. Maybe you've always wanted to be like a certain person—talk like them, be a good businessman or a good athlete. This can become jealousy, becoming the sin of comparing yourself to others and wishing you were like them. When you're jealous, nine times out of ten, you're also going to be angry.

We Are Proud

No wonder pride is at the top of the list of things God hates! It leads to a lot of other problems, one of which is anger.

He who is of a proud heart stirs up strife, But he who trusts in the Lord will be prospered (Prov. 28:25).

An angry man stirs up strife, And a furious man abounds in transgression (Prov. 29:22).

The same phrase, *"stirs up strife,"* is used for pride and for anger when you compare these two verses. There is a parallel statement in Proverbs 13.

By pride comes only contention [arguments], *But with the well-advised is wisdom* (Prov. 13:10).

When you put all this together, the angry person loses it and gets out of control and causes lots of divisions. What is the root of that? Proverbs tells us that it's pride. We're proud! That's why we're argumentative and angry.

Some things are worth fighting for and dying for, that's for sure. Face the problem! Most of the time it is our pride that leads us to be very angry in our lives.

We Do Not Like the Circumstances in Which We Find Ourselves

My son, do not despise the chastening of the Lord, Nor detest [a severe form of anger] *His correction; For whom the Lord loves He corrects, Just as a father the son in whom he delights* (Prov. 3:11-12).

Chastening, correction, is never a joyful thing; it is grievous and painful. Circumstances are going bad and we don't like what's happening. If you don't watch it, the changing circumstances can cause deep-rooted anger. We wonder why these bad things are happening to us.

Several years ago, I met a lady whose face looked very angry. You have to be careful not to judge by appearances—the person may just be sick or tired. Some people have lockjaw; they really can't smile! Some people just have a prune face that they were born with. We need to be careful.

This woman, however, I watched over a long period of time and I came to believe that I really saw bitterness and anger all over her face. One day, I was talking to her and another lady in the church office. The other lady asked her if she'd ever gotten that old problem solved from years ago. The lady just exploded! I stopped her and asked her what was really wrong. She didn't want to, but I got her to sit down for a moment. I asked her about the cause of the outburst.

"Who told you?" she turned on me fiercely. I didn't know anything so I told her that. "I have no idea, but there must be something or you wouldn't have gotten so angry." She had been treated badly by someone in that church forty-one years before and she had never gotten over it! The consequence of this unjust attack was that she was eaten up inside. She tried to hold it in, but in a pressured moment, she exploded. This often happens. You can hold it in for a long time and then it will explode. The pressure gets too great and you can't hold it anymore. Bitterness is a terrible thing.

Bitterness is rooted in the problem of anger. Anger is rooted in the problem of pride. It is our natural tendency and the enemy knows it, so we often need help in dealing with it.

WHEN IS IT RIGHT TO BE ANGRY?

I think that whenever I am angry, it is all right! Seriously, there are three simple ways to know if our anger is right.

When We Reflect the Righteousness of God

Matthew 18 is quite a story about forgiveness.

> "And his master was angry, and delivered him to the torturers until he should pay all that was due to him. So My heavenly Father also will do to you if each of you, from his heart, does not forgive his brother his trespasses" (Matt. 18:34-35).

Isn't it interesting that, in the story, the master who gets angry is the illustration of God the Father? There is a righteous anger that God Almighty has.

> "He who believes in the Son has everlasting life; and he who does not believe the Son shall not see life, but the wrath of God abides on him" (Jn. 3:36).

God has wrath. The Bible speaks of God's wrath many times.

> For the wrath of God is revealed from heaven against all ungodliness and unrighteousness of men, who suppress the truth in unrighteousness (Rom. 1:18).

> But if our unrighteousness demonstrates the righteousness of God, what shall we say? Is God unjust who inflicts wrath? (I speak as a man.) (Rom. 3:5).

The answer is, of course not! How would God judge, then? The judgment of God is rooted in His anger against sin and the unrighteousness of men. It's very important to see that there is a righteous cause rooted in the character of God.

> Let no one deceive you with empty words, for because of these things the wrath of God comes upon the sons of disobedience (Eph. 5:6).

So, when we reflect the righteousness of God, it is right for us to be angry.

When We Do Not Sin in the Process

Therefore, putting away lying, each one speak truth with his neighbor, for we are members of one another. "Be angry [a command!] and do not sin": do not let the sun go down on your wrath nor give place to the devil (Eph. 4:25-27).

There are two different words for anger here. The second one deals with a settled disposition that can become bitterness. God tells us to settle the things that are making us angry before we go to bed at night!

Be careful about sinning when you are angry. The text doesn't describe in great detail what that refers to. However, in verse 27, the sentence continues "nor give place to the devil". The devil uses our anger to cause us to sin. It is possible, therefore, to be angry and not sin.

When we're angry at that which is wrong, it is not wrong. In our narcissistic culture, it is terrible that we tolerate so much junk. Nobody ever seems to get mad about what's wrong. If something is not right, according to God, then it is perfectly right for us to be angry at sin. What happens is that we often also become angry at the sinner!

Parents know about this. Many of us discipline in anger because we get mad at what they did that was wrong and, before we know it, we get mad at them! In spanking them, we express the anger of the parent against the child rather than the balanced view of judgment for the sin that was done. This is a problem in parental discipline and, in later life, it leaves a more serious problem—a more complex human relationship between parent and child.

Sometimes parents don't separate the wrong from the child so the child feels that the anger is directed at them. The Bible teaches that parents should punish their children with a "rod". It says so very clearly in the Book of Proverbs. It tells you where to apply the rod-"in the middle of the back". It's not hard to find that spot! All spanking is applied to the bottom. Do you suppose a parent might be misapplying the Word of God by hitting the child anywhere else? You bet! It is well known by psychologists and sociologists that when a parent strikes a child across the face, it will stimulate anger. If the child is passive, they can hold it in for years and never forget it. You see this even in shopping malls. Parents clobber their kids in the head and slap them across the face. Maybe you were treated like this.

Parents often feel bad about this-hitting, pushing and shoving the kid when we're not supposed to. We are stimulating anger in our children. We are not getting mad at the situation, the sin, but we are getting mad at the child. This is a fine line here. Don't sin in the process of getting angry at sin. We always sin when the anger is applied to the individual rather than to what they did.

When We Are Angry for the Same Reasons as Our Lord Jesus Christ

> So when he had looked around at them with anger, being grieved [a very strong word] by the hardness of their hearts, He said to the man, "Stretch out your hand." And he stretched it out, and his hand was restored as whole as the other (Mk. 3:5).

It's interesting that Christ healed a man when He was mad. That blows the picture of Christ being only tender and loving. In this case, He was still compassionate toward the man who needed to be healed, but the Bible says he was angry! Nothing else here explains the situation. He just said, "Stick our your hand," and He healed it almost in defiance of their objections. The religious leaders were trying to accuse Him.

> Then they brought young children to Him, that He might touch them; but the disciples rebuked those who brought them, But when Jesus saw it, He was greatly displeased [really angry] and said to them, "Let the little children come to Me, and do not forbid them; for of such is the kingdom of God (Mk. 10:13-14).

I was at a Child Evangelism confrence and they used this text. They were talking about Jesus being so gentle—and He probably was—but He was angry! He said, "You let those kids come to Me right now for of such is the kingdom of heaven." I thought about a lot of people's attitudes about little children. Maybe we should get mad about that! There is righteous anger.

WHEN IS IT WRONG TO BE ANGRY?

When We Seek Revenge

Repay no one evil for evil. Have regard for good things in the sight of all men. If it is possible, as much as depends on you, live peaceably with all men. Beloved, do not avenge yourselves, but rather give place to wrath [anger] (Rom. 12:17-19).

I got a long letter from a lady who had committed adultery. She said that she was angry with her husband and decided to make him pay—he had been adulterous. It's wrong to be angry and to try to get revenge.

Do not say, "I will recompense evil"; Wait for the Lord, and He will save you (Prov. 20:22).

Don't take action! Don't try to settle the score! Don't do any of this. "Wait for the Lord, and He will save you."

When We Are Angry Without A Righteous Cause

Do not strive with a man without cause, If he has done you no harm (Prov. 3:30).

Some of us are just angry, and we don't know if it's jealousy or pride, or envy. Maybe we just don't like the person because they aren't like us. What wrong here? There is no righteous cause!

"But I say to you that whoever is angry with his brother without a cause shall be in danger of the judgment" (Matt. 5:22).

These are Jesus' words in the Sermon on the Mount and they are very clear. Just being angry isn't good enough.

When We Are Angry Because Others Are Treated Better Than We Are

In the story of the prodigal son, the older brother was unhappy about the way his brother was treated when he came home. After all, he had wasted his inheritance on *"riotous living"*.

"But he was angry and would not go in. Therefore his father came out and pleaded with him. So he

> answered and said to his father, 'Lo, these many
> years I have been serving you; I never transgressed
> your commandment at any time; and yet you never
> gave me a young goat, that I might make merry with
> my friends. But as soon as this son of yours came,
> who has devoured your livelihood with harlots, you
> killed the fatted calf for him.' And he said to him, 'Son,
> you are always with me, and all that I have is yours.
> It was right that we should make merry and be glad,
> for your brother was dead and is alive again, and was
> lost and is found'" (Lk. 15:28-32).

When you are angry because others are treated better
than you are, you are way off base. There is no righteous
cause there at all.

When We Are Bitter, Resentful, Speaking Evil of Others, and Argumentative

> A wrathful man stirs up strife, But he who is slow
> to anger allays contention (Prov. 15:18)

He stops arguments; he doesn't start them.

> It is better to dwell in the wilderness, than with a
> contentious [argumentative] and angry woman (Prov.
> 21:19).

Notice that argumentativeness and anger go together.

> Let all bitterness, wrath, anger, clamor, and evil
> speaking be put away from you, with all malice [the
> evil intent of doing harm] (Eph. 4:31).

These things all come together and behind it is malice.

> But now you must also put off all these: anger,
> wrath, malice, blasphemy, filthy language out of your
> mouth (Col. 3:8).

I was reading an article about the use of obscenity on TV
programs. Even TV Guide has dealt with the use of four-
letter words and swearing that is allowed now that wasn't
allowed ten years ago. The article I read analyzed the use of
four-letter words and it was insightful, even though I don't
believe the writer was a Christian. It said that when people
use four-letter words, behind it is usually anger.

People are angry at the way that people have treated them so they blow off and become as obscene as they possibly can. Behind that is a deep-rooted anger. All of this is wrong, according to God, and we need to get it out of our lives.

HOW DO WE CONTROL OUR ANGER?

Insufficient Solutions

People tell us to **count to ten.** It's a nice idea, but it doesn't work. Some people could count to a thousand and still be mad! Counting to ten is not God's way of dealing with anger. It's like running away from the truth.

"Take a cold shower," others will tell us. They think that will calm you down.

People actually advocate **throwing things** to control anger! It is supposed to make you feel better.

The classic, insufficient solution of all is to **blame someone else,** or something else.

Years ago, I drove home on a snowy day in Ohio. Snow piles up in front of your garage door. I first blamed the man who sold me the house facing the wrong way so that the snow piled up. I had to park my car to get all the snow out of the way to get the garage door up. The driveway was sloped and the car began sliding toward the street. No car came, so I got it and blocked it with a piece of wood in the hope of holding the car in the driveway. I also found myself blaming God for the snow! Eventually, I drove into the garage and got out of my car. I stepped on a rake facing the wrong way, and it hit me in the head! My first response was, "Who put that rake there?" I was the only one who used the rake so it was a terrible question. I was so mad that I threw the rake across the garage and it hit a piece of pottery and broke it. As I entered the screen door, I pulled it off the hinges! I flung the backdoor open and the lightbulb that was hanging down, hit me in the head. Now, I had a gash in my forehead and I was bleeding. I was furious! My wife said sweetly, "Hi, Honey!" Everything was wrong and I wanted to take it out on her!

Biblical Insights

However, there are some real solutions found in the Bible.

Don't Try to Defend or Justify Your Anger

You're wasting your time.

Who can say, "I have made my heart clean, I am pure from my sin"? (Prov. 20:9).

Obviously, no one can say that. Don't try to justify it. You will find victory, if you will confess it instead of trying to hide it. When you deny that you're angry, no one is convinced.

He who covers his sins will not prosper, But whoever confesses and forsakes them will have mercy (Prov. 28:13).

A young man who had had trouble with his temper, asked me about it. Later, he said that the best advice he ever received was to tell his famly when he was angry and ask them to pray for him. He didn't lose his temper for the next three months! God took control of it. He had been blaming, justifying, defending his anger. At the root of anger is pride. The moment you take the opposite tack, humility suddenly brings us God's answer.

When we humnble ourselves in the sight of the Lord, He lifts us up. How encouraging to see that the Lord will have compassion on us when we confess and forsake our anger.

Be Kind, Tenderhearted and Forgiving

Most people who are angry are not forgiving. When God tells us to get all anger out of our hearts, He tells us what to put in there.

Be kind to one another, tenderhearted, forgiving one another, just as God in Christ also forgave you (Eph. 4:32).

In my college Greek class, I saw in Ephesians 4:32 for the first time, that the word is not *"forgiving"*; it is the word *"grace"*. So the verse says, *"Be kind to one another, tenderhearted, gracing one another, just as God in Christ also graced you."* Grace gives to us what we don't deserve!

A lot of us are angry because we're thinking about whether people deserve things or not! God says, "I'll tell you how to handle the anger. Have so much kindness in your life that you grace people—give them what they DON'T deserve!" We are to *"grace"* others as God has *"graced"* us. That's the standard that ends all discussions!

Speak Softly

If you want to control your anger, speak softly.

A soft answer turns away wrath, But a harsh word stirs up anger (Prov. 15:1).

Learn to Overlook A Transgression

Is there something bad that someone has done to you and you can't get over it? That thing will build anger in you and in a moment you least expect, it will come out in a way that you didn't want to have happen.

The discretion of a man makes him slow to anger, And it is to his glory to overlook a transgression (Prov. 19:11).

Being slow to anger is equated with *"overlooking a transgression"* made against you. When you keep repeating it and bringing it up, you are stirring up your anger. It is a glory and an honor when you overlook it. You don't bring it up, anymore. You were treated wrongly. Somebody sinned against you. You've done all you can to handle it. They still won't do anything about it. Overlook it!

Some of us are hurt by the words of others, when they don't mean to be malicious at all. Sometimes, it is our perception of things. Because of our human nature, we can be very hurt and angry. We need to overlook the transgression. It is an honor to do so. It's at your discretion to be slow to anger and overlook a transgression against you.

Don't Get Into Arguments That Are Characterized by Strife

I did not say, "Don't argue!" The word, *"argument"* is used all the way through the Book of Acts concerning the Apostle Paul's ministry to lost people. If you're going to reach cults and people who have no Christian concensus, you must learn how to argue. Paul continually argued that Jesus is the Messiah. He spent a lot of time arguing with people the great facts of salvation. We're not just talking about arguments. We're talking about arguments that are characterized by strife. Behind that is a very bad spirit.

The beginning of strife is like releasing water; Therefore stop contention [arguments] *before a quarrel starts* (Prov. 17:4).

It is honorable for a man to stop striving, Since any fool can start a quarrel (Prov. 20:3).

It's not hard to get people upset. It's real easy!

Don't Become Friends With Angry People

The Bible is very clear that if you hang around with angry people, it will rub off.

Make no friendship with an angry man, And with a furious man do not go, Lest you learn his ways And set a snare for your soul (Prov. 22:24-25).

That's pretty powerful! However, the two most important ways to control your anger are these last two points.

Pray Constantly About It and Ask for the Lord's Help

"Watch and pray, lest you enter into temptation. The spirit indeed is willing, but the flesh is weak" (Matt. 26:41).

"Weak" here, means helpless. We started out by saying that getting angry is our natural tendency. We have a problem in our heart and the devil knows it, so he tempts us to get mad. There is nothing like prayer to help you control your temper. God answers prayer! When you're having a problem, get your friends and family to pray for you and with you about your anger. Every day pray for God's help to control your anger.

Be Filled With the Holy Spirit of God

When you get down to the bottom line, this is the only answer to any of our problems. There's a certain falseness in Christianity today that tries to get Christians to think they can conquer their problems without being controlled by God.

We can't control ourselves. We need to be filled with the Holy Spirit of God. You've got to be controlled by the Spirit.

The fruit of the Spirit is ... longsuffering [the opposite of getting angry] ..., self-control. If we live in the Spirit, let us also walk in the Spirit (Gal. 5:22-25).

Back in Galatians 5:16, we are told to *"walk in the Spirit"* but these two words for walk are not the same. In verse 25, it is a concept that comes from the Stoics. They were a Greek philosophical system that had standards and steps to follow in order to be good. They are the opposite of Epicureans who said, "Eat, drink and be merry for tomorrow we die!"

There is actually a warning in the admonition. Paul takes this word from the Stoics and puts it here. He is saying, "If you live in the Spirit," then take it a step at a time, please. If you go to a service where the Word is preached, you don't automatically get over your anger problem. We don't lick all of our spiritual problems by sticking a spiritual hypodermic needle into our arms.

Being filled by the Spirit, is the normal Christian life! We take life step by step, asking for God's help rather than trying to handle things ourselves. We should never assume that we can go three days without Jesus and then panic and get committed again.

The filling of the Holy Spirit is a continual process. No matter what we do in life, we need to take it a step at a time. If you've had a row with somebody, the thing to do is to go and ask for their forgiveness, apologizing for getting angry without a righteous cause. Ask that they pray for you so that you won't get mad like that again.

"Lord, You know my problem better than I do. I need Your help today!" Take one step at a time. Look at each situation in the light of God's Word and asking Him what He wants you to do in each one.

Don't be discouraged when you fall. Pick yourself up. Acknowledge your sin to God and start again to walk step by step with Him.

One writer said that a Christian with an anger problem could never expect to control it in his lifetime. I don't believe that! I don't believe that at all! Some Christians have been angry so long, however, that they have come to believe it. But you can start right now and God will give you victory over anger.

CHAPTER 9

THE PROBLEM OF LYING

Now the serpent was more cunning than any beast of the field which the Lord God had made. And he said to the woman, "Has God indeed said, 'You shall not eat of every tree of the garden'?" And the woman said to the serpent, "We may eat the fruit of the trees of the garden; but of the fruit of the tree which is in the midst of the garden, God has said 'You shall not eat it, nor shall you touch it [she added that part] lest you die.' And the serpent said to the woman, "You will not surely die [this was a lie]. For God knows that in the day you eat of it your eyes will be opened, and you will be like God, knowing good and evil." So when the woman saw that the tree was good for food, that it was pleasant to the eyes, and a tree desirable to make one wise, she took of its fruit and ate. She also gave to her husband with her, and he ate (Gen.3:1-6).

Ye are of your father the devil, and the lusts of your father you will do. He was a murderer from the beginning ... there is no truth in him. He is a liar, and the father of it (Jn. 8:44, KJV).

THE CAUSES OF LYING

When we look into the cause of lying, we have to start with the devil himself. He is the father of lies.

The Devil Himself

God is not a man, that He should lie (Num. 23:19).

...it is impossible for God to lie (Heb. 6:18).

So the cause of lying does not lie in the character of God. It is the devil that is called *"the father of lies"*.

As we move from the basic fact that God does not lie (it's impossible for Him to lie), and that the devil is the father of lies, we also begin to understand that man has a problem. There are reasons why he has a tendency to lie.

A faithful witness does not lie, But a false witness will utter lies (Prov. 14:5).

The Ten Commandments say, *"You shall not bear false witness..."* (Ex. 20:16).

A Lack of Faithfulness

Another way of looking at this is that a lack of faithfulness causes lying in our lives. We're not reliable. A lack of faithfulness, reliability and trustworthiness leads to telling lies.

A true witness delivers souls, But a deceitful witness speaks lies (Prov. 14:25).

Confidence in an unfaithful man in time of trouble Is like a bad tooth and a foot out of joint (Prov. 25:19).

Putting confidence in somebody that's unfaithful is a waste of time. Unfaithfulness leads to a lack of reliability, a lack of trustworthiness—speaking lies. The person you cannot trust to tell you the truth, is somebody who has not demonstrated dependability, faithfulness and consistency over a period of time—that's an insight. Many times we are misled and deceived by people whose lives haven't demonstrated faithfulness and reliability and dependability. They don't speak the truth in a moment of crisis, when we need it.

Hatred

Another reason we lie is because we have hatred in our hearts. We're really angry about something, or someone. There is bitterness and resentment. That leads to a lot of lying and deceit.

He who hates, disguises it with his lips, And lays up deceit within himself (Proverbs 26:24).

One who hates is actually deceiving himself and he doesn't even realize it. It is possible to live in a fantasy world and believe that you're speaking the truth when, in fact, you're lying. You're deceiving your own heart.

When he speaks kindly, do not believe him, For there are seven abominations in his heart; Though his hatred is covered by deceit, His wickedness will be revealed before the whole congregation. Whoever digs a pit will fall into it, And he who rolls a stone will have it roll back on him. A lying tongue hates those who are crushed by it, And a flattering mouth works ruin (Prov. 26:25-28).

The result of hatred in the heart is often deceit and lying. If we hate somebody and we try to say something nice to them, what we say is actuallly a lie. It's not the truth and it's not reliable, if, in fact, you hate that person. It can become so bad, that we deceive our own hearts. It's amazing how the depravity of our hearts causes confusion in us—emotional and mental confusion. Sometimes we don't even understand what we're saying or believing.

The heart is deceitful above all things, And desperately wicked [desperately sick]; Who can know it? I, the Lord, search the heart... (Jer. 17:9-10).

God knows us, but we don't know ourselves, and we're so deceitful inside that we're unable to deal with it in a truthful, open and honest way. Have you ever said, "I'm telling you the truth now." What does that mean? You don't tell the truth sometimes? "I swear on a stack of Bibles, I'm telling you the truth." Let's keep the Bible out of it!

Do not swear, either by heaven or by earth or with any other oath. But let your "Yes" be "Yes," and your "No," "No" (James 5:12).

When we speak, it ought to always be the truth. We're so deceitful that we can actually convince ourselves we are speaking the truth when, in fact, it's a lie.

The Fear of Others

Sometimes, we're afraid of somebody, intimidated, and therefore we lie. Perhaps, we're afraid of what they will think, and so we lie. You make up a story to try to impress them, but in fact, it's a lie. You try to make folks think that you're not as bad as they heard you were, or that you are better than what they thought. This is a natural tendency of our heart because we fear people. The fear of man is a snare and a trap.

We have a hard time telling the truth about ourselves. It's not easy to face that fact. We're all covering up for one reason or another because we fear man.

And of whom have you been afraid, or feared, That you have lied And not remembered Me? (Isa. 57:11).

If you'd only focus on the Lord, you could come clean and be honest about it.

The Old Sin Nature

"Do not lie to one another," says Colossians 3:9. The Greek grammar is more pointed and clearer. It is in a negative, dramatical form that in English literally means, "Stop doing it". It assumes that we have a natural tendency to lie. That makes all the difference in the world.

This is not a creative suggestion to people who are in "neutral gear", to lie or not to lie, and saying—please don't. It is saying, "Stop it! I know it's going on; I know all of you are doing it, now STOP IT!" That's the Greek text. I think it more adequately represents the problem, because the next statement in verse 9 says, *"...since you have put off the old man with his deeds, and have put on the new man who is renewed in knowledge according to the image of Him who created him* (Col. 3:9-10).

What is the *"old man"*? It is sometimes called *"the flesh"*, not meaning anything physical but a spiritual problem within us. *"The old man"* is our tendency, our nature to do evil that's in our hearts. It's because of sin. We were born in sin, and we sin because we are sinners. We have that *"old man"*. When we come to Christ, the Bible says (Romans 6) that our old man has been crucified with Christ. This principle of sin in my life, has been rendered inoperative—it no longer has the power to dominate and control my life. As a Christian, I don't need to let the old sin nature dominate and control my life. It's true, I have it, but I can live victoriously if I want to.

What are the causes of lying? Well, I can blame it on the devil—he's the father of lying. Because of the devil's lie, Adam and Eve fell into sin and, as a result, we all now have the problem. It's a problem of our sin nature.

One of the practical reasons we wind up lying is our lack of faithfulness, reliability and trustworthiness. We're not trustworthy in a crisis. Hatred and fear of man, these are all reasons. We need to deal with the fact that we have a tendency to lie. Every one of us has that in our hearts.

THE CHARACTERISTICS OF LYING

Let's take a look about lying as God reviews it for us in the Word.

The Lord Hates Lying

The Bible shows clearly that the Lord hates it. I think some people are in the game of lying, but it's not funny. I see little children that live in a fantasy world, who have wound up making it a practice to lie. Sometimes it carries over into adulthood, where we're lying and not understanding that it is lying, or that it's serious. Understand - the Lord hates lying.

These six things the Lord hates, Yes, seven are an abomination to Him: A proud look, A lying tongue...A false witness who speaks lies (Prov. 6:16-19).

Lying Is An Abomination to the Lord

Another characteristic of lying is that it is an abomination to the Lord. The word *"abomination"* always brings the judgment of God! Lying is an abomination.

Lying lips are an abomination to the Lord, But those who deal truthfully are His delight (Prov. 12:22).

God will bring judgment. One of the clearest judgments that comes to those who lie, an immediate judgment, is that you are found out. You're exposed; you're caught. That's very embarassing and worse. But it's even more serious than that!

A Liar Listens to Destructive Talk

One of the characteristics of lying is, that a person who lies, listens eagerly to destructive talk.

An evildoer gives heed to false lips; A liar listens eagerly to a spiteful [or destructive] *tongue* (Prov. 17:4).

If you are a liar and you hear somebody make a terrible remark about someone, you listen and love to perpetuate it. You don't stop and say, "Wait a minute, you don't have a right to say that. We need to check that out and go to that person and find out if it is true or not." A liar doesn't do that. A liar has a serious problem with gossip. He can't wait to spread the lie. It is a very dangerous problem.

Lying Is Worse Than Being Poor

What is desired in a man is kindness, And a poor man is better than a liar (Prov. 19:22).

To lie to somebody is not kind. It's disrespectful; it doesn't show them honor. You say that person is your friend, and you honor them—you respect them—you love them. Then don't lie to them. That is an attack upon that person's dignity, respect and integrity, and yet we do it—sometimes to protect ourselves.

Lying Oftens Comes in the Form of Boasting

Whoever falsely boasts of giving Is like clouds and wind without rain (Prov. 25:14).

Do not boast about tomorrow, For you do not know what a day may bring forth. Let another man praise you, and not your own mouth; A stranger, and not your own lips (Prov. 27:1-2).

For if anyone thinks himself to be something, when he is nothing, he deceives himself (Gal. 6:3).

What a simple point! The liar boasts, and falsely, about what he can do or what he's done or even about what he wants to do.

Even so the tongue is a little member and boasts great things. See how great a forest a little fire kindles! (James 3:5).

It's very common for us, because of this lying tendency in our hearts, to exaggerate and boast about things that have happened or we want to have happened. As a result, we wind up lying. The tongue has a natural tendency to boast and it causes tremendous problems.

But if you have bitter envy and self-seeking in your hearts, do not boast and lie against the truth (James 3:14).

If you're envious of somebody, you're jealous (for whatever reason) this is going to lead you into lying, whether you know it or not. Usually it will come by boasting. The Bible says don't boast. Stop it, and don't lie against the truth.

Whatever the truth is, it is, and nothing you say is going to change it. If you have self-seeking in your heart, you're trying to promote yourself, you're in a dangerous position because you're going to boast and lie about the truth.

I think one of the greatest examples of boasting is what we call (in business) your resume. It's incredible what's on peoples' resumes. It would be amusing, if it weren't so tragic. They put down anything. Promotions and honors and awards and trophies and all kinds of things-page after page of wonderful things. Then you read the bottom line and see that they're 30 years old. How did they get all of that in there in such a short period of time?

In conversation with people, we have a tendency to lie about who we are, and to present ourselves differently than another might describe us. Why? Because that tongue, that little member of your body, has a natural tendency to boast. Always remember that. Whenever we say anything, there is a tendency to boast, and to paint a different picture, and lie against the truth.

We need to be controlled. We're out of control, and we need something to control us, or we're going to wind up deceiving every time we talk to anybody.

Lying Is Failing to Live What We Believe

There is one other characteristic of lying I want you to focus on, and that is that we don't live what we claim to believe. We don't practice what we preach. It's a terrible thing to live a lie. There are some people who let their parents think that they are Christians, when in fact, they have never made any commitment to Christ. There are people who are church members, who went through all the motions and said all the right things, but in reality they have never been born again. They have been lying to everybody.

Our character is what we are in the dark, when no one knows. That's really what we are. Your reputation is just what people think you are. Your character is what God knows you to be. This is not easy to face sometimes.

If we say that we have fellowship with Him, and walk in darkness, we lie and do not practice the truth (I Jn. 1:6).

He who says, "I know Him," and does not keep His commandments, is a liar, and the truth is not in him (I Jn. 2:4).

All of us have to look at that with a sense of awe before God. "Lord, help me to speak truth, and to be truthful about who I am, and to live what I say I believe."

THE CONDITIONS WHEN LYING IS JUSTIFIED

There are several cases. We'll take a look at them.

In Exodus the midwives were told by Pharoah that when they delivered the Jewish baby boys, they were to kill them. When he asked them about it, they lied and said that the Jewish women delivered the babies before they could get there. They lied to spare those babies. Is that justified?

Another case is the case of Sampson in Judges 16. He lied several times, literally under the advice and direction of the Lord. Can you figure that out?

What about David and Jonathan? Jonathan lied through his teeth to his father, Saul, to spare David's life and God honored him for that.

What about the time that Samuel was going to anoint David, and was told by God to lie. That's a tough one. God said to tell him he came to sacrifice, then he wouldn't know what he was really there for. " Whoa! Wait a minute! I'm going to lie to him?" Samuel asked. God said, "Trust me." This is really tough, isn't it?

We read clearly in the Bible that *"Thou shalt not bear false witness."*

As you know, Isaac and Rebekah didn't have a child because Rebekah was barren even though they had prayed for a child. They were actually barren for twenty years. When the message came, it was given to Rebekah, not Isaac.

> And the Lord said to her: *"Two nations are in your womb, Two peoples shall be separated from your body; One people shall be stronger than the other, And the older shall serve the younger"* (Gen. 25:23).

So Rebekah knew clearly from God, that the older would serve the younger. The younger son, Jacob, was going to have the blessing and the birthright. She already knew that from God, while the children were still in her womb.

> And Jacob said to Rebekah his mother, *"Look, Esau my brother is a hairy man, and I am a smooth-skinned man. Perhaps my father will feel me, and I shall seem to be a deceiver to him; and I shall bring a curse on myself and not a blessing."* But his mother said to him, *"Let your curse be on me, my son; only obey my voice, and go, get them for me"* (Gen. 27:11-13).

Aren't we supposed to obey God rather than man? So if your parents tell you to lie, should you lie? Rebekah said to do what she told him to do. Since we are supposed to obey God, rather than man, and since Isaac is working to have Esau as his number one son, when Rebekah knows that the authority of God has already said that it is Jacob, then the proper thing is to obey God. In this case it is being expressed by the mother, and therefore the son should do what she said and deceive his father, who was way off base and away from the command of God.

So the higher authority does justify the lie to the lesser authority when it violates the authority of God. Are you with me so far?

> *And Jacob said to his father, "I am Esau your*
> *firstborn; I have done just as you told me; please arise,*
> *sit and eat of my game, that your soul may bless me."*
> *But Isaac said to his son, "How is it that you have*
> *found it so quickly, my son? And he said, "Because*
> *the Lord your God brought it to me"* (Gen. 27:19-20).

True or false? It's true. The Lord God was behind the whole thing. What was the lie, the deception? It was telling him that he was Esau. Does this trouble you?

> *Then he said, "Are you really my son Esau?" And*
> *he said, "I am"* (Gen. 27:24).

> *But he said, "Your brother came with deceit and*
> *has taken away your blessing"* (Gen. 27:35).

That's what Isaac said to Esau, when Esau found out what Jacob had done. Now, what's the problem here? Number one - did Esau or did he not, sell his birthright and blessing for a mess of pottage? Yes, he did. Did Esau marry pagan wives, directly against the commandment of God. Yes. He violated the command and the chain of command in God's program for the Messiah. Esau had forfeited everything by his lifestyle and his commitment. In Hebrews, chapter 12 it says Esau found no place for repentance, though he sought it with tears. The Bible says Esau had a root of bitterness in his heart, and Isaac was going along with it and supporting the very one to whom God said, "No".

Lying and deception can be justified when in fact, it honors the character and authority of God. To tell somebody you are not who the person thinks you are, to us sounds like a lie, but in reality, Jacob was obeying God and obeying his mother's instruction because of what God said. He's deceiving a father who has so deceived himself, that he thinks that Esau (in spite of what he had done) was still the Chosen One for the Messianic blessing. No way! Isaac is way off base, and Jacob and his mother are following the way of the Lord.

Jewish teaching on that subject has been consistent and never altered its opinion about it. Jacob is honored, he is never attacked for what he did. He's honored, because he honors the Lord. In Jewish history, when they refer to Jacob, he's always described as a man of truth. When you really understand it, there is more truth and more integrity in Jacob's life than there ever was in Isaac, his father, or in Esau. It's a tremendous insight into the whole problem of lying.

Is there a desire to go against the will of God? No. Is there a desire to disobey a known principle of the Word of God? No. Is there a desire to honor the truth as God had revealed it? Yes. Is that lying, then? Absolutely not. In other words, concealment of truth is not necessarily a lie. That's true in many cases. By the way, it's true with God. God tells us that He's concealed things from us.

God has not revealed everything to us, and no man will every really know all that God knows. Is God lying then, because He conceals truth from us? No. What he has revealed is always true, that's for sure, but God is hiding a lot of truth and knowledge from us. One day when we get to heaven we will know more than we know now, but even then we will never discover all there is to know about God. Is God lying to us because He hasn't told us everything about Himself? No. And neither are we, if we conceal the truth. Nevertheless, we need to be careful here.

In the case of Rahab in Joshua chapter 2, we have another example of somebody honoring the character of God, and submitting to the higher law, which deals with the sparing of human life. Let me give you an example. Suppose somebody comes into your house, and you've got kids upstairs in bed. They come in with assault rifles and say they're here to kill your children. I believe that it is perfectly honorable and right, based on the higher law of the protection of human life, to say to unbelievers, "No, they are not here." Dutch people and others who literally lied to the German Nazi soldiers to protect Jewish people, were honoring God. That happened time after time.

II Kings 6:13-23 says it's right to deceive the enemy. As a matter of fact, God told them to deceive the enemy, and they took the troops (after God struck them with blindness) to a different city than they had said at the beginning. It was a lie, but it was all set up by God to fulfill His purpose, and God told them to do that. Is it right to deceive the enemy in order to win the battle, and in order to accomplish the purposes of God? The answer is—absolutely! Every military man knows it.

Now Joshua the son of Nun sent out two men from Acacia Grove to spy secretly, saying, "Go, view the

*land, especially Jericho." So they went, and came to
the house of a harlot named Rahab, and lodged there.
And it was told the king of Jericho, saying, "Behold,
men have come here tonight from the children of Israel
to search out the country." So the king of Jericho sent
to Rahab, saying, "Bring out the men who have come
to you, who have entered your house, for they have
come to search out all the country." Then the woman
took the two men and hid them; and she said, "Yes,
the men came to me, but I did not know where they
were from* [lie number one]. *And it happened as the
gate was being shut, when it was dark, that the men
went out* [lie number two]. *Where the men went I do
not know* [lie number three]; *pursue them quickly, for
you may overtake them"* (Joshua 1:1-5).

I have read commentaries on this that do the most amazing gymnastics to get out of the fact that Rahab lied. I'm not
going to get out of it, Rahab did lie, and I say, "God bless her
memory."

*You see then that a man is justified by works, and
not by faith only. Likewise, was not Rahab the harlot also justified by works when she received the messengers and sent them out another way?* (James
2:24-25).

This passage is dealing with the issue of saving faith. If
you say you have faith and it doesn't do anything in your
life, that kind of faith doesn't save anybody. True saving
faith results in fruit being evidenced in the life.

Was Rahab lying? Yes or no? Absolutely, she was, and,
by the way, she married into the Messianic line. A Gentile
prostitute is in the line of the Messiah, all because she was
faithful to these spies and lied to the king of Jericho about
them.

Let me give you just one more to trouble you! I Samuel,
chapter 20, tells us the story of David and Jonathan.
Jonathan's father, King Saul, hated David and tried to kill
him.

*Now the king sat on his seat, as at other times, on
a seat by the wall. And Jonathan arose, and Abner
sat by Saul's side, but David's place was empty.
Nevertheless Saul did not say anything that day, for*

> *he thought, "Something has happened to him; he is unclean, surely he is unclean." And it happened the next day, the second day of the month, that David's place was empty. And Saul said to Jonathan his son, "Why has the son of Jesse not come to eat, either yesterday or today?" So Jonathan answered Saul, "David earnestly asked permission of me to go to Bethlehem. And he said, 'Please let me go, for our family has a sacrifice in the city, and my brother has commanded me to be there. And now, if I have found favor in your eyes, please let me get away and see my brothers.' Therefore he has not come to the king's table"* I Sam. 20:25-29).

Jonathan was lying through his teeth! Was he right or wrong?

> *Then Saul's anger was aroused against Jonathan, and he said to him, "You son of a perverse, rebellious woman! Do I not know that you have chosen the son of Jesse to your own shame and to the shame of your mother's nakedness? For as long as the son of Jesse lives on the earth, you shall not be established, nor your kingdom. Now therefore, send and bring him to me, for he shall surely die." And Jonathan answered Saul his father, and said to him, "Why should he be killed? What has he done?" Then Saul cast a spear at him to kill him, by which Jonathan knew that it was determined by his father to kill David. So Jonathan arose from the table in fierce anger, and ate no food the second day of the month, for he was grieved for David, because his father had treated him shamefully* (I Sam. 20:30-34).

Whether we like it or not, Jonathan lied, and it was a set up deal to expose the heart of wickedness in his father. Why did Jonathan do that? Once again, because he submitted to the higher authority. Jonathan knew that God had laid His hand on David to be the King of Israel. Jonathan knew what God had said, and he was watching to see if his father would react differently. He had to disobey his father, because he had to obey God rather than man.

Every time you dig just a little deeper, what you see in these supposed lies of the Bible (and they are lies), is that behind them is the motive and desire to honor the character of God and obey His authority. There are many examples in life where we ought to obey God rather than man. The deception is not because of a malicious motive to violate God's law, or to disobey God. The deception is rooted in a desire to please God, and to exalt his higher laws, of which the protection of human life is only one example.

THE CONSEQUENCES OF LYING

Let's now take a look at the consequences of lying. For one thing, **lying does not last.** People try to live a lie for a long time, but you can be sure your sin will find you out.

The truthful lip shall be established forever, But a lying tongue is but for a moment (Proverbs 12:19).

The lie won't last. If the deception is **not** rooted in obedience to God, honoring God's character, it's not going to last. It's going to be exposed. **The liar will not escape punishment.**

A false witness will not go unpunished, And he who speaks lies will not escape (Prov. 19:5).

A false witness will not go unpunished, And he who speaks lies shall perish (Prov. 19:9).

Getting treasures by a lying tongue Is the fleeting fantasy of those who seek death (Prov. 21:6).

A couple named Ananias and Sapphira (Acts 5) lied about the money they gave the Christians who were hurting in Jerusalem. Peter said to them they had not lied to man, but they had lied to God, and the result of their lie was that God killed them both on the spot. The sweeping consequences on the whole church were that the people began to fear the Lord and multitudes were added to the Lord. They saw that God doesn't mess around. **What we gain from lying will not satisfy us.** A lot of us lie, cheat, and deceive to get something we think we need or want, but it will not satisfy.

Bread gained by deceit is sweet to a man, But afterward his mouth will be filled with gravel (Prov. 20:17).

How vivid! It was sweet when you lied and got the result, but once you had it, it didn't satisfy and it turned sour.

The most serious consequence of lying is in the book of Revelation.

> But the cowardly, unbelieving, abominable, murderers, sexually immoral, sorcerers [drug addicts], idolaters, and all liars shall have their part in the lake which burns with fire and brimstone, which is the second death (Rev. 21:8).

> But there shall by no means enter it [the heavenly city] anything that defiles, or causes an abomination or a lie, but only those who are written in the Lamb's Book of Life (Rev. 21:27).

> But outside are dogs and sorcerers and sexually immoral and murderers and idolaters, and whoever loves and practices a lie (Rev. 22:15).

Obviously we commit sin, but anyone who continues in a practice of sin without repentance is described as a "liar". We do lie, but when you get into that habit and it's a constant lie—when you love the lie, you're continuing the lie, you cannot escape hell. When you are constantly immoral, when you are constantly a murderer, when you're constantly an idolater, and there's no repentance, you cannot escape **eternal judgment.** When you don't ask forgiveness from the Lord—there's no change of heart and you're continuing in sin, you will not escape hell. No way.

You can say all the right words to your friends, but if there's no change, no repentance, no attitude of remorse and getting right with God, then you have a hardened heart. You're giving evidence that you're not a believer—you're an unbeliever. God says the result will be hell.

THE CONTROL OF LYING

We control lying by loving people like we love ourselves. I don't have to tell you to love yourself; you already do. **Love people like you love yourself** and it will control lying.

> Owe no one anything except to love one another, for he who loves another has fulfilled the law. For the

commandments, *"You shall not commit adultery," "You shall not murder," "You shall not steal," "You shall not bear false witness," "You shall not covet," and if there is any other commandment, are all summed up in this saying, namely, "You shall love your neighbor as yourself"* (Rom. 13:8-9).

What a simple admonition! You just love people like you do yourself, and you'll start to control lying. I love you so much, I need to tell you the truth. What a simple statement.

I've found that's one of the hardest things to do in life. The Bible says, *"speak the truth in love"* (Eph. 4:15).

This brings me to the second way to control lying, and that is—**speak the truth.**

Therefore, putting away lying, each one speak truth with his neighbor, for we are members of one another (Eph. 4:25).

A lot of us don't sense our fellowship in the body of Christ. We're brothers and sisters in the Lord, so stop lying to each other; just tell the truth. If we love others as we do ourselves, and if we speak the truth, there will be a control of lying in our life.

A third thing I would recommend is to **pray for God's help.**

"Watch and pray, lest you enter into temptation. The spirit indeed is willing, but the flesh is weak" (Matt. 26:41).

The Greek word means *"without strength"*; helpless, not just sick. You can't do anything. The spirit is willing and your heart says, "I want to tell you the truth," but the flesh is totally helpless. It's geared toward lying and deceit, so we have a struggle.

What should we do to solve the problem? Jesus said to *"Watch and pray."* Be on the alert—be careful because you're always being tempted to lie. Pray, call upon the Lord and ask for God's help. Ask God to help you to speak the truth.

You may be aware of something that you're covering—some lie, some deceitful practice. Maybe it's with family, spouse, a friend at work. There's a lie there and it has come to your attention. Now you're faced with it. What are you going to do about it?

We all need to understand our need of the Lord's help to tell the truth. When we've been lying and we start to tell the truth, there is the danger of boasting of great things and coloring it again. Some people wind up lying again in a different way. How are we going to handle it without the Lord's help? Well, we're not. We need to pray and ask the Lord for help.

You desire truth in the inward parts, And in the hidden part You will make me to know wisdom. Purge me with hyssop, and I shall be clean (Ps. 51:6-7).

Hyssop is a plant like Yucca which is used to scrub the sores of lepers. You wouldn't use it on a normal hand, but in the sore of a leper there's no pain. It was used to get rid of the dead tissue and see if there was healing underneath. David takes that symbolism and compares leprosy to sin in our hearts, especially in the realm of lying. He said it makes you insensitive, like leprosy does, so you don't feel the pain anymore. So, he prays to the Lord and says, "Purge me with hyssop. Scrub me, Lord, and get this junk out of my life."

I pray that the seriousness of that prayer of David's in Psalm 51 might grip your heart. If you want to get victory, you had better call upon the Lord. "Lord, help me to tell the truth."

One last thing. We must **rely upon the Holy Spirit** in our lives as a regular habit.

Walk in the Spirit, and you shall not fulfill the lust of the flesh (Gal. 5:16).

How can a young man cleanse his way? By taking heed according to Your word. Your word have I hidden in my heart, That I might not sin against You (Ps. 119:9,11).

CHAPTER 10

THE PROBLEM OF LAZINESS

The problem of laziness is dealt with in Proverbs. One would almost think that this would be an unusual subject. Why would God bring this up in the Bible? Actually, there is quite a bit in the Bible about it. I believe it's well accepted that laziness is just a problem, not really a sin, especially if you happen to feel a little lazy every now and then. It's hard to know how to feel about this subject. However, the Bible has some strong condemnation for people who are lazy. There's also some good advice.

There are two Hebrew words used for "lazy", and one of them means "faint or feeble", but the other word (used 16 times) just means downright lazy! You don't feel motivated to do anything.

> Go to the ant, you sluggard! Consider her ways and be wise, Which, having no captain, Overseer or ruler, Provides her supplies in the summer, And gathers her food in the harvest. How long will you slumber, O sluggard? When will you rise from your sleep? A little sleep, a little slumber, A little folding of the hands to sleep - So shall your poverty come on you like a robber, And your need like an armed man (Prov. 6:6-11).

> I went by the field of the slothful, And by the vineyard of the man devoid of understanding; And there it was, all overgrown with thorns; Its surface was covered with nettles; Its stone wall was broken down. When I saw it, I considered it well; I looked on it and received instruction: A little sleep, a little slumber, A little folding of the hands to rest; So your poverty will come like a prowler, And your want like an armed man (Prov. 24:30-34).

The first time I heard about this was from my mother. I remember it well. I wanted to sleep in and I had a job to do, so my mother came into my room and woke me up. She read me this passage and walked out of the room. It bothered me all day—*"slothful ... sluggard ... lazy"*. God has a lot to say to us.

THE CHARACTERISTICS OF LAZINESS

I'd like to list for you some characteristics of laziness, the slothful person, the sluggard - the one who just isn't excited about anything. After you've worked hard, the bed can feel sweet, and many mornings we wake up wishing we could stay in it just a little bit longer. Is that laziness?

He Depends on Others to Give Direction

I hope this will demonstrate how all-encompassing the problem of laziness is in our midst. Verse 7 speaks of the ant, *"Which, having no captain, Overseer or ruler,"* does her work. An ant doesn't need anybody to give direction. One of the greatest needs we have among Christians today is for people who know what God wants them to do and who will do it without anyone telling them what to do. Happy is the parent whose kids do what they ought to do without being pressured, constantly "kicked in the pants" to get going for God.

We need to understand how motivation needs to come from our hearts before the Lord to do what God wants us to do and not wait for somebody to give us direction in doing it. It's a characteristic of a sluggish heart, a lazy heart when we depend on others for direction.

He Fails to Plan Ahead

We're to go to (and learn from) the ant who provides her supplies in the summer, and gathers her food in the harvest. So the ant is ready when there's cold in the winter and she can't go out looking for food. The ant is prepared ahead of time. A sluggard is someone who fails to plan ahead.

Someone, according to one magazine, paid $250,000 to a major company to find out how they could work more effectively in their corporation. The result of that study was a suggestion that each employee have a "things to do" list, and now, you can buy a little pad in the average stationery store that says, "Things to do".

We've been told over and over again about making a list, planning ahead, laying plans for the future. A sluggard never plans ahead. A sluggard just kind of cruises through life and lets it all happen. He doesn't think or plan at all.

He Neglects to Care For What He Has

You can always tell a sluggard by looking at his front lawn. Somebody has a sluggish heart.

I went by the field of the slothful, And by the vineyard of the man devoid of understanding; And there it was, all overgrown with thorns; Its surface was covered with nettles; Its stone wall was broken down (Prov. 24:30).

He neglects to care for what he has. That is a sluggard.

He Desires Things, But Does Not Work For Them

In an airline magazine, I read about how to get ahead in business. It said we have to work "smarter", not "harder". It said you can get a lot of things in life that you don't have to work for, if you just know how to do it. God has some words for that kind of a person.

The soul of a sluggard desires, and has nothing; But the soul of the diligent shall be made rich (Prov. 13:4).

God blesses hard work and diligence, and He condemns the person who just wants things, but doesn't do anything about it.

The desire of the slothful kills him, For his hands refuse to labor (Prov. 21:25).

That's why some people are eaten alive by desire that's unrealized. They never accomplish their goals in life. Their ambition far excels their desire to work, and I think that's basically true about all of us. We all would like to see wonderful things happen to us without any effort. Who wouldn't?

We say of some people, who seem successful, "Whatever he touches turns to gold". I recently read a report of a corporation in real estate. The young executive who manages this particular corporation has (before the age of 30) become a multi-millionaire. A new employee was curious as to how he had succeeded. He investigated, and the answer was hard work. He didn't stop. He kept at it all the time. Of course, there's always someone to come along and hand him an article about how dangerous it is to be a "workaholic". It's almost like we are on a crusade to prove that we can be successful with the least amount of effort.

In a recent business magazine, it said the number one desire of Americans in the work force today, is to have more leisure time. Time is now the great commodity, even more important than money. We want to work less hours and have more fun in between. Work is no longer a good thing. Work is an evil; work is something you tolerate in order to get your paycheck in order to buy the things that you want to get in life.

So we go to work on Monday morning with a bad spirit. We're downgrading the whole issue of work, but we ought to have (as believers) a desire to go to work. When we meet someone who has this eagerness to work, we hate them so much we don't know what to do! We feel like hitting them, or doing something to straighten them out!

A lazy person is one who desires a lot, but simply does not work for it. If you apply that to the spiritual realm, and you'll see the reason why a lot of us do not bear fruit in our lives.

He Puts Forth No Effort to Meet Basic Needs

Be sure to read carefully what I am going to say about the hungry and the homeless. I've met a lot of hungry and homeless people. There are some that are really in need, who really lost their job, but there are some of them that just won't work. I've met some right here in my community who have become professional panhandlers and love to laugh about it. Every time I see them now, they run the other way. I really get sick and tired of that, and so do you, but there are some real needy people who get hurt in the process.

There are a tremendous number of people who are hurting, and now I'm observing more families - women and children - that are hungry and homeless. Yet some of these

panhandlers make it tough for those of us who really want
to care. We run into these charlatan types, who sit around
and make money by doing nothing. Then they laugh and joke
about it. If you find them jobs, the first thing they say is
that they don't work for minimum wage. Are they really
hungry and homeless?

*A slothful man [a lazy man] buries his hand in the
bowl, And will not so much as bring it to his mouth
again (Prov. 19:24).*

I love God's vivid illustrations! Here's a guy that's going
to eat—he's got the bowl of food—but he sticks his hand in
it and is too lazy to bring the food up to his mouth. If that
isn't graphic, I don't know what is!

*The slothful man [slothful, sluggard, and lazy are
all the same Hebrew word] buries his hand in the
bowl; It wearies him to bring it back to his mouth (Prov.
26:15).*

*But we command you, brethren, in the name of our
Lord Jesus Christ, that you withdraw from every
brother who walks disorderly and not according to the
tradition which he received from us. For you yourselves know how you ought to follow us, for we were not
disorderly among you; nor did we eat anyone's bread
free of charge, but worked with labor and toil night
and day, that we might not be a burden to any of you,
not because we do not have authority, but to make
ourselves an example of how you should follow us.*

*For even when we were with you, we commanded
you this: If anyone will not work, neither shall he eat.
For we hear that there are some who walk among you
in a disorderly manner, not working at all, but are
busybodies. Now those who are such we command
and exhort through our Lord Jesus Christ that they
work in quietness and eat their own bread.*

*But as for you, brethren, do not grow weary in
doing good. And if anyone does not obey our word in
this epistle, note that person and do not keep company
with him, that he may be ashamed. Yet do not count
him as an enemy, but admonish him as a brother (II
Thess. 3:6 -15).*

That is a fascinating passage, isn't it? It relates to the whole business of society. We have scores and scores of people now, who do not want to work, but they want us to feed them. God says, if they don't work, they don't eat. That's different from somebody who can't get a job or can't work, but there are plenty of people who are able to work, and simply won't do it. It's embarrassing to take people to a business that will hire them and have them refuse to work when they find out it's a minimum wage job.

He Is Not Reliable

> As vinegar to the teeth and smoke to the eyes, So is the sluggard to those who send him (Prov. 10:26).

Someone sends him on a mission, and he's so lazy he won't carry through—you can't trust him to carry it out. It will not be accomplished.

He Does Not Respond When Facing Hardship

> The sluggard will not plow because of winter; Therefore he will beg during the harvest And have nothing (Prov. 20:4).

He won't plow because it's winter; it's too cold outside. It's snowing out there!

He Makes Excuses for His Lack of Involvement

> The slothful man says, "There is a lion outside! I shall be slain in the streets!" (Prov. 22:13).

Sometimes their excuses are really ridiculous.

He Lacks Understanding

He's not thinking clearly. He's certainly not thinking God's thoughts.

> I went by the field of the slothful, And by the vineyard of the man devoid of understanding (Prov. 24:30).

*The slothful man says, "There is a lion in the road!
A fierce lion is in the streets!"* (Prov. 26:13).

*As a door turns on its hinges, So does the slothful
turn on his bed. The slothful man buries his hand in
the bowl; It wearies him to bring it back to his mouth.
The sluggard is wiser in his own eyes Than seven men
who can answer sensibly* (Prov. 26:14-16).

He Thinks He Is Wise

A lazy person always thinks he is smart. He is wise in
his own eyes.

He Destroys the Work That Has Been Done

That's the sad thing. Someone might have worked hard
to do something for the Lord, or for his family, and a lazy
person can come in and destroy in short order what has been
done over a long period of time.

*He who is slothful in his work Is a brother to him
who is a great destroyer* (Prov. 18:9).

If I asked you if you knew or worked with someone who
is lazy, most of you would say yes. I wonder if the person
you're talking about would say the same about you!

He Does Nothing in Adversity

When things are really tough, you can't count on this person at all. An interesting comparison in Proverbs 17:17 is,
*"A friend loves at all times, And a brother is born for adver-
sity"*—but not a lazy person.

*If you faint in the day of adversity, Your strength
is small* (Prov. 24:10).

That's the tradgedy about a lazy person—you cannot
count on them in difficult times; they're not reliable—they
are lazy.

THE CONSEQUENCES OF BEING LAZY

One of the consequences is that you **sleep when it's time to work.**

Slothfulness casts one into a deep sleep, And an idle person will suffer hunger (Prov. 19:15).

If you're sleeping when it's time to work, you're going to pay a price for that.

Another consequence that we see often mentioned in the Proverbs, is also mentioned in Ecclesiastes—that's **deterioration.** Everything deteriorates, everything falls apart. That can happen in an organization. When you have somebody in the structure who is lazy, it all falls apart at that point. It deteriorates. You can have that in construction, as well. You can have a lot of guys working hard on a project, and put a lazy person in there and things will deteriorate.

Because of laziness the building decays, And through idleness of hands the house leaks (Eccl. 10:18).

In a community that I knew about several years ago, something happened that blessed my heart. It was a community that was going down—really deteriorating. I don't know if God just put all sluggards in one block or what, but it was really bad. Everybody's house was a mess. Every house needed painting. Every yard needed mowing. It was a disaster and it was getting worse. People called it a ghetto and pronounced judgments on those who lived there.

In that particular community God placed a dear couple who loved the Lord and saw the tragedy of all this. They were able to buy a place very cheap in the neighborhood. They started working every weekend, painting, cleaning, doing the yard, and so forth. One of the funny things which you could see driving through that neighborhood was that you could see other people standing outside with their hands in their pockets, watching these people. After a while, one by one they started fixing up their own places and soon the whole neighborhood was clean and nice looking—all because a few people decided to work instead of being lazy. Wouldn't it be great if people all over America, in every ghetto, decided to do that?

I was really challenged when I visited New York City for a radio rally in a facility that was in a bad neighborhood. It was in a church that had graffiti on it. I was challenged by the pastor and his people who went out there and rubbed it off and painted it every time there was graffiti. They had done it 35 times in one month! I asked him if he wasn't tired of doing it, and he said, "Yes, but we're not going to stop." I thought to myself - there's a man who has no laziness in his blood. There's a man who knows what to do. The inspiration, everything in that church and its ministry was booming, because that man was not lazy. He saw a problem, and he was there; "he was born for adversity". I watched the effect that had on the community and the people. It was really powerful.

Understand that laziness produces deterioration—always—whether it's in buildings and properties, or in personal lives. Be careful!

Here is another consequence of laziness—**thorns in the way**; trouble in the path that God has for you.

The way of the slothful man is like a hedge of thorns, But the way of the upright is a highway (Prov. 15:19).

The way that a slothful man walks is a hedge of thorns, nothing but problems in it. It needs to be cleared away. Thorns are used as an allegory, or an illustration.

Thorns and snares are in the way of the perverse; He who guards his soul will be far from them (Prov. 22:5).

Obviously, thorns take on a spiritual impact; this is not simply the literal thorns in our way. He's talking here about our lives. Thorns can tear at your soul. *"He who guards his soul will be far from them."* If you don't guard your soul, you're lazy about your spiritual life. There will be thorns, traps, and snares in your way.

Isn't it interesting what the next verse says [if you're a parent, take note!]

Train up a child in the way he should go ... (Prov.22:6).

In Proverbs, the way the Lord wants you to go is contrasted with the way of the wicked; the way of the righteous compared with the way of the wicked. The way of the diligent is the opposite of the way of the slothful. The way of the perverse is contrasted with the way of character and integrity. That's what we see here: The way of the perverse is in verse 5, the way of the Lord is in verse 6.

Parents are to train their children. They are not to be lazy and slothful in training their children, otherwise there will be thorns and snares in the path of the child. There is a terrible consequence if you're so lazy that when you come home at night, you don't have time to spend with the children. You're lazy and indifferent if you don't have time to discipline a child when he needs it (in a godly manner). If you don't have time to teach the child the way of the Lord, you're lazy! Many parents don't know that what Proverbs is about is laziness and how it can affect the life of your child.

I've compared my generation and how we raised our kids with the way I was raised. Then I look at the way kids are being raised today. It's like America is on a slide—we're getting more lazy all the time. I remember at age ten, I went out and got a job. I also remember going to school one day, and a kid showed me his allowance. I didn't even know what it was! I went home and asked my dad about an allowance, and he asked what they did to get it. I didn't know, so he told me to find out. I went back and asked, and the kid said he did nothing for it. When I told my dad, he said, "Well, that's going to ruin their life. You wouldn't want me to do that for you, would you?"

So, I went out and got a job! I've known from age ten on that I should work and I believe that it was a blessing in life. I've watched this in society and noticed that things are on a slide. How are we going to turn this around? Parents have got to stop being lazy in training their children *"in the way they should go"*.

One of the most frequent characteristics of laziness is the matter of **poverty and need**. Why are so many people in need? Could it be that there is laziness in the background?

> *So shall your poverty come on you like a robber,*
> *And your need like an armed man* (Prov. 6:11).

It will come as a surprise; you won't believe it! "What did I do to deserve this?" you'll say. Plenty! You've been lazy for quite a while. Are you getting the message that God blesses the person who works hard?

*The soul of a sluggard desires, and has nothing;
But the soul of the diligent shall be made rich*
(Prov.13:4).

*The sluggard will not plow because of winter;
Therefore he will beg during the harvest And have
nothing* (Prov. 20:4).

The consequence of laziness is poverty and need.

*So your poverty will come like a prowler, And your
want like an armed man* (Prov. 24:34).

There is one other consequence that our Lord Jesus
pointed out that is really convicting to me. Jesus points out
that there will be a **loss of reward**. I wonder how many
believers are affected by this. We have a parable that begins
in Mathew 25:14 of a man who was going to a far country.
He called his servants together and gave different amounts
of money to each one. To one he gave five talents; to another,
two; and to another, one.

*"But his lord answered and said to him, 'You wick-
ed and lazy servant, you knew that I reap where I
have not sown, and gather where I have not scattered
seed.   Therefore you ought to have deposited my
money with the bankers, and at my coming I would
have received back my own with interest. Therefore
take the talent from him, and give it to him who has
ten talents. For to everyone who has, more will be
given, and he will have abundance; but from him who
does not have, even what he has will be taken away'"*
(Matt. 25:26-29).

That's almost a paradox! Doesn't that seem unfair? It
says the fellow who does not have, will have it taken from
him. Wait a minute! He had one talent, what didn't he
"have"? What he didn't have was any use for the talent that
he had. He didn't do anything with it, so the Bible says that
God will take from the one who does not produce, all that
He gave him. The person who went out with the five talents
and worked hard, had ten talents when the master came
back because he really worked hard. He got the other
fellow's one talent.

One of the difficulties about this parable is verse 30.

> *"'And cast the unprofitable servant* [the lazy ser-
> vant] *into the outer darkness. There will be weeping
> and gnashing of teeth.'"*

You can see that if I'd begun this study with the talents
representing salvation, we would have a fellow losing his salvation. If the talents were to represent salvation, then we'd
have a person able to work to improve his salvation, so we
would walk into a performance-oriented salvation.

We could argue that the talents are simply the rewards
for the service we do for God involving the use of our gifts
and how we use all the resources God has given us for the
Lord. Then the one fellow who doesn't do anything with what
God gave him is not just losing the reward, he is lost in hell!
Either way you go, you're in trouble on this one!

If the talents represent the abilities and gifts that God has
given us, and if we're so lazy we haven't used what we've got,
that text says that we're going to wind up with "weeping and
wailing and gnashing of teeth". That's a description of hell.
Does it mean you lose your salvation because you don't serve
the Lord? That's pretty serious, isn't it? You're probably
saying that you don't believe that. I can understand why
you don't want to, but it still sits there, staring us in the face.

Is it possible that we're trying to make this parable walk
on all fours! Is it possible that this servant has never been
saved in the beginning? He's not one of the Lord's children
at all. What else did he use besides the word "lazy" in
describing this servant? He called him, "Wicked," a term
that Jesus Christ never uses of the saved, only of the lost.

Read carefully. Laziness, in terms of doing what God
wants us to do, is the number one mark of an unbelieving
heart. I don't believe you can lose your salvation, but laziness is a mark, a characteristic, of an unbelieving heart. He
was a wicked, lazy, unprofitable servant, and he won't get
away with it.

I looked at that and wondered if there were a challenge
here for the believer. Yes, there is. There is strong teaching
from Paul, and we have to think it through carefully. In I
Corinthians 3, Paul tells us to really work.

> *"I planted, Apollos watered, but God gave the in-
> crease. So then neither he who plants is anything, nor
> he who waters, but God who gives the increase. Now
> he who plants and he who waters are one, and each*

one will receive his own reward according to his own labor. For we are God's fellow workers; you are God's field, you are God's building. According to the grace of God which was given to me, as a wise master builder I have laid the foundation, and another builds on it. But let each one take heed how he builds on it. For no other foundation can anyone lay than that which is laid, which is Jesus Christ. Now if anyone builds on this foundation with gold, silver, precious stones, [here's another category] *wood, hay, straw, each one's work will become manifest; for the Day* [presumably the Day of God's judging hand] *will declare it, because it will be revealed by fire; and the fire will test each one's work, of what sort it is.* [Obviously, the wood, hay and straw would be burned up.] *If anyone's work which he has built on it endures, he will receive a reward.* [The precious metal would endure.] *If anyone's work is burned, he will suffer loss; but he himself will be saved, yet so as through fire* (I Cor. 3:6-14).

What do you think? It seems to me, first of all, that if any of us gets to heaven, it's by the skin of our teeth! We only make it, because of the grace of our Lord Jesus Christ, and not because of any merit of our own. That's for sure. Thank God, he rescued us out of the pit of hell, and set our feet on a solid rock.

I think there is another thread here. Not a single one of us can walk away without saying, "Serving the Lord is more serious than I thought!" God puts no premium on laziness. There is a consequence to it and that's a loss of reward. Sometimes I think of standing in front of Jesus and hearing Him say, *"Well done, thou good and faithful servant. Enter into the joy of the Lord."* I want to hear that, don't you? Jesus said to *"work for the night is coming when no one can work".* Work while it's day. Are you still breathing? God has a job for you.

THE CURE FOR LAZINESS

God's cure is three simple things. We could say, "Go out and get a job!" or make up a long list of things, but let me give you what God says.

Learn From the Ant

Why not learn from an elephant or a lion? Give me something good! An ant, you're kidding me! The first thing it suggests is the need for humility, doesn't it? How stupid we are. Learn from the ant!

It also suggests that a little creature that crawls along our sinks has a lot of intelligence that we don't seem to grasp as human beings. Learn from the ant. *"Consider her ways and be wise."*

One day when I was a little boy, I was sitting on the sidewalk watching an ant carry a load that was five times its size. I put my finger up as a block to see if that would discourage the ant. No way, the ant persisted no matter what I did. Even carrying a huge load, it didn't quit.

What do we do? We ask for a lighter load! What we ought to ask for is stronger shoulders to carry the burdens that we ought to be carrying. The Bible says, *"Bear one another's burdens, and you'll fulfill the law of Christ."* Most of us say, "No way, I've got too much now. I need a break." Really? God knows when you need a break.

There is a general tendency not only in our secular society, but in our Christian communities to do as little as possible for the Lord. You know that, and I know that. However, there is a positive side of serving the Lord! That's what is coming. The joy of God is in your heart when you're serving the Lord. Serving the Lord until you get tired is a lot better than doing nothing well rested.

Observe the Consequences of Laziness

When I saw it, I considered it well; I looked on it and received instruction (Prov. 24:32).

Solomon said, "I looked at this field and saw the consequences of somebody who is lazy. I sat there and studied it well, and I received instruction. Lord, don't let that ever happen to me!"

Serve the Lord With Your Whole Heart

We are to serve the Lord with our whole heart.

...not lagging in diligence, fervent in spirit, serving the Lord (Rom. 12:11).

When I tell all believers to go out and serve the Lord, everyone agrees, but if I say that the only ones who will be accepted by our Lord are the ones who serve Him with their whole heart, the number who agree is reduced. I'm talking total dedication, intensity, your whole heart. A lot of us just do what we can to get by.

You don't have to answer to me; it's Him we have to answer to. Serve with your whole heart. *"Don't lag behind in dililgent service. Be fervent in spirit, serving the Lord."*

Servants, obey in all things your masters according to the flesh, not with eyeservice, as men-pleasers, but in sincerity of heart, fearing God. And whatever you do, do it heartily, as to the Lord and not to men, knowing that from the Lord you will receive the reward of the inheritance; for you serve the Lord Christ. But he who does wrong [does not serve the Lord with a whole heart] will be repaid for the wrong which he has done, and there is no partiality (Col. 3:22-25).

You're going to suffer the consequences of laziness or half- heartedness in the work of the Lord. It's going to come from the Lord. Whatever you do, do it heartily, with your whole heart, and do it unto the Lord, not to other people. Do whatever you can, and if someone doesn't think it is as good as it should be, forget it! Don't listen to that. If you've done it with all your heart and done the best that you can, it's no disgrace. Even if you fail, it's not a sin. The sin is to do less that your best.

It's a sin for us to do less than our best, and we'll experience the consequence of that. However, if we've done the best we can, and we fail, it is no disgrace. One day, we shall be rewarded by our Lord Jesus Christ, no matter what, because we served Him with our whole heart.

"Turn your eyes upon Jesus.
Look full in His wonderful face,
And the things of earth will grow strangely dim,
In the light of His glory and grace."

CHAPTER 11

THE PROBLEM OF GOSSIP

In our study of Proverbs, we now come to a very serious matter—the problem of gossip. We'll deal first with the characteristics of a person who gossips. Then we'll look at the consequences of gossip, and the control of gossip. Every one of us has a natural tendency to listen to gossip and to repeat it.

> Lord, who may abide in Your tabernacle? Who may dwell in Your holy hill? He who walks uprightly, And works righteousness, And speaks the truth in his heart; He who does not backbite with his tongue, Nor does evil to his neighbor, Nor does he take up a reproach against his friend; In whose eyes a vile person is despised, But he honors those who fear the Lord; He who swears to his own hurt and does not change; He who does not put out his money at usury [interest], Nor does he take a bribe against the innocent. He who does these things shall never be moved (Psalm 15).

It is interesting to note the things that are concluded in this passage about what kind of people walk with the Lord. It mentions gossip, and backbiting, and *"taking up a reproach against a friend"*. This literally means somebody put your friend down and you accepted what they said, and did not defend your friend. You did not challenge and confront what was said. There are a lot of interesting things in this Psalm.

One week, I decided to count up the rumors and gossip I heard that could have hurt some people. There were five incidents. In each one of them, the people involved (some were lay people, some were ministers) believed that what they were saying was the truth, and in each case, it was not the truth. I have discovered that it is a lot easier to repeat that which is not true than to find out what is true. I have found out that something about us wants to hear the failure, the trouble, the suffering and the heartache of other people without ever investigating it as to whether it is the truth or not. It is a terrible thing in the Christian world. Sometimes it is prefaced with these unique, spiritual-sounding words- "I want you to pray about something." Doesn't that make it sweet! But you had no right to share it. Once you find out what the Bible says, you'll see how many times, we have no right to do that, and we should be defending and protecting each other a lot more than we are.

THE CHARACTERISTICS
OF A PERSON WHO GOSSIPS

How do you spot a gossip? How do you recognize it in your own heart? There are six basics that I would draw to your attention from the book of Proverbs.

Whoever hides hatred has lying lips, And whoever spreads slander is a fool (Prov. 10:18).

Isn't that an interesting thing? You didn't neccesarily tell a lie, but you really had hatred in your heart and you covered it up. God says you've got lying lips. That's what we call a parallism in the poetic usages in Proverbs—the second statement is like the first, so **spreading slander** is the same thing as hiding hatred.

"What I'm saying is in strict confidence, something we can pray about," and similar statements show a symptom of a problem of gossip. We wouldn't even do that unless we had the problem. So we set it all up, and then before we know what's happening, slander is being spread. God says the root is that there is hatred in your heart, otherwise you wouldn't do that. If you loved them, you would cover the situation completely. That's hard to face because you don't want to say, "I hate that guy so I'm just trying to inform you, so you can be more intelligent in your prayer life." Really? The Bible says, *"Whoever spreads slander is a fool."*

Whenever anything puts down a brother or a sister in the Lord, immediately check it, no matter who it is. If the information makes somebody who is a believer in the Lord look bad, check it immediately. Then ask the person reporting the situation if they have been to that person to try to help. That's one way to deal with it.

A second characteristic of a gossip is that he **reveals secrets.**

A talebearer [gossip] *reveals secrets, But he who is of a faithful spirit conceals a matter* (Prov. 11:13).

You and I both know that this is a very important point in counseling and in the legal profession, where we are not to betray confidences. This is a poetic device by contrast, not parallelism. The contrast is between one who conceals what he knows and one who reveals what he knows. One of the surest characteristics of a gossip, or a slandering spirit, is when you immediately reveal things. You want to tell somebody, instead of protecting it.

He who goes about as a talebearer [a gossip] *reveals secrets; Therefore do not associate with one who flatters with his lips* (Prov. 20:19).

"Flattering with your lips" in this context is interesting, because you're actually revealing secrets, but doing it in a way that deceives the person that you're talking to. So you wind up being a gossip. You may be very good at it. You may be able to cover it up, but in reality, because you revealed a secret, you're telling something that you don't have a right to share. That makes you guilty of gossiping.

Another characteristic of a person that gossips is that he **stirs up and sows strife** and division among the people of God. There's an example of this in I Corinthians, chapter 1, verse 10 and following, about division in the church in Corinth. It says that *"contentions"* had been reported by those of Chloe's household. Somebody had spread a rumor and caused division in the body of Christ. That happens so often.

Many believe that that's what Paul is referring to in Philippians, chapter 4, when he said, *"I implore Euodia and I implore Syntyche to be of the same mind in the Lord."* Some believe that they were spreading rumors, or it could be that they were just upset with one another and talking against one another to others. Paul said to stop it because they were causing division among the members of the body of Christ.

Hatred stirs up strife, But love covers all sins (Prov. 10:12).

It's hatred in our hearts that stirs up strife. Love covers all sins. One of the hardest things that a Christian must bear is when he learns about another fellow Christian that has fallen. That's very hard, and even when it's the truth and it has been handled properly, it's very hard not to bring it up again. Love will cover it.

A perverse man sows strife, And a whisperer separates the best of friends (Prov. 16:28).

Where there is no wood, the fire goes out; And where there is no talebearer, strife ceases (Prov.26:20).

If you were attending a church seminar on church relationships and somebody asked you, "How do you stop division and strife in the church?" Proverbs tells you to find out who the gossip is, and stop it right there. If you don't have a gossip around, no talebearer, then it will stop.

It was interesting to me to discover that when truth is communicated to you, it does not mean that you are to tell it to somebody else. It is bad enough when you hear something that is a rumor and you don't know if it is the truth or not, but even when truth is shared with you, you aren't automatically to tell another person what you just learned. If there is love in your heart, it might cover what the truth is, so that it can be properly resolved and handled.

When an issue in the life of somebody is very serious - they have fallen into sin, but then they get right with the Lord, and somebody hears the fact that they've fallen into sin and then says, "Did you hear that so-and-so fell into sin?" It spreads, but the problem was solved months ago. I've seen more people's lives hurt because we do not apply love to people. It's easy to believe that we are under divine responsibility to share that truth. No we aren't. That's not what the Bible teaches. Sometimes it's necessary, but certainly not always.

A fourth characteristic simply that a gossip is one who **repeats a matter.** They have no business to repeat it, it is not necessary to repeat it, they just do.

He who covers a transgression seeks love, But he who repeats a matter separates the best of friends (Prov. 17:9).

Now in this particular case, looking at the poetry of that passage, we know that the matter under discussion is a transgression. It is honorable to cover it, even though it has been a transgression against you. Some of the highest honor belongs to members of the body of Christ who have had transgressions committed against them, who refuse to tell anyone else. They simply confront the one who transgressed against them and wait patiently for the Lord to solve it, and if He never does, they still will not seek revenge. That is godliness.

The desire to tell others about a transgression that has taken place is very strong. We feel we need to get it off our chests. We begin by asking the other person not to tell what we're about to say. Hey, don't even promise! Many times somebody will tell you something that you must tell such as a crime. So, just say you will not tell anybody unless it is necessary according to the Bible to do so. If they say they won't tell you unless you promise, so be it. However, a lot of us (because we like to hear something) will "promise". What's the matter with us? If we would only become stronger in our desire to protect, stronger in our desire to defend, stronger in our desire to have only those people deal with it who really need to deal with it, we would see more healing in the body of Christ than hurt. The rest of us should stay out of it.

There are people who are badly hurt, who are not even ministering any more, and are worshipping in church, but don't want to get involved with anybody's life. I understand that, but it grieves me. We can destroy people's lives so quickly by what we share. We need to be very careful.

A false witness shall perish, But the man who hears him will speak endlessly (Prov. 21:28).

God is going to deal with a man who is a false witness, but the one who hears the false witness, *"speaks endlessly".* The rumor keeps going and going, and it was all based on a false report. It was not true, but it spread like wildfire. One writer on gossip says that "error dressed up in partial truth, spreads more rapidly than the truth itself." I think that's true.

The fifth characteristic of a person who gossips, is that they **do evil to their friends.**

He who does not backbite with his tongue, Nor does evil to his neighbor, Nor does he take up a reproach against his friend (Ps. 15:3).

It's a commendation to a godly man who doesn't do that. There we see the characteristic of a gossip-they do evil to the person who obviously is their friend. They spread the rumor, they tell the matter without any authority to do so, or any accountability involved. That is a terrible thing to do to your friend.

This last characteristic of a gossip is that he **likes to hear it.** Here's where we need to deal with ourselves. We like to hear gossip. The more influential that person is to you, the more likely you will spread a rumor. Maybe that will help us decide why we're doing what we're doing. There is something in us that needs to be dealt with.

The words of a talebearer are like tasty trifles, And they go down into the inmost body **(Prov. 18:8).**

It's hard to accept the fact that we enjoy hearing about or telling about things that are none of our business. The Bible is true, and what we say is not always true. We need to confront ourselves with this.

The words of a talebearer are like tasty trifles, And they go down into the inmost body **(Prov. 26:22).**

When a Proverb is repeated **exactly** (cf. 18:8 and 26:22 above), it is done for emphasis. It is crucial. When you say something about someone, even when it's not true, the untruth goes down into you. The rumor gets into you, and the rumor affects your relationship with that person. Even when the issue has been dealt with, people have a tendency to believe the rumor rather than the truth.

THE CONSEQUENCES OF GOSSIP

What are some of the consequences? For one thing, **gossip destroys a reputation.**

The hypocrite with his mouth destroys his neighbor, But through knowledge the righteous will be delivered (Prov. 11:9).

The hypocrite obviously is not giving correct information. That's the point of the Proverb, and he has hypocrisy in his heart because he is falling into the gossip trap. He doesn't want to help. He's destroying, the Bible says, and he does it with his mouth. You can destroy a person's reputation and character by the things that you say. Did you know that our Lord Jesus warned us about this? He did. It's going to happen. People are going to slander you, misrepresent you, falsely judge your motives, criticize you about things that are not true, and Jesus said that you will be blessed and your reward will be great in heaven. You talk about destroying a person's reputation and life!

> *Do not go hastily to court; For what will you do in the end, When your neighbor has put you to shame? Debate your case with your neighbor himself, And do not disclose the secret to another; Lest he who hears it expose your shame, And your reputation be ruined* (Prov. 25:8-10).

What is the consequence of gossip? You destroy a person's reputation. If you have suffered some hurt in this regard, let me give you a little statement I learned in college that has stuck with me and it means a lot. Your reputation is what people think you are. Your character is what God knows you to be.

A second consequence that we've already seen in a few verses, is that **gossip separates friends from each other.** Have you ever sensed something wrong in a relationship, and there is not an obvious reason? After reading the Proverbs on this, I believe this problem of gossip is a major reason why friends are separated from each other. Somebody believed a rumor, and it ruined somebody's life.

> *... a whisperer separates the best of friends* (**Prov. 16:28**).

If you start spreading rumors and slander, you'll separate the best of friends.

> *He who covers a transgression seeks love, But he who repeats a matter separates the best of friends* (**Prov. 17:9, cf. 16:28**).

A third characteristic is that **gossip causes anger.**

> *The north wind brings forth rain, And a backbiting tongue an angry countenance* (Prov. 25:23).

Often, the people who cause it say, "Well, don't get mad." Wait a minute. You caused it. What did you expect? All of us better be careful, because we're causing the problem by telling what we shouldn't tell and it produces anger.

The fourth consequence of **gossip is that it will not go unpunished.** You will not escape.

Whoever secretly slanders his neighbor, Him I will destroy; The one who has a haughty look and a proud heart, Him I will not endure (Ps. 101:5).

God says He will destroy the person who gossips.

A false witness will not go unpunished, And he who speaks lies will not escape ... shall perish (Prov. 19: 5 and 9).

Whoever digs a pit will fall into it, And he who rolls a stone will have it roll back on him (Prov. 26:27).

Do not malign a servant to his master, Lest he curse you, and you be found guilty (Prov. 30:10).

God makes it very clear—if you spend your time gossiping, tearing down, spreading rumors, criticizing others verbally, you're going to suffer the consequences for it.

THE CONTROL OF GOSSIP

Let's get to the hope. How do we control this problem? If someone says, "Have you heard ... ?", we need to stop them. "Am I supposed to hear this?" "Is there something I can do about it?" "Why are you telling me this?" "Does it involve me?" There are a lot of things being said, especially among Christians that ought not to have ever been said. They don't do anybody any good. They don't help anybody at all. How do you control gossip? I want to use the word, **"desire"**, and I want you to think about your own heart.

Do you have **a desire to protect**? If you have a desire to protect, you'll start controlling your gossip.

Hatred stirs up strife, But love covers all sins (Prov. 10:12).

"... he who is of a faithful spirit conceals a matter (Prov. 10:13).

A prudent man conceals knowledge, But the heart of fools proclaims foolishness (Prov. 12:23).

He who covers a transgression seeks love, But he who repeats a matter separates the best of friends (Prov. 17:9).

An interesting verse in the "Love Chapter" (I Cor. 13:7) says, Love *"bears all things, believes all things, hopes all things, endures all things."* When it says, *"bears all things",* that's the Greek word that is used in modern Greek for the roof of a house. Love *"covers"* all things. That's right from the Proverbs! That's what God's love is about. When it controls your life, there is a desire to protect people, not to hurt them - not to spread rumors.

The second way of controlling gossip is to have **a desire to forgive.** If you have tasted deeply of the Lord's grace in your life, then the desire to forgive will be evident. That will be your immediate response, no matter what somebody has done. Is your first response to jump all over a person, to point out how terrible they are and that they don't deserve anything that God's giving them, or is there in your heart a desire to forgive? This doesn't exclude confrontation and accountability, but what goes on in our hearts is often very critical.

The discretion of a man makes him slow to anger, And it is to his glory to overlook a transgression (Prov. 19:11).

The desire to forgive is the mark of a godly person who does not want to be dominated by spreading gossip, or listening to it.

When you want to control gossip, there is **a desire to know the truth.** When you're walking with the Lord, you want to know the truth—it doesn't matter what was shared. Sometimes it is difficult to find out.

The lips of the wise disperse knowledge [spread knowledge], *But the heart of the fool does not do so* (Prov. 15:7).

The person who walks with the Lord—who has the wisdom of God, always wants to know the truth.

The heart of him who has understanding seeks knowledge, But the mouth of fools feeds on foolishness (Prov. 15:14).

If you have a heart of understanding, you're going to seek knowledge; you want to know the truth.

The heart of the prudent acquires knowledge, And the ear of the wise seeks knowledge (Prov. 18:15).

Over and over again in Proverbs, it is shown that people who walk with the Lord and are godly and wise, are always ones who want to know the truth. They do not accept hearsay, rumor and gossip, and they do not want to spread it.

There is **a desire to heal** in the heart of a person who wants to control gossip. Gossip hurts.

There is one who speaks like the piercings of a sword, But the tongue of the wise promotes health [healing] (Prov. 12:18).

When you speak about something in a delicate matter, is there a desire to know the truth and a desire to heal and restore the situation? If we walk with the Lord, we're going to find out what is true. We're going to go after that truth, and protect everybody until we find out what the truth is. Our whole goal is to heal the relationship—to restore the relationship and not let the rumors keep going.

If you're going to control gossip, there is **a desire to know all sides of an issue.** This is a very delicate matter.

The first one to plead his cause seems right, Until his neighbor [friend] *comes and examines him* (Prov. 18:17).

The first person to tell you something always seems right, until you hear the other side. We need to be wise. Not that we're questioning and doubting what somebody says, but that we are careful with a desire to protect, to love, to forgive, and to heal. We want to know all sides of an issue; however, sometimes we need to ask ourselves why we even feel the need to know. Are we really involved?

In order to control gossip, we need **a desire to be careful.**

> *The lips of the righteous know what is acceptable,
> But the mouth of the wicked what is perverse* (Prov.
> 10:32).

The words *"appropriate"*, *"proper"*, or *"acceptable"* are very
important words. Some people don't like them because they
they think you should "Tell it like it is!" However, we're not
always to tell it like it is. We're always to tell the truth, but
the way we say something is important. A righteous man
knows what is acceptable, what is appropriate, what is
proper, and what is fitting. That's very important to understand. Be careful what you say about someone else. People
can change by the grace of God and the Holy Spirit, so don't
judge them by something that happened in the past. It is
possible that they have changed by the power of God. We
can all change—at any age.

> *The heart of the righteous studies how to answer,
> But the mouth of the wicked pours forth evil* (Prov.
> 15:28).

A righteous person thinks about it before he speaks.

> *Whoever guards his mouth and tongue Keeps his
> soul from troubles* (Prov. 15:28).

That is really true. Troubles come because you didn't put
a guard over your mouth, and you told somebody something
that you shouldn't have, and then you later learn that it
wasn't the truth. That is an embarrassment. When something like that happens, you should go back and confess
what you did to everyone you told, and ask for forgiveness.

If we are going to control gossip, we need **a desire to love
others.** Sometimes I have to ask myself if I really love other
people. It is not something we boast or brag about, is it? Do
you really love other people? In God's law, this business of
loving other people is associated with gossip.

> *"You shall do no injustice in judgment. You shall
> not be partial to the poor, nor honor the person of the
> mighty. But in righteousness you shall judge your
> neighbor. You shall not go about as a talebearer
> among your people; nor shall you take a stand against
> the life of your neighbor: I am the Lord. You shall not
> hate your brother in your heart. You shall surely
> rebuke your neighbor, and not bear sin because of*

him. You shall not take vengeance, nor bear any grudge against the children of your people, but you shall love your neighbor as yourself: I am the Lord" (Lev. 19:15-18).

If want to control gossip, it is obvious that we need to love other people. Jesus took this teaching and said to His disciples the night before He went to the cross, *"A new commandment I give unto you ...."* It wasn't new from the standpoint of time; it had been given way back in Leviticus 19. The Greek word is not *"new"* meaning new in time. It's a word *"new"* meaning fresh. Here is the key. He said, I'm giving you a *"fresh"* commandment about this—that you love one another [here comes the freshness] as I loved [past tense] you. This phrase is repeated in the epistles, repeated in the gospels, repeated in the writings of John many times—all rooted in the cross. Jesus was saying, "Whenever you want to love somebody, just think of what I have done for you. Whenever you want to spread a rumor, think of the day I died on the cross because of what's wrong with you." When you think of a wrong that's been done to you—a transgression, a hurt, something said to you, a criticism—Jesus said to remember that He died on the cross for you.

"You forgive them, like I forgave you. A new [fresh] commandment I give to you, that you love one another."

CHAPTER 12

THE PROBLEM OF LEADERSHIP

There are two interesting illustrations in the Book of Proverbs showing those who don't need any leaders—ants and locusts! The rest of us need leaders.

These also are proverbs of Solomon which the men of Hezekiah king of Judah copied (Prov. 25:1).

Chapter 30, verse 1, speaks of *"Agur"*, and chapter 31, verse 1, mentions *"King Lemuel"*. Are there three guys here or is there one guy with a couple of other names?

The words of Agur the son of Jakeh, his utterance. This man declared to Ithiel—to Ithiel and Ucal (Prov. 30:1).

Now I don't know what that means to you—probably nothing, but there is no mention of Ithiel and Ucal anywhere else in the entire Bible. Why do we have these two fellows mentioned, telling us that this utterance was given to them? Who in the world are they? And who cares? Let's come back to that. For now, let's concentrate on Proverbs 30.

[The first analogy] *The leech has two daughters, Crying, "Give! Give!" There are three things that are never satisfied, Four things never say, "It is enough": The grave, The barren womb, The earth that is not satisfied with water, And the fire that never says, "It is enough." The eye that mocks his father, And scorns obedience to his mother, The ravens of the valley will pick it out, And the young eagles will eat it.*

[The second analogy] *There are three things which are too wonderful for me, Yes, four which I do not understand: The way of an eagle in the air, The way of a serpent on a rock, The way of a ship in the midst of the sea, And the way of a man with a virgin. This is the way of an adulterous woman: She eats and wipes her mouth, And says, "I have done no wickedness."*

[Analogy three] *For three things the earth is perturbed, Yes, for four it cannot bear up: For a servant
when he reigns, A fool when he is filled with food, A
hateful woman when she is married, And a maidservant who succeeds her mistress.*

[Analogy four] *There are four things which are little on the earth, But they are exceedingly wise: The
ants are a people not strong, Yet they prepare their
food in the summer; The rock badgers are a feeble folk,
Yet they make their homes in the crags; The locusts
have no king, Yet they all advance in ranks; The spider*
[some translations say lizard] *skillfully grasps with
its hands, And it is in kings' palaces.*

[Analogy five] *There are three things which are
majestic in pace, Yes, four which are stately in walk:
A lion, which is mighty among beasts And does not
turn away from any; A greyhound, A male goat also,
And a king whose troops are with him. If you have
been foolish in exalting yourself, Or if you have
devised evil, put your hand on your mouth. For as the
churning of milk produces butter, And as wringing the
nose produces blood, So the forcing of wrath produces
strife* (Prov. 30:15-33).

LEADERS NEED RIGHTEOUSNESS
They need to have a godly lifestyle.

*When it goes well with the righteous, the city
rejoices; And when the wicked perish, there is shouting. By the blessing of the upright the city is exalted,
But it is overthrown by the mouth of the wicked* (Prov.
11:10-11).

*Righteousness exalts a nation, But sin is a
reproach to any people* (Prov. 14:34).

*It is an abomination for kings to commit wicked-
ness, For a throne is established by righteousness*
(Prov. 16:12).

*A wise king sifts out the wicked, And brings the
threshing wheel over them* (Prov. 20:26).

These things also belong to the wise: It is not good to show partiality in judgment. He who says to the wicked, "You are righteous," Him the people will curse; Nations will abhor him. But those who rebuke the wicked will have delight, And a good blessing will come upon them (Prov. 24:23-25).

Take away the wicked from before the king, And his throne will be established in righteousness (Prov. 25:5).

When the righteous are in authority, the people rejoice; But when a wicked man rules, the people groan (Prov. 29:2).

If a ruler pays attention to lies, All his servants become wicked (Prov. 29:12).

Leaders need righteousness—they must do what is right.
LEADERS NEED JUSTICE
We see a lot of social and political and civil injustice in our world, and Proverbs is very strong on this.

Even though divination is on the lips of the king, His mouth must not transgress in judgment. A just weight and balance are the Lord's: All the weights in the bag are His work. It is an abomination for kings to commit wickedness, For a throne is established by righteousness. Righteous lips are the delight of kings, And they love him who speaks what is right. As messengers of death is the king's wrath, But a wise man will appease it. In the light of the king's face is life, And his favor is like a cloud of the latter rain (Prov. 16:10-15).

The king establishes the land by justice, But he who receives bribes overthrows it (Prov. 29:4).

The king who judges the poor with truth, His throne will be established forever (Prov. 29:14).

Many seek the ruler's favor, But justice for man comes from the Lord (Prov. 29:26).

LEADERS NEED MERCY

Mercy and truth preserve the king, And by lovingkindness he upholds his throne (Prov. 20:28).

The word, *"lovingkindness"*, is the Hebrew word, *"mercy"*, and this is certainly a proper application of it. *"Mercy ... preserves the king. By mercy and compassion he upholds his throne."* Leaders need mercy.

LEADERS NEED UNDERSTANDING

It is the glory of God to conceal a matter, But the glory of kings is to search out a matter. As the heavens for height and the earth for depth, So the heart of kings is unsearchable (Prov. 25:2-3).

A ruler who lacks understanding is a great oppressor, But he who hates covetousness will prolong his days (Prov. 28:16).

You see there is a lot in Proverbs about leadership, and what we have in chapter 30 is apparently instruction about a leader. The question is—who is Agur? Who is the son of Jakeh? Who is Jakeh? Who is Ithiel? Who is Ucal? And why does that passage open with that? And what about chapter 31, *"the words of King Lemuel"*? There is instruction here about leaders and what they're supposed to do. Are these different men, or are they one in the same?

I'm going to quote out of one Bible teacher's commentary on Proverbs 30. He said, "This text is hopelessly corrupt." Why would he come to that conclusion if he believes the Bible? I believe if you keep searching you will discover an answer. In the Greek translation of Proverbs 30, verses 1 - 9 are back in chapter 24, placed after verse 22. The rest of the passage comes after verse 34 in chapter 24.

Let's go to Jewish teaching, because the rabbis study very carefully. Jewish teaching says that Agur is an allegorical term for Solomon. The word Agur means *"gatherer"*. We do know that Solomon gathered together many proverbs and songs. They believe that it is simply an allegory for King Solomon, and that he wrote the whole book. The word Jakeh they see as a name for David because it means *"obedient"* or *"pious"*. What they see here is an allegory of King Solomon. Solomon is saying he has gathered all of this and that he is the son of he who is obedient and pious, which is the theme of the book. His dad (King David) was an example of many of these principles.

It's interesting that the name Agur and the other names in verse one don't appear in the Greek translation at all. The Greek translation sees this, not as proper names, but as a continuous sentence. The Greek translation of verse one is: *"My son, reverence my words, and receive them and repent. Thus saith the man to them that believe in God, and I cease."*

In the Syriac translation, the word Ucal is translated as *"prevail"*, and the word Ithiel doesn't appear twice, but only once. It seems that the placing of the Hebrew vowels in the text has confused things in terms of how this should be translated.

After looking at all this together, I agree with my Jewish friends. I believe that what happens here is that Solomon himself gives us an analogy that illustrates what he's doing in the book of Proverbs, and he pulls it all together and gives us five analogies to show us what life is all about. Although it's in the context of his own leadership, it is a lesson for every one of us. I also think the rabbis are right on chapter 31—Lemuel is another term for Solomon. Solomon is the one who wrote the entire book. These are simply two other designations for him. I believe the term *Jakeh* in verse one could very well be referring to his own father.

If you think about it, how is the book of Proverbs organized? It's primarily a father saying to his son, "I want you to listen to my instruction, and I want you to follow my commands." Over and over again, the relationship of father and son is in the book of Proverbs. It makes sense, therefore, to find Solomon referring to himself as the one who gathered all this together, and he is the son of a man who was pious before God and honored by God-a man after God's own heart.

The greatest example of leadership that Solomon ever had in his life was his own dad. His dad was not without problems, and neither are any of us, but there was never a leader like King David. King David never showed partiality. He took people that nobody wanted. They were in debt, they were depressed, they were discouraged, and they had lost their ability to function, and David gathered them together and made them into one of the mightiest armies ever known in the history of the world. Israel never (from that day till now) has ever had the territory or kingdom that they had under King David. This man was a leader of all leaders.

He was the leader that inspires all of Israel's leaders today to do something that very few military machines in the world ever do- they put their generals on the front line. It was King David who fought with his men. It was King David who refused to be honored as a king and a leader among them. It was King David who stripped himself of all vestiges of appearing to be the king so the enemy wouldn't know him as they went into battle and fought.

It was King David who (**after** he had been selected in God's timing to be the king of Judah, but had not **yet** been crowned) refused to lay his hand against the anointed King Saul. He knew Saul was after him, trying to kill him, and David had the chance to kill Saul, but he didn't! It was King David who (when a group of youths stood on a hillside, seeing him as he came back from the battle and mocked him) said to his armed men to leave them alone. It was King David who was criticized more than anybody that is mentioned in the Bible, and perhaps more than any in all of history.

I believe that what Solomon does here is to tell us about his father in five analogies.

In each one, I'm going to tell you there is a problem. And in each one, we're going to look at God's answer.

THE PROBLEM OF SATISFACTION

We see in Proverbs 30:15—"... *three things that are never satisfied"* and in verse 16, *"The earth that is not satisfied with water."* The problem is satisfaction, and is that ever a problem among leaders in this world! We are encouraged to set goals, and we are warned if we do not, we will never really accomplish much for the Lord. It seems to me, the problem, if we examine our hearts, is that of satisfaction. It affects all of us in our Christian life.

There are four illustrations to impress that fact upon us— the grave, the barren womb, the earth and fire. It was all introduced by a leech that has two daughters that say, *"Give! Give!"* There is a warning in verse 17—a warning of the danger of compromise and disobedience in order to meet the unsatisfied goals and ambitions of one's heart.

What is it that we are after? Sometimes we look for satisfaction in "busyness" and activity; sometimes we pursue a career, or seek a certain level of income, a position or a title, but, once we get it, we realize there was nothing there. The sad commentary of the great, wealthy people of the world is that it did not satisfy their hearts.

The problem of satisfaction hits the leader as well as the non-leader. Society tells us that there is something out there that we ought to have. We're bombarded with advertising giving us the message that everything that we have is old, worn-out, broken, or unsatisfactory in terms of new technology. They tell us we need something else to bring happiness into our life. All of life is like that.

GOD'S ANSWER: CONTENTMENT

God's answer has always been contentment.

"In whatever state [we] are," Paul says in Philippians 4:11-12, 19, *"to be content.... I have learned both to be full and to be hungry, both to abound and to suffer need.... My God shall supply your need."* I Timothy 6:7-8 says, *"We brought nothing into this world and it is certain we can carry nothing out. And having food and clothing, with these we shall be content.... For the love of money is a root of all kinds of evil."* It's so clear!

The problem of satisfaction in life is only answered by a real peace and contentment that is settled in the sovereignty of God and His purposes for your life. If we have that, it doesn't matter what we have or don't have, or whether somebody else has something better.

Contentment is resting in the Lord, and thanking Him for all things.

THE PROBLEM OF UNDERSTANDING

The second problem we face (verse 18) is the problem of understanding. The reason I chose this is because in verse 18 it says, *"There are three things which are too wonderful for me."* The Hebrew word, *"wonderful"*, means *"difficult to comprehend."* The parallel phrase says there are four things *"which I do not understand."* Don't worry about it saying **three** things, then **four** things; that's just a poetic device.

There are four things here that are too difficult to understand—the way of an eagle in the air, the way of a serpent on the rock, the way of a ship in the midst of the sea, and the way of a man with a virgin. It is talking about tracing a path. You can't trace the path of an eagle flying, or show where a snake has come across a rock; there is no path made. There is no evidence of where a ship has gone through the water, nor comprehending how romance develops.

Verse 20 makes it clear that the specific issue here is moral direction and knowledge. It says, *"This is the way of an adulterous woman: She eats and wipes her mouth, And says, 'I have done no wickedness.'"* All of these four illustrations show some form of adultery. Interesting! The problem of understanding deals with morality.

GOD'S ANSWER: OBEDIENCE

We can't trace the path of everything. We can't explain how we feel, or why we're motivated to sin against God. We cannot trace the path of how that works through the human psyche and personality. In fact it is so bad, that people can sin against God and act like it was not a sin at all. The problem that leaders have (as well as everyone else) is that we can't trace how and why things are happening as they are, and the answer is that we are to be obedient to God at all times. We are to do what we know is right, even though we don't feel like it, and we don't understand.

THE PROBLEM OF STRESS

For three things the earth is perturbed, Yes, for four it cannot bear up: For a servant when he reigns, A fool when he is filled with food, A hateful woman [a hated one] when she is married, And a maidservant who succeeds her mistress (Prov.30:21-23).

The Bible says the earth can't stand this, it can't bear up under the problem of stress. I like to phrase it this way—what to do when things don't turn out the way you counted on. This is a question of what to do about hard-to-bear situations that do not seem right or fair.

It doesn't seem right that a servant should reign. It's the leader, the king who should reign.

It doesn't seem right that a fool should be completely satisfied, and all his needs met. After all, he's a fool, and the fool in Proverbs is a wicked man—he deserves judgment. Why is he being blessed? Have you ever asked that question? Why do the wicked prosper, and the righteous suffer?

A woman (when she's hated and she's married) it doesn't seem fair, it doesn't seem right. You'd think when she got married, she would be loved. The world can hardly stand that. You're married, and yet you're hated. In some cases, these passages are almost too real to back away from and take a look at them. There are people who are married and feel hated by their spouses, and it is a terrible stress.

What about the maidservant who succeeds her mistress? Just go back and read the story of Abraham, Sarah, and Hagar to know about the stress of that. What do we do when things don't turn out the way we were counting on? What is God's answer to these trials and all of these difficulties?

God's answer to the problem of satisfaction is **contentment**. God's answer to the problem of understanding is **obedience to God**—no matter what. What is God's answer to the problem of stress?

> *My brethren, count it all joy when you fall into various trials, knowing that the testing of your faith produces patience. But let patience have its perfect work, that you may be perfect and complete, lacking nothing* (James 1:2-4).

GOD'S ANSWER: PATIENCE

God's answer to the problem of stress is patience. You'll need patience when a servant reigns. You'll need patience in a rough marriage where there's no love and you feel hated. You'll need patience if you have to deal with a foolish man who is being blessed and it doesn't seem fair. You'll need patience when a gal succeeds her own boss.

You see, all of life doesn't turn out the way we want, and God says to count it all joy when you fall into these situations—not IF you fall into an undesirable situation, but WHEN! It is only a question of time until we're going to run into situations like this, so how do we handle it? Leaders can become impatient trying to solve that which is apparently unsolvable. What is needed is patience.

The way we get patience is through stress and difficult situations. That's the way God produces it. You can't get patience unless you're in situations that are hard to cope with. Have you got something you can hardly stand? Is there something where you work that needs to be straightened out and hasn't been? Does it keep going and nobody does anything about it? What do we need? We need patience.

THE PROBLEM OF ABILITY

We all want to be capable. We all want to do our job. Leaders want to be capable.

There are four things which are little on the earth, But they are exceedingly wise: The ants are a people not strong, Yet they prepare their food in the summer; The rock badgers are a feeble folk, Yet they make their homes in the crags; The locusts have no king, Yet they all advance in ranks; The spider skillfully grasps with its hands, And it is in kings' palaces (Prov. 30:24-28).

What is this analogy all about? They're little, but they're wise. It deals with abiltiy. Do you remember that in Mark 4 Jesus told about a small mustard seed that will become a large plant? Let's look at each of these, and ask why are they so wise—we know they are little.

Let's take ants. We can smash them with our finger. They are small and weak compared to us, and yet they can carry things many times their own weight and they prepare ahead for what's coming. Nobody tells them what to do, they just do it. Do you?

The rock badgers are another example. These little things can be wiped out by any animal in the wilderness. They don't fight back, they just run. They make their homes in the clefts of the rock, little holes too small for other animals to get into. The Bible says they are smarter than we are! Sometimes we don't see our own weakness like God does. The Psalmist spoke about *"hiding ourselves in the cleft of the rock"*, our Lord Jesus Christ. We're not called to act like we can handle everything. The smart and wise thing to do is to know our vulnerability and weakness and flee to the safety of the rock of our Lord.

What about the locusts? They don't have any leader at all yet they all go out in groups. When a locust plague comes, farmers try to predict where they're going. I found out that the locusts go with the wind currents. Do you do that? You might say that sounds like compromise. Just go the way the wind blows? I ask you, if you don't have any leader, how shall you be guided in your life?

It is WIND that is used over and over to describe the Lord's direction in our life. It even comes to be an exact translation of the Holy Spirit of God, guiding, directing us—going where the Lord would have us go. Not thinking we know what to do—that we know which path to take. People say, "What's the will of God for my life?" Leaders say, "This is the way—let's walk in it." Wait a minute! Sometimes, the Lord takes us in a direction we never thought. We need to follow the Lord. *"Be not like the horse and mule,"* says Proverbs and Psalms, *"which have no understanding."* They think they know, but they need a bridle so that we can control them. Instead, trust the Lord, with all your heart. Follow the Lord.

"I will lead you, I will guide you with My eye," the Lord said. Follow Him, trust in the Lord with all your heart. *"Don't lean to your own understanding,"* said Proverbs 3. *"In all your ways acknowledge Him, and He shall direct your paths."*

How about the spider? Some say lizard, but I don't see the lizard grasping like this with its hands. It says, *"The spider skillfully grasps with its hands, And it is in kings' palaces."* Are you? A lot of us are not where God wants us to be. We aren't in the positions we think we should be in order to affect this world for Christ because we don't even understand a spider!

Why is the spider in kings' palaces? Because it skillfully grasps with its hands. When I was a little boy, I was fascinated watching the spider build intricate webs. Then I would pull the web down, and watch the spider build it again. This would go on and on—and the spider won! He would not give up no matter how many times I destroyed his web. I thought about that—the problem of ability. The spider gets into places of prominence by constant perseverence. He does not give up. God says, *"Be not weary in well doing, for in due season you will reap, if you faint not."* Spiders may be small, but they are exceedingly wise. We all need to learn from that.

GOD'S ANSWER: WISDOM

Every one of these creatures presents God's wisdom. What we need is God's wisdom. The problem of our inability and our incapacity to be what we want to be (or what we think God wants us to be) is solved by His wisdom. In fact, Proverbs 6 says to go to the ant and learn from him. You can compare that passage to this to understand the point. It's God's wisdom that we need.

"If any of you lacks wisdom, let him ask of God, who gives to all liberally and without reproach, and it

*will be given to him. But let him ask in faith, with no
doubting, for he who doubts is like a wave of the sea
driven and tossed by the wind. For let not that man
suppose that he will receive anything from the Lord;
he is a double-minded man, unstable in all his ways"*
(James 1:5-8).

Come and ask God for wisdom. "Lord, I don't know what
to do. Lord, I'm not capable of handling this." That delights
the heart of God. "Lord, I'm not sure what direction to go."
God is pleased. "Lord, I need your wisdom."

THE PROBLEM OF SELF-CONFIDENCE

*There are three things which are majestic in pace,
Yes, four which are stately in walk* (Prov. 30:29).

A lion doesn't turn away from anyone, nor does a
greyhound, a male goat or a king whose troops are with him.
That just fascinates me!

*If you have been foolish in exalting yourself, Or if
you have devised evil, put your hand on your mouth.
For as the churning of milk produces butter, And as
wringing the nose produces blood, So the forcing of
wrath produces strife* (Prov. 30:32-33).

That's the problem of self-confidence. It's a leadership
problem as well as a follower's problem. Self-confidence is
described as *"majestic in pace"* (verse 29), *"stately in walk"*.
Match that with verse 32—*"exalting yourself"*. The
greyhound in Hebrew refers to a strutting cock. Have you
ever seen a peacock spread those feathers? They think
they're hot stuff! Pride in appearance.

The lion doesn't turn away from anyone, and the male
goat will fight anyone or any animal on the face of the globe,
and try to ram them. It's a stupid animal—it will ram a wall,
if it thinks it moves. Talk about dumb! Don't laugh too
much, because we do the same thing in our pride and arrogance. We can't back down.

"A king whose troops are with him," is the last phrase. I
like the way the Greek translates it—instead of troops, it says
"when speaking publicly." The point is, the king has a terrible problem of self-confidence and pride. He feels stronger

when he's got an army with him, and when he's speaking publicly, he can "snow" everybody.

Pride is most often manifested by anger and that produces strife. There's only one answer from God.

GOD'S ANSWER: HUMILITY

Where do wars and fights come from among you? Do they not come from your desires for pleasure that war in your members? You lust and do not have. You murder and covet and cannot obtain. You fight and war. Yet you do not have because you do not ask. You ask and do not receive, because you ask amiss, that you may spend it on your pleasures. Adulterers and adulteresses! Do you not know that friendship with the world is enmity with God? Whoever therefore wants to be a friend of the world makes himself an enemy of God. Or do you think that the Scripture says in vain, "The Spirit who dwells in us yearns jealously"? But He gives more grace. Therefore He says: "God resists the proud, But gives grace to the humble." Therefore submit to God. Resist the devil and he will flee from you. Draw near to God and He will draw near to you. Cleanse your hands, you sinners; and purify your hearts, you double-minded. Lament and mourn and weep! Let your laughter be turned to mourning and your joy to gloom. Humble yourselves in the sight of the Lord, and He will lift you up (James 4:1-10).

CHAPTER 13

THE PROBLEM OF DISCIPLINE

And you have forgotten the exhortation which speaks to you as to sons: "My son, do not despise the chastening of the Lord, Nor be discouraged when you are rebuked by Him; For whom the Lord loves He chastens, And scourges every son whom He receives" (quoted from Prov. 3).

If you endure chastening, God deals with you as with sons; for what son is there whom a father does not chasten? But if you are without chastening, of which all have become partakers, then you are illegitimate and not sons. Furthermore, we have had human fathers who corrected us, and we paid them respect. Shall we not much more readily be in subjection to the Father of spirits and live? For they indeed for a few days chastened us as seemed best to them, but He for our profit, that we may be partakers of His holiness. Now no chastening [discipline] seems to be joyful for the present, but grievous; nevertheless, afterward it yields the peaceable fruit of righteousness to those who have been trained by it (Heb. 12:5-11).

THE PURPOSES OF DISCIPLINE

This is not simply a study for young families as to how to discipline their children. There will be things that deal with that. But what I see in this is two parallel lines: one of discipline in the family; the other of discipline in the Christian life. The way God disciplines us is illustrated by the way we are to discipline our children.

You may ask, Why does God use discipline in our lives? How do I know it's coming from God? I'm going to tell you.

When we look at the Bible, it is very obvious that God intends to discipline His children. That's very clear. You are not going to live without discipline. If, in fact, you are living without discipline, it is only a matter of time until you get His discipline in your life. If you are totally without discipline, you are not a believer—that is very clear in this passage. All of God's children are going to be disciplined—that's clearly taught in the Bible. What is the purpose of it?

AS IT RELATES TO WISDOM

Evidently, we can't be smart, unless we're disciplined. A lot of people who manifest foolishness probably have never been disciplined by God. That's why they don't have wisdom.

Foolishness is bound up in the heart of a child, But the rod of correction will drive it far from him (Prov. 22:15).

Parents believe that is the truth! Discipline is necessary to get rid of foolishness which is the opposite of wisdom. Parents must be careful not to use this verse out of its context and the entire teaching of the book of Proverbs. For instance, it is natural for a kid to be a kid. Sometimes, parents discipline kids incorrectly when the kids are just having fun. If they do something that bothers you, ask yourself if you are willing for God to discipline you on the same basis!

We are to love our children, not consider them to be burdens- to be "seen and not heard". That's nonsense! We ought to love our children, they are to be part of our family gatherings and present with adults. I have a lot of strong feelings about this. Don't exclude our children as though they can't identify with adulthood. At the same time, don't impose your adulthood on the kids.

The Lord Jesus taught us many wonderful things about children and it is apparent that God loves kids. We ought to appreciate the fun-loving side of kids and enjoy it. Please do not interpret the word, "foolishness," as meaning frivolity, fun-loving, or acting like a kid. That is not foolishness! Foolishness is the way of wickedness in the book of Proverbs.

A fool, in Proverbs, is one who has no regard for the things of the Lord. The fool is headed toward hell, not heaven. The fool is contrasted with the wise-who are in tune with the Lord. What drives foolishness, which is the way of wickedness, out of the hearts of God's children, is discipline. God wants us to be wise. That's means that we live for Him and get the wickedness out of our lives. Discipline is the thing God uses to deal with that.

> *The rod and reproof give wisdom, But a child left*
> *to himself brings shame to his mother* (Prov. 29:15).

Once again, the whole point of discipline in the life of a believer is illustrated by a parent with a child. If you don't spank the child, don't discipline him, he will bring shame to you at some time. Today, they are calling almost all spanking "child abuse", but that's not how God sees it.

AS IT RELATES TO LOVING PROTECTION

God brings discipline into our lives because He wants to protect us. He's not trying to keep us from having fun. He is using His love to protect us. Again, this can be illustrated in the discipline of a family.

> *Do not withhold correction from a child, For if you*
> *beat him with a rod, he will not die. You shall beat*
> *him with a rod, And deliver his soul from hell* (Prov.
> 23:13-14).

There's a loving protection here that is designed to keep us from ruining our lives. God doesn't want us to make a mess of our lives. He wants us to go to heaven, not hell. If you understand the purposes of discipline, it helps you to accept it when it comes.

AS IT RELATES TO FAMILY HAPPINESS

> *Correct your son, and he will give you rest; Yes,*
> *he will give delight to your soul* (Prov. 29:17).

Discipline is intended by God, to bring peace and happiness to the family. In the family of God, those who are disciplined will bring much more happiness than those who are undisciplined. That's for sure!

AS IT RELATES TO GOD'S LOVE

> *My son, do not despise the chastening of the Lord,*
> *Nor detest His correction; For whom the Lord loves He*
> *corrects, Just as a father the son in whom he delights*
> (Prov. 3:11-12).

This was quoted in Hebrews 12. It demonstrates love.

I once asked a fellow how things were going. He told me that what was happening in his life was unbelievable. He began to describe it. I said, "Man, the Lord must really love you!" He looked at me with a glare and suggested that he'd be glad to have the Lord love someone else for a while.

The Bible understands this and doesn't want us to act like nothing is wrong. *"No chastening for the present seems joyous,"* says Hebrews 12. It is painful! Nevertheless, it is an evidence of the love of God for you. That's very important to understand. God is not trying to put a heavy trip on you. He's not trying to wipe you out with one blow. In fact, He is showing you His love. That's hard!

Discipline is never interpreted as love by the one who is being disciplined, but God teaches us that it is love. Once again, that is shown in a family.

He who spares his rod hates his son, But he who loves him disciplines him promptly (Prov. 13:24).

Discipline, when it comes, relates to love. The opposite is true: If you let somebody go on and ruin their life, love has not been shown to them. Love says, "Stop!"

If a child runs into the street, chasing a ball, it is NOT loving to say, "I believe you should find your full potential. Find out who you are." Love says, "Stop!" and runs out and grabs the child in time. That's what love does. That's the way God works with us.

God loves us so much that He disciplines us to teach us things we can never learn any other way.

AS IT RELATES TO SUBMISSION AND RESPECT

We all have a problem with submission and respect in life. It is so widespread that we hardly know where to begin to talk about it.

A few years ago, a schoolteacher in the public high school thought I should see what was happening in there. So, I went to the school with him and we had lunch in the kids' lunchroom. Afterward, I sat in the back in a couple of the classes. When I saw what was going on, I could hardly believe it. Some public schools are like warzones. It's a battle over submission and respect and authority. There are plenty of kids who have not been disciplined and will not submit to any kind of authority, no matter who it is.

The Bible says that if we sow the wind, we reap the whirlwind. When we raise a generation of kids who are not disciplined at home, the school is helpless. They are reaping the problems caused by the lack of discipline at home. In the Bible, we are to be disciplined by our fathers.

There are problems caused by the lack of a father in the home. Single parents know what I mean. Also, there are a lot of fathers who have been in the home, but have never done one thing to discipline their children. No wonder we suffer in our spiritual life! If that hasn't existed or a child has never seen how a father should discipline the children in love, he will have difficulty in relating to the way God disciplines His children. If he has been abused, he not only will have a difficult time responding to human authority, but he will also have problems in relating to God. Discipline teaches us submission and respect.

Furthermore, we have had human fathers who corrected us, and we paid them respect (Heb. 12:9).

That doesn't make us warped! I had a healthy fear of my father. I did not lack discipline when I was a child. A lot of people think I must have needed it, and that is true. However, I loved my father-I loved everything about him. My hero in life was my Dad. When he died, it was a very difficult time for me. I never had anybody that was such a guide, and friend, and counselor. He was an encouragement to me. My Dad never got out of the sixth grade, so he never helped me with my homework, by the way. My Dad loved me and I got spankings from him. I just hurt thinking about it.

My Dad hit me in the place the Bible teaches and it taught me a lot. That taught me respect. Parents today are trying to "con" their kids into loving them, it seems to me. They do this instead of being real parents and providing loving discipline in the home. Discipline didn't make me dislike my Dad-it caused me to fall in love with him! I understood what authority is and that I need to submit to authority in my life. We all need that and the discipline of God that continues after we're grown, it's for the same purpose.

AS IT RELATES TO A GODLY LIFESTYLE

Shall we not much more readily be in subjection to the Father of spirits and live? For they indeed for a few days chastened us as seemed best to them, but

He for our profit, that we may be partakers of His holiness (Heb. 12:9).

My Dad wasn't always right in his reasons for disciplining me; however, there were times when I got by with things. When our kids were growing up, I'd say to my wife, "I know they need a spanking." I didn't always know exactly what they had done, but I could feel it in my bones. What God is saying is that our fathers had their own reasons for punishing us. However, God always does it for our profit. He does it for our holiness—separation from a sinful lifestyle.

Submission is vitally related to holiness in the Christian lifestyle. James 4 says, *"Submit to God. Resist the devil and he will flee from you. Draw near to God and He will draw near to you. Humble yourselves in the sight of the Lord and He will lift you up."* Submission is always related to walking with the Lord. Submitting to God is not easy.

We're told to submit to every ordinance of man—all the human authorities that are placed in our lives. This is the will of God to submit. We don't even like the word! Submission is the key to walking with the Lord.

"No chastening seems to be joyful for the present, but grievous; nevertheless, afterwards it yields the peaceable fruit of righteousness to those who have been trained by it" (Heb. 12:11).

A godly lifestyle is the result of spiritual discipline. When we are disciplined, however it comes to us, there is a painful struggle involved. It is spiritual gymnastics of the Lord as we learn how to walk with the Lord.

THE PROBLEMS OF DISCIPLINE

There are really just two problems of discipline—neglect and abuse. If you neglect discipline, you will pay a terrible price.

He who spares his rod hates his son, But he who loves him disciplines him promptly (Prov. 13:24).

Any parent knows that you discipline a child as close to the offense as possible. Of course, it should be private so that there is no embarrassment in front of other people. That's not easy, especially in a public place. But discipline needs to be given in private—always! There is a serious problem in neglecting correction.

> *Do not withhold correction from a child, For if you beat him with a rod, he will not die. You shall beat him with a rod, And deliver his soul from hell* (Prov. 23:13-14).

Don't neglect discipline—it will deliver the child's soul from hell!

> *The rod and reproof give wisdom, but a child left to himself brings shame to his mother* (Prov. 29:15).

Without discipline, we also bring shame to our Heavenly Father. We have a Bible illustration in I Samuel, chapter two. We're talking here about the sons of Eli, a priest, into whose home Samuel came. His sons were wicked boys.

> *Therefore the sin of the young men was very great before the Lord, for men abhorred the offering of the Lord* (I Sam. 2:17).

They were having sex with the young women who came to the temple. This was not only wicked, but it was well known and people were making a mockery of the sacrifices of the temple because of what the sons of the priest, himself, were doing.

> *"Why do you kick at My sacrifice and My offering which I have commanded in My habitation, and honor your sons more than Me, to make yourselves fat with the best of all the offerings of Israel My people?"* (I Sam. 2:29).

Would God say that to today's parents who refuse to discipline them in the name of "loving" them?

> *"For I have told him that I will judge his house forever for the iniquity which he knows, because his sons made themselves vile, and he did not restrain them"* (I Sam.3:13).

Eli did not rebuke them or restrain them, he let it go. He did nothing. He didn't deal with it. Many parents throw up their hands and say, "What can you do?" Our secular world today is telling us that parental confrontation is necessary to break the bad habits of a child. In therapeutic sessions dealing with drug addiction and alcohol, they are telling people of the necessity of family members being involved in confrontation and discipline. We need discipline in life. If we neglect it, we will pay a terrible price.

Eli's sons made themselves vile and he didn't rebuke them, and he didn't correct them. I know the kids will hassle you for it. We've suffered through it ourselves. We parents aren't sure we've ever done anything right. We fight about what time the kids will be home, where they go, and who their friends are. Thank the Lord, if He gave you enough sense to ask your kids what they were doing.

I'm thankful that my parents wanted to know what time I would be in and they were really ticked, if I wasn't home when I said I would be. I'm glad I didn't grow up in a home where my parents didn't care where I went or when I got home. The kids may broadcast that they think it's cool to have parents who don't care, but I'm glad my parents cared! If you, as a believer, are living without discipline, then Hebrews 12 tells you that you are, in fact, not a believer because God disciplines His children. God doesn't neglect it.

We also know that there is a problem of abuse and we're told in Ephesians 6:4, *"Fathers, do not provoke your children to wrath."* Again, in Colossians 3:21, fathers are told not to make their children discouraged. Those are the two results of improper discipline—anger or discouragement. Anger comes from injustice in the discipline that is given. Discouragement breaks the spirit of the child and makes him think he can't ever do anything right. Perhaps discipline is given without love.

Abuse is a terrible thing! I believe that child abuse is whenever a child is hit anywhere except *"the fleshy area in the middle of the back"* which was divinely ordained by God. We should never hit a child in the face, or shove them or kick them. That's child abuse. The proper way to discipline a child is to spank his bottom. I've said that a lot of times and it has gotten me into a lot of trouble. Even workers from the state Department of Child Welfare sit across from me at my desk and accuse me of fostering child abuse.

I never justify child abuse! If you are hitting your child anywhere but on their bottom, get counsel right now! Seek the child's forgiveness and stop it right now!

THE PROCESS OF DISCIPLINE

What is the process that God uses? One thing that is discipline from God as seen in the Bible, is physical illness. Not all sickness is intended for that purpose but it definitely can be a discipline from the Lord. Emotional stress is also a discipline from the Lord. Financial problems can be used of God to discipline us. Not that every financial problem is for that reason, but God can use anything and everything—and He has!

He used a lot of things with Job. Your house can burn down, as Job's house did. Sometimes these things are the discipline of the Lord. It's hard to understand that sometimes. It helps to see the causes behind all of this.

The Fall of Man brought a curse on the world and some of our problems stem from that curse. We had one of the most beautiful backyards when I was a kid that I have ever seen. My dad loved to give barbeques for a couple hundred people at a time. The walkways were lined with rosebushes and I loved to pick the roses. But the bushes have thorns! "Why are there thorns on the roses?" I asked my father one day. He said, "That's because of the curse God tells us about in Genesis."

> For I consider that the sufferings of this present time are not worthy to be compared with the glory which shall be revealed in us. For the earnest expectation of the creation eagerly waits for the revealing of the sons of God. For the creation was subjected to futility, not willingly, but because of Him who subjected it in hope; because the creation itself also will be delivered from the bondage of corruption into the glorious liberty of the children of God. For we know that the whole creatiron groans and labors with birth pangs together until now (Rom. 8:18-22).

The thorns remind us that man sinned and God placed a curse upon the earth. It gives us hope to remember that He will also one day deliver us (and the earth) from the curse and its consequences.

Let me show you an example. I got up the other day and I was tired and dragged my feet out of bed, hitting the bedframe on the way. It hurt! I have to be careful about things that are not as tall as I am. The other day, I ran right into something I was trying to miss. That hurt, too! I wondered why that happened since I manage to miss it almost every day. That was the discipline of the Lord as it relates to the curse.

The truth is that our bodies don't make the grade. The older we get, the more we realize it. We try to eat right and exercise, but eventually we know that even that is not working. What positive benefit could God be giving me in this? The answer is that He is building our anticipation of heaven! It's as simple as that. In God's special love for us, He sometimes even puts us in the hospital, laying flat of our back so we can think about heaven and look forward to it!. As our bodies fall apart, we think of heaven.

There are also a lot of problems in society that make us look forward to heaven.

The second cause of these problems is "self". The Bible says in I Peter, chapter two, that we are sometimes *"beaten for [our] faults."*

> For what credit is it if, when you are beaten for your faults, you take it patiently? But when you do good and suffer for it, if you take it patiently, this is commendable before God (I Peter 2:19-20).

What is the cause of our troubles? Maybe it's our own fault. We sometimes blame God, but the truth is that we may have done it to ourselves by failing to follow good principles. We can be *"beaten"* for our own faults as much as we suffer at the hand of God for His reasons. It's important to understand that we can suffer because of our own stupidity.

The third cause of discipline in our lives is the devil. All of the trouble in our lives does not come from the devil; however, there is trouble that comes from him.

> Lest I should be exalted above measure by the abundance of the revelations, a thorn in the flesh was given to me, a messenger of Satan to buffet me, lest I be exalted above measuure. Concerning this thing I pleaded with the Lord three times that it might depart from me. And He said to me, "My grace is sufficient for you for My strength is made perfect in weakness" (II Cor. 12:7-9).

When we wonder why God lets Satan beat up on us, we need to remember that God wants us to trust Him—

not ourselves. God allowed Satan to inflict punishment on Job, but Satan could do nothing more than God permitted. That's true for all of us. If I'm reading the Bible correctly, God is using Satan to bring discipline to believers. That's God's joke on Satan who thinks he's being mean to us! God uses it to help us and Satan can't do anything that God doesn't allow. God allows Satan to inflict punishment on His children so that we will learn to trust the Lord.

> *Be sober, be vigilant; because your adversary the devil walks about like a roaring lion, seeking whom he may devour. Resist him, steadfast in the faith, knowing that the same sufferings are experienced by your brotherhood in the world. But may the God of all grace, who called us to His eternal glory by Christ Jesus, after you have suffered a while* [the attacks of Satan], *perfect, establish, strengthen, and settle you. To Him be the glory and the dominion forever and ever* (I Peter 5:8-11).

God uses satanic pressure and attack in this spiritual warfare, not to weaken us, but to make us stronger. How interesting! So Satan can inflict discipline, but God is behind Satan, using him to strengthen us.

God, Himself, is the fourth source of discipline in our lives. One thing that many evangelicals hesitate to say is that God causes physical problems. That's a hard question. Physical illness is traced to the curse but not all illness is due to specific sin in the lives of believers. In John 9, the disciples and Jesus met a man who had been born blind. They asked Jesus who sinned to cause this blindness. Jesus said, "Neither! It was so that the works of God would be manifested in him." He wasn't born blind because of sin.

When God called Moses to lead the Children of Israel, Moses said he was *"slow of speech"* (a lie). Let's pick up the story in Exodus 4.

> *So the Lord said to him, "Who has made man's mouth? Or who makes the mute, the deaf, the seeing, or the blind? Have not I, the Lord?"* (Ex. 4:11).

Does God cause physical deformity? Yes! I tell that to parents who have a deformed child. I believe we never get peace and freedom in our hearts until we recognize that God is not doing this because of a specific sin of the parents or of the child. God is doing it for His purposes which are far greater than I understand at the moment, but God has allowed that to exist. God knows what He is going to do with it. We have to praise Him—no matter what! It is hard teaching, but it deals with the sovereignty of God and the fact that He is in control of everything.

Does God cause physical difficulties? Yes. Does God use Satan to accomplish His purposes? Yes.

Having said all of that, let's go back to the process of discipline.

VERBAL INSTRUCTION AND WARNING

Can we be disciplined by words? Yes. We can be warned and parents are disciplining their children when they do. Verbal instruction absolutely can discipline.

My son, hear the instruction of your father, and do not forsake the law of your mother (Prov. 1:8).

"*My son, if sinners entice you, Do not consent*" (Prov. 1:10). That is verbal instruction.

"*My son, do not forget my law, But let your heart keep my commands*" (Prov. 3:1). More verbal instruction is given in these words.

I want to ask you if you are aware that the Bible is filled with the Lord's verbal instructions to us for our lives. We'd be wise to listen to it.

A SPECIAL INSTRUMENT IS USED

In the case of the family, in Proverbs this instrument is called, "*a rod*". Does the Bible teach that God has a rod? Yes, it does. The "*rod of God*" is frequently referred to.

It is proper to use an instrument to discipline a child and your hand should be an instrument of love. The Bible talks about using a rod. When you put your hand on a child, they shouldn't back away but know that **you are showing love** to them by your hand. Use an instrument to punish your child.

He who spares his rod hates his son (Prov. 13:24).

The rod of correction will drive it [foolishness] *far from him* (Prov. 22:15).

If you beat him with a rod, he will not die. You shall beat him with a rod, And deliver his soul from hell (Prov. 23:13-14).

The rod and reproof give wisdom (Prov. 29:15).

The rod is for the back of him who is devoid of understanding (Prov. 10:13).

The Bible teaches that we should use an instrument, and we should use it in the *"middle of the back"* the Hebrew says.

Judgments are prepared for scoffers, And beatings for the backs of fools (Prov. 19:29).

Again, it says the *"middle of the back"* in Hebrew.

A whip for the horse, A bridle for the donkey, And a rod for the fool's back (Prov. 26:3).

This one says, *"the backside"*. The rod should be our first response—not our last resort! We should use the rod on the middle of the back. If you wonder where that is, use a tape measure and you'll find that it hits right on the fleshy part we call "the bottom". It's very clear that parents should use an instrument on the bottom—nowhere else! Don't miss!

God uses an instrument with us. He speaks about the *"rod of His anger"*. If we don't listen to the verbal instruction of the Lord, He uses the rod of circumstances—difficulties and trials—as His rod. The rod of God's own character is applied to our lives so that we will learn by it.

Could we learn if we just obeyed the verbal instruction? Yes, we could. Could we avoid being disciplined by the Lord by being obedient to Him in what He said? Yes, but when we disobey and decide to go our own way, God will use many circumstances, difficulties and trials.

DIVINE INTERVENTION AND CHASTENING

God many times directly steps in and disciplines instead of using something else in our lives.

My son, do not despise the chastening of the Lord, Nor detest His correction; For whom the Lord loves He corrects (Prov. 3:11-12).

God uses physical death to discipline a believer who continues to sin without repentance. God can move in and cause that person's death. He can withdraw His breath from a person in an instant and remove him, because of continual sinning in his life. If he refuses to repent, God can use physical death.

We all need discipline. God is doing it for our good. He doesn't just try to keep us from enjoying life. He disciplines us for a good purpose. He wants us to be all that we have ever dreamed of being. Discipline is used to make us into something wonderful. Without it, we wouldn't have completed our education or performed a worthwhile job. Without discipline, we would not see God's blessings in our lives.

CHAPTER 14

THE PROBLEM OF ALCOHOL

Alcohol has ruined more marriages and families than any of us would like to admit. It has destroyed people's lives—physically, emotionally and spiritually. It is a serious problem which is growing, not diminishing in our society.

> *Who has woe? Who has sorrow? Who has contentions [arguments]? Who has complaints? Who has wounds without cause? Who has redness of eyes? Those who linger long at the wine, Those who go in search of mixed wine. Do not look on the wine when it is red, When it sparkles in the cup, When it swirls around smoothly; At the last it bites like a serpent, And stings like a viper. Your eyes will see strange things, And your heart will utter perverse things. Yes, you will be like one who lies down in the midst of the sea, Or like one who lies at the top of the mast, saying: They have struck me, but I was not hurt; They have beaten me, but I did not feel it. When shall I awake, that I may seek another drink?* (Prov. 23:29-35).

There is no subject that brings such controversy among Bible teachers as the subject of alcohol and wine. I'd like to say to you that the reason for that is because we're not clear as to the meaning of the Bible terms. In the Old Testament twelve different words are used in 251 different places, not even counting the word, *"drink"* which is associated with alcoholism. It's not a small subject. In the New Testament Greek, we have three words. Acts 2:13 uses the word, *"glucose,"* where it says that those who were filled with the Holy Spirit on the Day of Pentecost appeared to be *"filled with new wine"*.

Another word which means "a wine press" is used five times. The primary word used for wine in the New Testament is used 36 times. The problem is that this primary word is used for all stages of wine—from the grape itself to the most fermented stage. Because of loose interpretation, some have used this ambiguity to take some positive passages about wine to justify the usage of wine in our day. Let's get something straight! In ancient times, fermentation began immediately—within a 24-hour period with a slight foam appearing on the grapes placed into wine vats.

Jewish tradition tells us that it is available immediately for the *"wine tithe"* which is spoken of in the Old Testament. After a week, certain violent processes that have been going on will subside. The wine is usually tranferred to jars or wineskins at that stage. At that point, it is called *"new wine"*. Up to forty days, this wine was suitable for use as the *"drink offering"* in the Old Testament days. After that, the wine was deteriorating so rapidly that Jews taught it was unacceptable for religious purposes.

The longest wines were ever kept in ancient times was three years, then all of it was destroyed. The term *"old wine"* seems to refer to that which is at least one year old. The wine that is served at Passover was always mixed with three parts water to make sure that it was not an alcoholic beverage.

The issues that trouble us which are in the Bible, we need to deal with. These are what appear to be positive statements concerning the drinking of wine.

ALCOHOLIC BEVERAGES ARE DANGEROUS

The Bible is clear on this; they are dangerous for anyone.

Wine is a mocker, Intoxicating drink arouses brawling, And whoever is led astray by it is not wise (Prov.20:1).

"Intoxicating drink" defines the kind of wine being discussed here. It is alcoholic.

Your eyes will see strange things, And your heart will utter perverse things [twisted things apart from God's truth] (Prov.23:33).

Harlotry, wine, and new wine enslave the heart (Hosea 4:11).

Wine, in the Bible, is often connected with immorality. Alcoholic beverages are dangerous because they begin to control your heart, your attitudes, your thinking processes.

Woe to him who gives drink to his neighbor, Press-
ing him to your bottle, Even to make him drunk, That
you may look on his nakedness! (Habakkuk 2:15).

Don't try to avoid the meaning and intent of this statement by saying that the motives here were wrong. The Bible
says, *"Woe to him who gives drink to his neighbor."* That's
what it says.

"But take heed to yourselves, lest your hearts be
weighed down with carousing, drunkenness, and
cares of this life, and that Day come on you unexpec-
tedly" (Luke 21:34).

Alcoholic beverages are obviously dangerous in terms of
"carousing, drunkenness" and also in terms of being un-
prepared for the Second Coming of Christ.

Thieves, nor covetous, nor drunkards, nor revilers,
nor extortioners will inherit the kingdom of God (I
Cor.6:10).

Now the works of the flesh are ... drunkenness ...;
of which I tell you beforehand, just as I also told you
in time past, that those who practice such things will
not inherit the kingdom of God (Gal. 5:19-21).

Is this serious? Of course it is! People who get drunk,
according to the Bible, are living very dangerously, if they
call themselves Christians. Drunkards *"will not inherit the*
kingdom of God". It is a very serious matter.

I realize that this deals with unrepentant hearts and it
deals with habits of mind and lifestyles that are totally away
from the Lord. I understand that. However, I believe we
must speak of the danger of alcoholic beverages and stop
trying to justify them. They are dangerous.

ALCOHOLIC BEVERAGES ARE DENIED TO CERTAIN PEOPLE

No matter what stage the wine is in, there are some people
who are denied wine in the Bible. Who are these people?

Priests

> "Do not drink wine or intoxicating drink, you, nor
> your sons with you, when you go into the tabernacle
> of meeting, lest you die. It shall be a statute forever
> throughout your generations" (Lev. 10:9).

If there's nothing wrong with drinking wine, then why
such a prohibition?

Nazarites

> "He shall separate himself from wine and similar
> drink; he shall drink neither vinegar made from wine
> nor vinegar made from similar drink; neither shall he
> drink any grape juice, nor eat fresh grapes or raisins"
> (Num.6:3).

The vow of a Nazarite was taken for a period of time in
which a man was committed totally to the Lord, not doing
his other occupation. That was really separation—not even
grapes or raisins!

Prophets

> Woe to the crown of pride, to the drunkards of
> Ephraim, Whose glorious beauty is a fading flower ....
> But they also have erred through wine, And through
> intoxicating drink are out of the way; The priest and
> the prophet have erred through intoxicating drink,
> They are swallowed up by wine, They are out of the
> way through intoxicating drink; They err in vision,
> they stumble in judgment (Isa. 28:1,7).

The Bible teaches that prophets should not drink wine.
Priests while they are worshipping in the Lord's temple
should have nothing to do with it.

Kings and Princes

> It is not for kings, O Lemuel, It is not for kings to
> drink wine, Nor for princes intoxicating drink; Lest
> they drink and forget the law, and pervert the justice
> of all the afflicted (Prov. 31:4-5).

Alcoholic beverages dull the senses and cause us not to
think objectively. Then we pervert and twist the justice that
people need. When we drink, we lose our inhibitions and
forget ourselves—we act differently.

Some people drink just because they have problems in their lives. On television, one study reported a phenomenal number of drinks shown during one week. They showed them because they were depicting someone with an emotional problem they couldn't handle! "Get a drink to calm yourself!" was the message. But the Bible forbids kings and princes from drinking any intoxicating drink.

Elders and Bishops

A bishop [elder] must ... not [be] given to wine (I Tim. 3:2- 3). (That's also repeated in Titus 1:7.)

Deacons

Likewise deacons must be reverent, not double-tongued, not given to much wine, not greedy for money (I Tim. 3:8).

At this point, you will find a most amazing exegesis by some people who say that the bishop and elder cannot drink at all, but the deacon can take a little drink now and then! They quote, *"not given to much wine."* That is a categorical statement to stay away from it! To argue that the use of an adjective in verse eight (*"much"*) cancels what it says in verse three, is utter nonsense! The same phrases are used in literature outside of the Bible and this is a strong statement to stay completely away from it.

Literally, it says not to be *"beside the wine"* and some people who are in favor of social drinking, argue that it's picturing a drunk. No way. It is telling you not to even get close. God forbade it to His leaders in the Old Testament, and the same applies in the New Testament.

John the Baptist

You may be getting the idea that I'm against alcohol!

"For he will be great in the sight of the Lord, and shall drink neither wine nor strong drink. He will also be filled with the Holy Spirit, even from his mother's womb. And he will turn many of the children of Israel to the Lord their God" (Lk. 1:15-16).

Stay completely away from it, God said. It ought to be **clear** to those of us who want to be used of God, and who believe that God desires to use us—we ought to stay away from alcoholic beverages completely.

ALCOHOLIC BEVERAGES ARE DESIGNED TO HELP PEOPLE FORGET THEIR MISERY

> *Give strong drink to him who is perishing, And wine to those who are bitter of heart. Let him drink and forget his poverty, And remember his misery no more* (Prov. 31:6-7).

Do you think there is any positive blessing connected with drinking in the Bible? There are some statements that we are going to look at. We'll see whether or not they apply to alcoholic beverages.

The statements given in the Word of God which have to do with mixing grains to make the alcoholic content greater are all very clear in that we should have nothing to do with it. Don't even look at it! That's what Proverbs 23:31 says! It's only for those who are dying and want to "end it all".

ALCOHOLIC BEVERAGES ARE DEVELOPED TO A STAGE OF FERMENTATION THAT IS NOT RECOMMENDED IN THE BIBLE

I want to repeat this because people attack this point. The Bible is very detailed, practical and clear.

> *Who has woe? Those who linger long at the wine, Those who go in search of mixed wine. Do not look on the wine when it is red, When it sparkles in the cup, When it swirls around smoothly* (Prov. 23:29-31).

There is a lot of debate over what the translation here really implies, but there is one thing that is very obvious— it is talking about a strong stage of fermentation where the wine is very active. God says, Don't even look at it! Stay away from it completely.

There are a lot of questions that come into people's minds, so I want to go into this a little further. I've said that alcoholic beverages which are developed to the stage that we have them today, is never recommended in the Bible. But there are some positive statements in the Bible.

They Are Not the Wine That Reminds Us of the Blessing of the Lord

He causes the grass to grow for the cattle, And vegetation for the service of man, That he may bring forth food from the earth, And wine that makes glad the heart of man, Oil to make his face shine, And bread which strengthens man's heart (Ps. 104:14-15).

There! That justifies alcoholic beverages, some people say. No, it doesn't! It's talking about that which God created; it's not talking about the processes of man which follow His creation. It's not talking about stirring in extra grain in order to ferment it. He's talking about the product of God's own creation! It is a perversion of the Word of God to use this verse to justify alcoholic beverages.

Go, eat your bread with joy, And drink your wine with a merry heart; For God has already accepted your works. Let your garments always be white, And let your head lack no oil (Eccl. 9:7-8).

Remember that *"wine"* refers to all stages of grapes from the fresh fruit to the most fermented stage. Only the context can help us. The context here goes on to talk about living joyfully with your wife. It is talking about bread and wine and the basic things of life. It means that God supplies our basic needs. There is not a Jewish commentary in the world that authorizes fermented alcoholic beverages as the interpretation of this passage. It is a beverage we would drink like water, long before any fermentation takes place.

It is talking about God providing for all of our needs. We are to be thankful and to praise the Lord that He's taking care of us. It has nothing to do with the promotion of alcoholic beverages as we know them today.

They Are Not the Wine Created by Jesus at the Wedding in Cana

One gentleman who was quick to accept social drinking said to me, "The wedding at Cana of Galilee is all the proof I need!" Really! At that wedding, we have the first of the miracles that Jesus did. His disciples and He attended the wedding and they ran out of wine. The mother of Jesus came and said, "They have no wine." Jesus performed an amazing miracle!

There were six waterpots of stone and they contained twenty or thirty gallons apiece. He said, *"Fill the waterpots with water,"* and when they drew it out, here's what happened.

> *When the master of the feast had tasted the water that was made wine, and did not know where it came from (but the servants who had drawn the water knew), the master of the feast called the bridegroom. And he said to him, "Every man at the beginning sets out the good wine, and when the guests have well drunk, then that which is inferior; but you have kept the good wine until now"* (Jn. 2:9-10).

The practice was to let the guests get into a state where they didn't care whether the wine was good or bad before bringing out the lesser wine. But what I want you to see here is that *"good wine"* has a special meaning.

The grapes are thrown into the winevat when they bring them in from the field—they are going to trample them out. The sheer pressure causes juice to seep down into a pan they put underneath the vat. You can still see it done that way today. The workers will run in from the field and drink the juice straight from the pan before they ever start pressing out the grapes. They fight over it! That's *"good wine."*

Can you imagine how many grapes the men would have had to gather to make enough *"good wine"* to fill all those stone jars. How did they have the time to do that? It was an obvious miracle of the Lord and no magical tricks here at all. It was a sensational miracle.

That *"good wine"* was the only kind of wine that the rabbis would even consider for the *"wine tithe"*. They never used strongly fermented wine as we know it today.

They Are Not the Wine that Relieves Stomach Problems

> *No longer drink only water, but use a little wine for your stomach's sake and our frequent infirmities* (I Tim. 5:23).

People often use this verse to justify drinking alcoholic beverages. I don't know if you know this or not, but in Israel, the medical profession does not recommend alcoholic beverages for stomach problems! If you have the flu, they

recommend pure grape juice. You can still go into res-
taurants in Jerusalem where they put bottles on your table
to look like wine. I've seen this many times and I've tasted
it. It is not wine at all, it is pure grape juice!

Why do they recommend grape juice for your stomach's
sake? They teach that the nutritional value that will help our
stomach is strongest when it is grape juice. As the process
of fermentation goes on, it is losing its nutritional value because fermentation is a process of decay. This only takes a
little thinking for us to understand it. The whole process of
fermentation in the Bible is as a sedative! It is not teaching
that wine has nutritional value for your stomach problems.
That is not what Paul recommended. He recommended
grape juice as they still do today.

They Are Not the Wine Used in the Worship of the Lord

*"You shall eat before the Lord your God, in the
place where He chooses to make His name abide, the
tithe of your grain and your new wine and your oil, of
the firstlings of your herds and your flocks, that you
may learn to fear the Lord your God always"* (Deut.
14:23).

If alcoholic processes were as harmless as some people
try to tell us, then God wouldn't be distressed about having
them used in worship. In fact, there is only one kind of wine
ever used in worship. How do we know what stage of fermentation is meant here? The Hebrew word is very clear
and it only refers to wine less than forty days old and, usually, it only refers to pure grape juice.

As we look over the evidence of the Bible, we learn that
alcoholic beverages are dangerous; it is denied to certain
people; it is designed to help some people forget their misery,
like a sedative given to those who are dying; it is at a stage
of fermentation that is never recommended in the Bible.

ALCOHOLIC BEVERAGES ARE DESCRIBED AS DRINKS THAT CAUSE EMOTIONAL, PHYSI-CAL, AND SPIRITUAL PROBLEMS

Go back to Proverbs 23:29. Look at the list! Who has
woe, sorrow, arguments, complaints, wounds without

cause, redness of eyes? We could add—flushed faces, bad livers and other things. We don't need to argue over this! All you need is a little bit of medical background to tell you about the destructive action of alcoholic beverages on your body. That is without counting the emotional turmoil involved as indicated by verse 29.

In Ephesians 5:18, we are commanded to be filled with the Holy Spirit and that verse says, *"Do not be drunk with wine wherein is excess; but be filled with the Spirit"* (KJV). The most obvious point here is that *"being drunk with wine"* is the OPPOSITE of *"being filled with the Spirit"* even though it illustrates it.

Someone who is filled with "spirits" is NOT filled with "the Spirit"!

> *Therefore, since Christ suffered for us in the flesh, arm yourselves also with the same mind, for he who has suffered in the flesh has ceased from sin, that he no longer should live the rest of his time in the flesh for the lusts of men, but for the will of God. For we have spent enough of our past lifetime in doing the will of the Gentiles—when we walked in licentiousness, lusts, drunkenness, revelries, drinking parties, and abominable idolatries. In regard to these, they think it strange that you do not run with them in the same flood of dissipation, speaking evil of you. They will give an account to Him who is ready to judge the living and the dead* (I Peter 4:1-5).

The very term, "party time," is associated with drinking. It is also associated with drugs and with sex. What a sad thing that a very wholesome, healthy word that should describe joy and blessing ("party") has suddenly become a destructive term. Our kids use the term, "party," to mean drinking, drugs and sex. That doesn't say that everyone who goes to such a party has participated in any of that. However, the sad truth is that drinking is a serious problem on both junior high and high school campuses and is very prevalent on elementary school campuses. One out of every seven children in fourth through sixth grades has a drinking problem—not "has a drink". I said, "... has a drinking problem!"

In homes where either one or both parents drink regularly, there is a 75-80% chance that the child will also drink. It should be obvious to parents who realize the dangers of alcoholism that the best tactic (even if we didn't have all this Bible evidence) is to stay away from the stuff, if you care about your children. Get it out of your house!

In order to be as practical as possible, I want to say that a person who fools around with social drinking does not really care about this problem. When you compromise and argue that it is OK for you, you are not caring about the one person in twelve who cannot stop after they have taken their first drink. Some of us have a chemical balance in our systems that makes it impossible to "handle" drinks! One person can put down a six-pack of beer and not be affected at all. Another person can take one and already be severely affected emotionally, physically and mentally.

Why would any Christian, who says they love the Lord Jesus Christ, even get close to alcohol? It's beyond me! What should we do about this? We'll make it as simple as we possibly can for all of us—kids, students, adults.

Stop drinking alcoholic beverages!

Remove all alcoholic beverages from your house! Some of you ladies like to cook with alcohol and you have some of it in the refrigerator—hidden behind something. After the heartache I have seen caused from alcohol, I have come to the conclusion that even that has to go. In the name of protecting all of us, let's get it out of our home.

Why should the world have to bombard us with, "Say NO to drinking?" Shouldn't we have been saying that to ourselves for a long time? Get it out of your home. If you have a wetbar, turn it into a study! Get it out of your home! If you don't understand, hear it again—**Get It Out Of Your Home!**

A colonel in the army had an alcohol problem. I worked with him for a long time and he told me he had complete victory. We went to lunch one day and stopped by his house. I asked him if he had any drinks in the house. He said, "What?" (That's Freudian for "Yes"!) "No," he answered hesitantly. "You don't mind if I look, do you?" People who haven't had experience in looking for this stuff, look in the refrigerator. That's dumb. Are they going to put it in the refrigerator, if they don't want you to know they are drinking? I found six bottles in the most unbelievable places! One was in the toilet tank!

I don't always recommend what I did on that occasion. I said, "You want to get this out of your life, right?" "Oh, yes. I don't know what I was thinking!" I stopped him. "Yes, you did! You took the time to hide those bottles ... just in case! We're going to take care of this." We stood in front of the sink and poured all of it down the drain.

His first statement was, "I paid good money for that!" He lost it. "I'll tell you how to get victory-don't ever buy it again!" I told him. Then, I suggested that he call someone immediately to whom he was accountable the first moment he was tempted to turn back to it. We try to help people that have a drinking problem.

What's the matter with us? How can we help them if there are lots of Christians fooling around with social drinking? Lives are being torn apart.

There are many people who have gotten victory over alcohol addiction and they can thank God that they are finally sober. People are going to programs and paying lots of money to get this out of their systems and somehow get their lives back together. And you're going to mess around with a little social drinking? In the name of compassion, and love, and commitment to Christ, get it out of your life.

Encourage others to stop drinking, too, no matter how much or how little they drink.

I ran into a young couple at a local shopping center and the fellow had a beer can in his hand. It was so funny! He saw me coming and put it behind his back! To my knowledge, he has never heard me speak on alcohol. I said, "What's that behind your back?" (I'm very terrible that way.) "It's a light beer," he said. "No, it's not! It's regular beer," I went on. "I usually drink light," he mumbled. "Do you have a problem?" I inquired. "No, I only have a pack a day." "That's six cans a day! I wouldn't want you to drive me home," I levelled with him.

Then, he asked what was wrong with it! I offered to tell him but he really didn't want to know. Within two weeks, that guy made a complete break and no longer has anything to do with it. The blessing that has come to his life since then is incredible!

Don't you know that drinking is hurting you? It hurts you spiritually, emotionally, physically, mentally. It's hurting you! Your life could be turned around just like that, if you'd stop. You'd have new life, new joy, new zeal, new attitude, new victory, if you'd stop it. Encourage people to stop it, wherever you are.

Refuse to Participate in Activities that Promote, Encourage or Allow Drinking

This is tough! People say they want to win people to Christ, so they drink. It is like smoking—I don't have to smoke in order to win a non-believer to Christ. People have offered me cigarettes at different times and, when I say, "No thank you," they have never said that I was missing out on one of the greatest thrills of life! Normally, people say, "Boy! I wish I could quit!" You don't need to do these things in order to win people to Christ.

I have gotten up and walked out of activities where Christians were allowing and promoting the use of alcoholic beverages. Yes, it's embarrassing! Yes, it hurts people, but I'm going to continue to do it until Jesus comes. I don't want anything to do with alchol. I want people to know that I don't want anything to do with it and I hope you'll join me in that.

Offer Help, Support and Accountability to Those Who Are Addicted and Want to Stop

We've got to care for people. If you've ever tried to help someone with a serious alcohol problem, you know it's not easy. The world tells them that the chances of them going back into drinking are very strong even if they stop. There are parents who have seen their home torn apart by alcohol. It breaks our hearts to see our kids who have been trained in the ways of the Lord, drinking. Alcoholics in their early twenties often look like they've been drinking for twenty or thirty years. We've got to start caring!

There is hope and there is help. Our Lord Jesus does not abandon somebody because of a drinking problem. We need to help by taking a stand against it. We also need to help by letting someone who has a drinking problem be accountable to you. It doesn't matter what time of day, let them call you the first time they feel like they want a drink. Go and stay with them until the problem is settled. We need to help each other.

> *And such were some of you. But you were washed, but you were sanctified, but you were justified in the name of the Lord Jesus and by the Spirit of our God* (I Cor. 6:11).

It is not hopeless! God can change your life! Drunkenness is not a sin that cannot be conquered. *"Such were some of you. But you were washed!"* How sweet to sense that you

are clean! That may be what you were, but no more! God
sets people free!

We need compassion for a person who has gone through
that and falls back into such a habit. *"Restore such a one,"*
Galatians 6:1, *"in a spirit of gentleness, considering
yourself lest you also be tempted. Bear one another's
burdens, and so fulfill the law of Christ."*

I'm asking you to care!

CHAPTER 15

THE PROBLEM OF FEAR

Problems abound in our lives but there's one thing that comes to us all at one time or another—that's fear. You can soften it with the word, "anxiety," but it's still fear. You can say you're "concerned," but it's fear. A lot of us are afraid of relationships. Some of us are afraid of passing time. We can fear problems of health, finances, or a multitude of things. Most damaging of all is the fear of death.

> *Then they will call on me, but I will not answer; They will seek me diligently, but they will not find me. Because they hated knowledge And did not choose the fear of the Lord, They would have none of my counsel And despised all my reproof, Therefore they shall eat the fruit of their own way, And be filled to the full with their own fancies. For the turning away of the simple will slay them, And the complacency of fools will destroy them; But whoever listens to me will dwell safely, And will be secure, without fear of evil* (Prov. 1:28- 33).

There are five different Hebrew words all translated *"fear"*. It's not a small subject. The most common word appears 420 times! Almost 600 times in the Bible, it deals with the subject of fear. I have divided the subject into three areas.

IT IS AN EXPECTED RESULT
OF NOT TRUSTING THE LORD

We may not want to face it, but we should expect fear to happen when we are not trusting the Lord. We open a "Pandora's box" of fear when we stop trusting the Lord.

It Results in Emotional Traps

When you decide that you're not going to trust the Lord, or you just stop trusting Him, you'll fall into emotional traps.

> *The Lord is my shepherd; I shall not want. He*
> *makes me to lie down in green pastures; He leads me*
> *beside the still waters. He restores my soul; He leads*
> *me in the paths of righteousness For His name's sake.*
> *Yea, though I walk through the valley of the shadow*
> *of death, I will fear no evil* (Ps. 23:1-4).

The fear of evil is a result of not trusting the Lord. Some
of us are afraid of evil, itself, no matter what form it takes.
That is an emotional trap.

> *Hear my voice, O God, in my meditation; Preserve*
> *my life from fear of the enemy* (Ps. 64:1).

A military man certainly understands **the fear of an
enemy,** but that can happen to anybody at any time in your
life. You can be afraid of the opposition, afraid of the enemy.
Might I add that the greatest enemy we have is Satan and
there are plenty of Christians who are afraid of Satan.
However, the Bible never once tells us to be afraid of him!
The Bible tells us to resist him. The Bible tells us, *"Greater
is He that is in you than he that is in the world."* A lot of us
are afraid of Satan. He is powerful, but we have no reason
to be afraid of him because we trust the Lord. The "shield
of faith" will quench all his fiery darts. "The sword of the
spirit" will stab him good! It is totally contrary to trusting
the Lord to let the latest movie or TV show or what we read
cause us to be afraid of Satan.

Perhaps it is more practical to talk about **the fear of man.**
This hits home more than the fear of evil or of an enemy.

> *The fear of man brings a snare* [a trap], *But*
> *whoever trusts in the Lord shall be safe* (Prov. 29:25).

A human person intimidates you. Regardless of their influence or power or authority, a human person should never
intimidate the child of God. Never! *"I will not fear what man
can do to me,"* the Bible says. So, the actions of man, his
anger, his attitude—the fear of man is indeed an emotional
trap. Some of us can go to work and have to face someone
that we fear—someone who intimidates us, threatens us,
makes us feel uncomfortable.

Sometimes we do this to ourselves more than the other
person does it to us. In order to justify our failure to trust
the Lord, we sometimes speak of someone who intimidates

us. No matter what anyone says or does to you, no person on the face of this globe can intimidate the child of God who trusts in the Lord. The fear of man is a trap!

I can fear a man's presence just by looking at him. For instance, the sight of the defensive linemen in the National Football League is awesome. But not even that sight can intimidate the child of God who trusts the Lord.

> *All the children of Israel murmured against Moses and Aaron, and the whole congregation said to them, If only we had died in the land of Egypt! Or if only we had died in this wilderness! Why has the Lord brought us to this land to fall by the sword, that our wives and children should become victims? Would it not be better for us to return to Egypt? So they said to one another, "Let us select a leader and return to Egypt." Then Moses and Aaron fell on their faces before all the assembly of the congregation of the children of Israel. And Joshua and Caleb the son of Jephunneh, who were among those who had spied out the land, tore their clothes* (Numbers 14:1-6).

The Children of Israel were listening to the ten men who said there were giants in the land instead of listening to Joshua and Caleb who were telling them it was a very good land—"It's flowing with milk and honey, and God promised this land to us. Let's go and get it!" The Israelites were thinking about the giants. I find there are always people around to remind us of *"the giants"*.

> *And they spoke to all the congregation of the children of Israel, saying: "The land we passed through to spy out is an exceedingly good land. If the Lord delights in us, then He will bring us into this land and give it to us, 'a land which flows with milk and honey.' Only do not rebel against the Lord, nor fear the people of the land, for they are our bread; their protection has departed from them, and the Lord is with us. Do not fear them." And all the congregation said to stone them with stones* (Num. 14:7-10).

Just because we speak the truth, everybody isn't going to bow down and say, "Amen, brother!" No way! They were afraid, so they wanted to stone Joshua and Caleb. All fear is an emotional trap. Here it is the fear of man, yet the challenge came, *"The Lord is with us. Don't fear them."*

If the Lord is for us, who can be against us?
(Rom.8).

We either believe it or we don't.

There is one fear (if the Lord tarries) that all of us will face. **The fear of death** has bothered some of God's greatest servants who serve God with all their hearts, trust His Word, and have been instrumental in leading many to Christ.

Do you know there is a blessing in having an unexpected heart attack and suddenly going home to be with the Lord? Have you ever thought about it? Some say, "That is such a shock!" I know the loved ones are stunned, but I have seen the difference between dying quickly and having a terminal illness-being told you are going to die. Being incapacitated over a long period of time, produces an agonizing fear that continues with you every single day. It's a blessing to die quickly.

Inasmuch then as the children have partaken of flesh and blood, He Himself likewise shared in the same, that through death He might destroy him who had the power of death, that is, the devil, and release those who through fear of death were all their lifetime subject to bondage (Heb. 2:14-15).

Bondage refers to a trap! The fear of death is the last enemy. The Bible says it will be destroyed—we are going to be resurrected from the dead, but we have to take it by faith. What is the opposite of faith? Fear! Faith trusts the Lord for what He says. Why would I be afraid of death? Death is a release into God's presence. *"Absent from the body and present with the Lord!"* Paul calls it an exodus—a way out!

I'm looking forward to going home to be with the Lord. Why would we want to stay around in this miserable world? We only want to stay, if the Lord wants us to, so that we can win others to Christ.

The other day, I was talking to a fellow about the difference between evangelism and edification. I believe in both, but I believe that evangelism is more important than edification because whether people are edified or not, evangelism means the difference between heaven and hell. We know that theologically. We're here on earth to take people to heaven with us, by whatever means possible. We even edify one another so that we'll have our act together so that we can talk to lost people without being intimiated. We want to be loved, encouraged and built up in the body of Christ so we can go out there into the world and tell someone about Jesus so they can get to heaven and escape hell.

We're so afraid and death can be an awesome threat to our emotional security. All of these emotional traps are to be expected as a result of not trusting the Lord.

It Results in Personal Trembling

"And there will be signs in the sun, in the moon, and in the stars; and on the earth distress of nations, with perplexity, the sea and the waves roaring; men's hearts failing them from fear and the expectation of those things which are coming on the earth, for the powers of heaven will be shaken. Then they will see the Son of Man coming in a cloud with power and great glory. Now when these things begin to happen, [believers] *look up and lift up your heads, because your redemption draws near"* (Lk. 21:25-28).

We heard about servicemen, on their way to the war zone, scurrying around trying to find a Bible in order to find an answer to the terrible panic that can hit someone at such a time. These verses in Luke extend that into the Tribulation period. Unbelievers' hearts will fail them in utter panic while believers are unafraid, expecting the return of the Lord.

I heard an interview of some Israelis who experienced the "scud" missile attacks. They had to deal with fear and panic. These men said they were no longer so fearful because they think they have run out of "scud" missiles. Wait a minute! Doesn't that reveal our problem? We're only OK as long as there is no serious threat that we can foresee on the horizon.

"Men's hearts failing them for fear" results in trembling and losing control—utter panic. It is the expected result for those who don't trust the Lord.

It Results in Spiritual Timidity

We are intimidated by the world around us. We are fearful even to share the gospel with people.

"Therefore do not fear them. For there is nothing covered that will not be revealed, and hidden that will

not be known. Whatever I tell you in the dark, speak in the light; and what you hear in the ear, preach on the housetops. And do not fear those who kill the body but cannot kill the soul. But rather fear Him who is able to destroy both soul and body in hell" (Matt. 10:26-28).

He's talking about hell. He's talking about the world and being intimidated and not standing up for what you believe—backing down.

A lot of us are afraid to speak up. Maybe we're afraid that people will mock us or reject us. Maybe they will think we're religious "nuts". Or maybe we really want to identify with wordly people in a way that is not biblical. Maybe we really don't want to be their friends to win them to Christ, but we want to be like them, so we are afraid to let them know that we are Christians. Maybe we're afraid we'll lose our job, or our influence or something else. We're afraid to say that we are Christians. I like that shirt that says, "I'm the Christian the devil warned you about!" Some of us need those shirts to start conversations because we are spiritually timid.

However, no one spoke openly of Him for fear of the Jews (Jn. 7:13).

This verse brings that point out. They were afraid of the Jewish leaders. They would be ostracized; they couldn't buy or sell. It was going to cost them something. They decided to be quiet so they could get along.

You can see evidences of the Holocaust all over Jerusalem. Many Jews, because of fear, never spoke up, but there was a worse problem! There were many Christians who were afraid to speak against Hitler, who used Christianity to deceive the people. He told them abortion and euthanasia were right and needed. He wanted to select the very best among them to live and Christians by the scores, by the thousands, refused to stand up! Talk about spiritual timidity! The same thing can happen to us as we watch the armies of evil march straight through the values that we know the Bible teaches and none of us say anything.

Then, the same day at evening, being the first day of the week, when the doors were shut where the disciples were assembled, for fear of the Jews, Jesus came and stood in the midst, and said to them, "Peace be with you" (Jn. 20:19).

That's a good way to handle fear. *"If God be for us, who can be against us?"*

Timothy was a man who had been trained and discipled to be a leader in God's church. I believe he was an evangelist who was responsible for an area. First and Second Timothy and Titus are not manuals for pastors, but for evangelists in trying to plant churches and see God's work thrive. Here's a young man who had stomach problems, and evidently, he was fearful. Here he was hanging around with one of the boldest guys in human history-the Apostle Paul. You can imagine how intimidated he was.

In Paul's last epistle, not written from the guardhouse in Rome but rather from the Mamertine Prison which was a dungeon below ground. I have been there and sat down in the present Mamertine Prison. I wouldn't want to sit there for very long! It is a rat-infested, mudhole that stinks to high heaven.

That was where they put people they were going to execute. That's why Paul said, *"The time of my departure is at hand. I am now ready to be offered."* It was all over, and Paul knew it, but he said that the *"crown of righteousness was laid up"* for him *"that the Lord, the righteous judge would give on His appearing and to all those who love His appearing."* What confidence this man was putting into this young leader, Timothy!

> *Therefore I remind you to stir up the gift of God which is in you through the laying on of my hands. For God has not given us a spirit of fear, but of power and of love and of a sound mind. Therefore do not be ashamed of the testimony of our Lord, nor of me His prisoner, but share with me in the sufferings for the gospel according to the power of God, who has saved us and called us with a holy calling, not according to our works, but according to His own purpose and grace which was given to us in Christ Jesus before time began, but has not been revealed by the appearing of our Savior Jesus Christ, who has abolished death and brought life and immortality to light through the gospel, to which I was appointed a preacher, an apostle, and a teacher of the Gentiles. For this reason I also suffer these things; nevertheless I am not ashamed [timid], for I know whom I have believed and am persuaded that He is able to keep what I have committed to Him until that Day* (II Tim. 1:6-12).

That's strong stuff for the soul! God NEVER gives us a spirit of fear. He gives us the Holy Spirit of *"power, and of love, and of a sound mind"*. Fear is the expected result of not trusting in the Lord.

FEAR IS AN EMOTIONAL RESPONSE TO GOD HIMSELF

If you have studied the Bible or even read it much, you are aware of the fact that it tells believers to *"fear the Lord"*. That's hard to understand. Some English translations try to help us by speaking about having reverence for the Lord. I appreciate what they are doing, but the Bible is talking about something more than a godly respect for God.

One time, after studying the word *"fear,"* I wrote, "I have come to the conclusion that it is a very complex, difficult thing to understand. After going over all the Hebrew and analyzing the word studies, I have come to the conclusion that what 'fear the Lord' really means, is—fear." We're almost searching for a clue to get off the word, *"fear"*. The longer you study it, the more you realize that He means *"fear"*. It is healthy to fear God; it is unhealthy to fear man. It is an emotional response of my heart to God.

It Refers to God's Law

> The law of God is perfect, converting the soul; The testimony of the Lord is sure, making wise the simple; The statutes of the Lord are right, rejoicing the heart; The commandment of the Lord is pure, enlightening the eyes; The fear of the Lord is clean, enduring forever; The judgments of the Lord are true and righteous altogether (Ps. 19:7-9).

If you back up, you have *"law,"* *"testimony,"* *"statutes,"* *"commandment,"* *"judgments,"* and *"fear"* all meaning the same thing. If I fear the Lord, I have a healthy respect and understanding of the importance of my obedience to what God says. It refers to the Law of God and that has an effect upon me. That is what Psalm 19 is saying.

It Realizes God's Judgments

If you have this fear of God, you realize the awfulness of God's judgments. It sees holiness and righteousness in God and realizes that judgment is the natural result of God's holy, righteous character. Do you believe that God judged Jesus Christ when He died on the cross? He certainly didn't judge Jesus for any sin He did! But God judged Jesus, in the sense that He bore our sins on the cross. The judgment of God against sin, all the wrath of God against sin, Jesus endured when He died on the cross. That's why the Bible calls it, *"enduring the cross"*. It was not for what He had done, but for what we have done. He experienced the justice and judgment of God.

Does God excuse your sin and mine? No, never! Does He sweep it under the rug and say it isn't important? No, that is not the gospel! The gospel is that the penalty has been paid. Don't ever think that the penalty was not endured. Don't ever think that the judgment of God has never been brought against sin. It has! Either you accept what Jesus did, or you will experience the judgment of God in the future-and you will deserve it! God, by His own nature, must judge sin and wrong.

> *My flesh trembles for fear of You, And I am afraid of Your judgments* (Ps. 119:120).

This was David, a believer, talking. When we fear the Lord, and not man, it is an emotional response to God Himself when you learn the character of God.

I read in a book of encouragement for believers that we are not supposed to be afraid of God and what He does. I appreciate what they were trying to do, but I don't believe that. I've seen too many Scriptures that say just the opposite! It is right, healthy and proper for us to fear God! His holy and righteous character will bring judgment. The psalmist uses strong words in Hebrew (Psalm 119). He is *"trembling"*; he is *"afraid"* of God's judgments in his life!

It Recognizes God's Anger

> *Now therefore, be wise, O kings; Be instructed, you judges of the earth. Serve the Lord with fear, And rejoice with trembling. Kiss the Son, lest He be angry, And you perish in the way When His wrath is kindled but a little. Blessed are all those who put their trust in Him* (Ps. 2:10-12).

This is the gospel in the Old Testament. It doesn't say, "Kiss the Father!" It says, *"Kiss the Son. Blessed are all those who put their trust in Him."* That's the gospel.

Does God get mad? Perhaps our English common usage is not appropriate; however, I think there is a tendency for us not to believe in the anger of God. This verse says, *"Kiss the Son, lest He be angry ... His wrath ..."* It's important to understand that you do recognize God's anger if you are relating to God correctly.

It Remembers God's Holiness

Oh, worship the Lord in the beauty of holiness [separate from all else]! *Tremble before Him, all the earth* (Ps. 96:9).

We tremble before Him because we know how separate He is from us. His holiness demands that our sin be dealt with, so our emotional response to God is to remember God's holiness—always. Peter wrote, *"Be ye holy, for I am holy, says the Lord."* We are told to live holy lives, separate from sin, because God is holy and we ought to tremble at the thought. To think that we can somehow get away with something, in the light of God's holiness, is incredible!

It Responds to God's Mercy

But as for me, I will come into Your house in the multitude of Your mercy; In fear of You I will worship toward Your holy temple (Ps. 5:7).

Understand that mercy, or compassion, means that God is holding back what we deserve. We come with fear and trembling, understanding that mercy, alone, is what allows us to come into His presence. Lamentations 3:22 says, *"It is of the Lord's mercies, that we are not consumed because His compassions fail not."*

A person growing in faith, walking close to the Lord, understands why he fears the Lord. If it were not for the **mercy** of God, His **holiness** and **righteousness** would wipe us out! If there were no problem, we wouldn't need mercy.

It Rests on God's Protection

I sought the Lord, and He heard me, And delivered me from all my fears. They looked to Him and were radiant, and their faces were not ashamed. This poor man cried out, and the Lord heard him, And saved him out of all his troubles. The angel of the Lord encamps all around those who fear Him, and delivers them (Ps. 34:4-7).

We fear the Lord and we seek Him, and He delivers us out of all our fears! The fear of man can be taken out of your heart when you fear the Lord. "The angel of the Lord encamps all around those who fear Him." Isn't that beautiful?

It Relies on God's Provision

Oh, taste and see that the Lord is good; Blessed is the man who trusts in Him! Oh, fear the Lord, you His saints! There is no want to those who fear Him. The young lions lack and suffer hunger; But those who seek the Lord shall not lack any good thing. Come, you children, listen to me; I will teach you the fear of the Lord (Ps. 34:8-11).

It is saying that God will take care of you, if you fear Him! *"Blessed is the man who trusts in Him."* We get an insight into the **meaning of fear**, in this context. We said that the fear of man is the expected result of not trusting in the Lord. Now I learn that the fear of the Lord means trusting in the Lord rather than my fears. It's almost a paradox! If I trust in the Lord, I will not fear man. If I don't trust in the Lord, I will fear man. Trusting in the Lord IS fearing the Lord!

IT IS AN ESSENTIAL REQUIREMENT IN OUR RELATIONSHIP TO GOD

We can't leave out the fear of the Lord! To show you that it is an essential thing, I want to show you that it is commanded by God. It is not an option. It is a command to Christians. Ecclesiastes says, *"Fear God and keep His commandments."*

It Is Commanded

My son, fear the Lord and the king; Do not associate with those given to change; For their calamity will rise suddenly, And who knows the ruin those two can bring? (Prov. 24:21).

It is a command to fear the Lord.

It Is Connected With the Knowledge of God

The fear of the Lord is the beginning of knowledge (Prov. 1:7).

> *Then you will understand the fear of the Lord and find the knowledge of God* (Prov. 2:5).

> *The fear of the Lord is the beginning of wisdom, And the knowledge of the Holy One is understanding* (Prov. 9:10).

> *The fear of the Lord is the instruction of wisdom, And before honor is humility* (Prov. 15:33).

Frankly, we're not smart unless we fear God! We're not smart at all. It is an essential requirement in our relationship to God. It's commanded and it's connected with the knowledge of God Himself.

It Is Controlled by a Hatred of Sin

If we really fear God, it is controlled by a hatred of sin.

> *Do not be wise in your own eyes; Fear the Lord and depart from evil. It will be health to your flesh, And strength to your bones* (Prov. 3:7-8).

What an encouragement! What an awesome reminder!

> *The fear of the Lord is to hate evil; Pride and arrogance and the evil way And the perverse mouth I hate* (Prov. 8:13).

What does it mean to fear the Lord? It means to hate sin! Don't hate sinners—hate sin.

> *A wise man fears and departs from evil, But a fool rages and is self-confident* (Prov. 14:16).

What does it mean to fear the Lord? It means to stay away from sin.

> *In mercy and truth Atonement is provided for iniquity; and by the fear of the Lord one departs from evil* (Prov. 16:6).

Take the fear of God out of our hearts and we will sin.

> *Do not let your heart envy sinners, But in the fear of the Lord continue all day long; For surely there is a herafter, And your hope will not be cut off* (Prov. 23:17-18).

Once again, what is the fear of the Lord and why is it an essential requirement in my relationship to God? It is commanded; it is connected with the knowledge of God Himself and it is controlled by a hatred of sin.

It Is Characterized by Strong Confidence and Trust

Do not be afraid of sudden terror, Nor of trouble from the wicked when it comes; for the Lord will be your confidence, And will keep your foot from being caught (Prov. 3:26-26).

In the fear of the Lord there is strong confidence, And His children will have a place of refuge (Prov. 14:27).

If you fear the Lord, it brings confidence of refuge from all that is a threat and an intimidation in your life. Beautiful!

The fear of the Lord leads to life, And he who has it will abide in satisfaction; He will not be visited with evil (Prov. 19:23).

What a wonderful promise! If we fear God, He will protect us! He's our strong confidence and our trust.

It Is Compared to Wealth, Honor, and Life

The Bible teaches that the fear of the Lord is essential in our lives because it is compared with wealth, honor and life.

The fear of the Lord is a fountain of life, To avoid the snares [traps] *of death* (Prov. 14:27).

Better is a little with the fear of the Lord, Than great treasure with trouble (Prov. 15:16).

It is compared to wealth and there is no contest!

By humility and the fear of the Lord Are riches and honor and life (Prov. 22:4).

Charm is deceitful and beauty is vain, But a woman who fears the Lord, she shall be praised (Prov. 31:30).

This refers to that woman Solomon loved. Here the fear of the Lord is compared to honor.

It Is Contrasted With Disobedience and a Lack of Convictions

What is the fear of God? It is the OPPOSITE of disobedience to God and a lack of moral conviction.

Abraham said, "Because I thought surely the fear of God is not in this place; and they will kill me on account of my wife" (Gen. 20:11).

Here a man who feared God recognized that there was no moral conviction in a pagan place about murdering his wife.

He who despises the word will be destroyed, But he who fears the commandment will be rewarded (Prov. 13:13).

In Romans 3:10-18 the fear of God is contrasted with disobedience and immorality.

As it is written: "There is none righteous, no, not one; There is none who understands; There is none who seeks after God. They have all gone out of the way; They have together become unprofitable; There is none who does good, no, not one. Their throat is an open tomb; With their tongues they have practiced deceit; The poison of asps is under their lips; Whose mouth is full of cursing and bitterness. Their feet are swift to shed blood; Destruction and misery are in their ways; And the way of peace they have not known. There is no fear of God before their eyes."

It is Committed to a Godly Lifestyle

When we talk about the fear of God being the essential requirement in our relationship to God, it is *"the sum of the whole matter"* (Ecclesiastes). You can put it all together—everything God wants you to know—in one simple statement: **Fear God and keep His Word.** What is the fear of God? It is a commitment to a godly lifestyle.

And now, Israel, what does the Lord your God require of you, but to fear the Lord your God, to walk in all His ways and to love Him, to serve the Lord your God with all your heart and with all your soul, and to keep the commandments of the Lord and His statutes which I command you today for your good? You shall fear the Lord your God; you shall serve Him, and to

*Him you shall hold fast, and take oaths in His name.
He is your praise, and He is your God, who has done
for you these great and awesome things which your
eyes have seen* (Deut. 10:12-13, 20-21).

*He who walks in His uprightness fears the Lord,
But he who is perverse in his ways despises Him*
(Prov. 14:1).

Who is the man who fears the Lord? It is the man who
walks in His uprightness; a man who lives a godly lifestyle;
who wants to be obedient to God in all things.

*Therefore, having these promises, beloved, let us
cleanse ourselves from all filthiness of the flesh and
spirit, perfecting holiness in the fear of God* (II Cor.
7:1).

Look at it again. The reason we are to cleanse ourselves
is because of *"all these promises"*. What promises? Paul has
just been writing about not being yoked together with unbelievers and the promises are found in verses 16 and 17:

*"I will dwell in them And walk among them. I will
be their God, And they shall be My people ... I will
receive you. I will be a Father to you, And you shall
be My sons and daughters."*

The number one reason for us to clean up our act is because we are children of the King. We belong to Him and we
want His blessing in our lives. We believe in Who He is. We
understand His character and we want to live for Him. We
have the promises ... therefore ... *"let us cleanse ourselves."*

Don't we often try to get out of the obvious? It says to
CLEANSE OURSELVES. God wouldn't have said it that way
if it were not possible! That means that you and I can
change. Some people say, "I'm helpless! I can't do it!" If you
are a Christian, you can change yourself because you have
the power of the Holy Spirit within you. You can do it.

How MUCH trouble should you clean out of your life? *"All
of the filthiness of the flesh"* refers to the things that you do.
"... and spirit" alludes to our attitudes and disposition of the
heart. How much? ALL of it!

How do these things change? YOU DO IT, God says!

What is the result? You will finally arrive at what God wants you to be—holy in His sight! And that holiness is a product and a result of the fear of the Lord.

It is in the secret places of our own hearts that we win the battle. Our character is what we are in the dark, when no one else knows. Our reputation is simply what people think we are.

All of us need to take a look at this question, Does God tell us that we can clean up our act? Absolutely! **This is what it means to fear the Lord.**

CHAPTER 16

THE PROBLEM OF COUNSEL

The proverbs of Solomon the son of David, king of Israel: To know wisdom and instruction, To perceive the words of understanding, To receive the instruction of wisdom, justice, judgment, and equity; To give prudence to the simple, To the young man knowledge and discretion-A wise man will hear and increase learning, And a man of understanding will attain wise counsel, To understand a proverb and an enigma, The words of the wise and their riddles. The fear of the Lord is the beginning of knowledge, But fools despise wisdom and instruction (Proverbs 1:1-7).

Most of Proverbs is all about counsel. The whole practice of counseling has exploded across our culture and it's easy to see why this has happened. There are many broken marriages and families. Some studies say that 80-90% of all counseling deals with marriage and family problems.

WHY DO WE NEED COUNSEL?

Some of us prefer to walk alone. We don't want anyone's advice and we don't think we need counseling. For such a person, it is an offense to tell them they need counseling. We need a biblical understanding of the subject of counseling. We need to understand how it should be done and who should give it.

It Is the Wise Thing To Do

The Bible says that we need counsel because it is the wise thing to do. In each case, you avoid something undesireable if you seek counsel.

The way of a fool is right in his own eyes, But he who heeds counsel is wise (Prov. 12:15).

You can write it down—it is wise because you **avoid trusting yourself.** *"The way of a fool is right in his own eyes"* tells us that he believes he knows what to do, so he trusts himself. One of the reasons we need to seek counsel is because, in fact, we do not want to trust ourselves. We want to trust the Lord and one of the ways God communicates His truth to us is through wise counsel. It is a wise thing to do.

> *Listen to counsel and receive instruction, That you may be wise in your latter days. There are many plans in a man's heart, Nevertheless the Lord's counsel—that will stand* (Prov. 19:20-21).

We should never let anyone put us down because we have gone for counseling. The truth of the matter is that God encourages that.

Getting counsel **avoids the problem of losing a battle.**

> *Every purpose is established by counsel; By wise counsel wage war* (Prov. 20:18).

It Is the Safe Thing To Do

> *Where there is no counsel, the people fall; But in the multitude of counselors there is safety* (Prov. 11:14).

Some people get to the point that they trust one particular person and perhaps that person is worthy of that trust and is competent to counsel. The Bible is very clear, however that we should seek counsel from more than one source. It is a safe thing to do.

If we want to avoid trusting ourselves, we will get counsel. If we want to avoid a battle, we will get counsel. If we want **to avoid a fall,** we will get counsel. It is the safe thing to do.

I wonder how many people are making colossal mistakes in their families and marriages because, in fact, they do not seek counsel and don't want it. Yet Proverbs 1 says that the whole point of this book is to get wise counsel—*"The fear of the Lord is the beginning of knowledge."*

It Is the Good Thing To Do

People sometimes say that counseling is not a good thing. Perhaps it is because of some of the abuses they have seen in this area. However, that is not what the Bible says.

> *Without counsel, plans go awry, But in the multitude of counselors they are established. A man has*

joy by the answer of his mouth, And a word spoken in due season, how good it is! (Prov. 15:22).

On the old "Honeymooners" series, Jackie Gleason used to say, "How sweet it is!" I feel like saying that here about counseling. How good it is when the right word comes from the Lord and it is just what we need! **We avoid having our plans fail.** It is good, indeed, and without it, all our plans are going to go awry.

It Is the Pleasant Thing To Do

Incline your ear and hear the words of the wise, And apply your heart to my knowledge; For it is a pleasant thing if you keep them within you; Let them all be fixed upon your lips, So that your trust may be in the Lord; I have instructed you today, even you. Have I not written to you excellent things Of counsels and knowledge, That I may make you know the certainty of the words of truth, That you may answer words of truth To those who send to you? (Prov. 22:17-21).

They received counsel **to avoid error.** Sometimes we need to face the fact that we, in ourselves, cannot see things clearly. Our perspective is messed up and we will have error and deceit in our lives, and our perspective will be wrong without counselors. We need them to keep us on the right track.

WHO SHOULD GIVE US COUNSEL?

The Lord is Our Counselor

This is where we are having trouble. The FIRST ONE we should turn to is the Lord, Himself.

There are many plans in a man's heart, Nevertheless the Lord's counsel—that will stand (Prov. 19:21).

We need to hear from the Lord, and one of the primary ways that we hear from the Lord is in the Scriptures.

Whatever things were written before were written for our learning, that we through the patience and comfort of the Scriptures might have hope (Rom. 15:4).

The word, *"comfort"*, here is the Greek word, *"counsel"*. We have counsel from the Scriptures. When the Lord brings us counsel, it is all written for our learning. The verse obviously refers to the Old Testament, so don't leave that out! It's all God's message. *"The Lord's counsel will stand."* That's Who we shoud be hearing from.

Believers Only

> *Blessed is the man Who walks not in the counsel of the ungodly, Nor stands in the path of sinners, Nor sits in the seat of the scornful* (Ps. 1:1).

It is very clear in the Word of God that we are not to walk in the counsel of the ungodly.

> *The thoughts of the righteous are right, But the counsels of the wicked are deceitful* (Prov. 12:5).

There is more trouble caused by ungodly, unbelieving counselors among God's people than you can shake a stick at. I can't believe the trouble that Christians get into, listening to unbelievers give counsel. Let me give you some of the ways we get used to this:

- Talk shows are a place where people pool their ignorance. Incompetent people tell us all sorts of crazy things, and we listen! Some of us listen for the humor in it, but we need to be warned about listening to any of that king of thing. Be careful what you are listening to, even when you are making fun of it. Make sure you don't listen to bad counsel as a regular habit in your life.

- Soap operas succeed because people watch them. Advertisers pay for those spots because they know you are watching. Surveys show that more people watch soap operas than watch primetime television. We have a problem! In soap operas, we are having wrong counsel communicated to us by unbelievers.

- Novels and literature written by unbelievers are also sources of bad counsel. In these books, we are receiving counsel whether we know it or not. The counsel of the wicked is deceitful. We're being told by the stories created in fiction, how to deal with life's problems. Do you think you're just fascinated by the stories? Really! We need to be careful.

- Television and movies send us counsel. It is always directly opposite to the Word of God and to what we believe as Christians. This is a constant problem in our society.

God says, "*Don't walk in the counsel of the ungodly,*" and "*Remember that the counsel of the wicked is deceitful.*" Believers only should counsel us. When we go for professional counseling, it is our right (and we should exercise it) to ask, "Would you please explain to me how you came to know Jesus Christ as your Savior and Lord. Also, explain to me how you put your trust in the Bible and in Jesus Christ as your Lord and Savior. I'll not pay you a dime until I hear what your personal faith is all about."

Believers Who Are Filled With Goodness

Not every believe is trustworthy in the area of counseling. Be careful! They may be carnal; they may not be walking with the Lord; they may have a hidden agenda; there may be something wrong in their lives.

> *Now I myself am confident concerning you, my brethren, that you also are full of goodness, filled with all knowledge, able also to admonish one another* (Rom. 15:14).

The word, "*admonish,*" is dealing with a word in counseling that Dr. J. Adams popularized called, "neuthetic counseling." It refers to "the mind" and "to place"; hence, to place in the mind. It is a kind of counseling mentioned in the Bible and often translated "*warn*" or "*admonish*". Instead of sitting and listening to someone tell you their problems, it is to place in their minds the warnings given in them Bible. Some counseling is more CONFRONTIVE than it is CONSOLING. We need to understand that since the world's view is a therapeutic, or consoling, approach. In the Bible, there is a confrontive approach whereby we are being warned.

If there is someone in your life who is willing to give you Scripture that contradicts what you are doing, you should get on your knees and thank God that they are still around. We need more counselors who are filled with the knowledge of God's word and with all goodness. They intend to do what is right. They're not interested in wearing their hearts on their sleeves and getting strokes from the counselee. They're not interested in making sure that you come back in order that their fee be paid. They are interested in giving you the truth. That's a Bible counselor!

Believers Who Are Filled With Wisdom

Him [Christ] *we preach, warning* [the same word—counsel, admonish] *every man and teaching every man in all wisdom* (Col. 1:28).

Let the word of Christ dwell in you richly in all wisdom, teaching and admonishing [counseling—putting into someone's mind] *one another in psalms and hymns and spiritual songs, singing with grace in your hearts to the Lord* (Col. 3:16).

I think of an incident some years ago. A lady who was experiencing great distress came for counseling. She had a strong tendency to depression and she came to the church to receive counsel, and no one was there except a person in the music department. So, this dear lady from the music department sat down to talk with her and she said, "When was the last time you sang a song of praise to the Lord?" The lady said, "I came in here for counseling!" "I know," replied the other lady, "I'm just asking." "I don't feel like singing," she replied. But Colossians says that we are to counsel one another *"in psalms and hymns and spiritual songs, singing with grace in our hearts to the Lord."* That woman, just by the use of praise and music, got her heart turned around for God! Today, she says that God delivered her from depression by the music of praise and thanks to the Lord. What are you listening to in your home?

This is a very serious matter. What is on our car radios? Interesting, isn't it, that counseling is to be done by believers who are filled with wisdom.

Believers With the Spiritual Gift

God has given certain people spiritual gifts and one of these gifts is counseling. Not simply the professionals who have been trained in school are qualified, there are also believers in the church who have the gift of counseling.

Having then gifts differing according to the grace that is given to us [whatever we have, God gave to us so don't get proud], *let us use them: if prophecy* [preaching], *let us prophesy in proportion to our faith* [our confidence has to be in the Word of God]; *or ministry* [the gift of service], *let us use it in our ministering* [do something!]; *he who teaches, in teaching* [refers to teaching God's Word]; *he who exhorts* [counsels], *in exhortation* [this is a warning to stick to the Word of God] (Rom. 12:8).

If folks have told you that you have the gift of counseling and have been able to help and encourage them by what you've said, then it would be wise to learn as much as you can about it. I would hope that all people who are in professional counseling who are Christians also have the gift. That would help. If you have the gift, you've got maximum effectiveness with minimum weariness. If you don't have the gift, it's a hassle and you can't wait to get through the day. The only reason such a person endures all these people with problems is because they need the money. That's a problem!

Even though people in this field have to charge fees in order to sustain the ministry to people, please understand that we don't do it for that reason. Make sure your heart is clear. Make sure you have the gift and you're doing it for the Lord. Your intention must be to put people's lives back together regardless of whether they pay you or not. That's very important.

Believers With a Father's Heart

I do not write these things to shame you, but as my beloved children I warn you [admonish, counsel, put into their minds]. *For though you might have ten thousand instructors in Christ, yet you do not have many fathers; for in Christ Jesus I have begotten you through the gospel* (I Cor. 4:14).

Those who counsel need a father's heart, Paul says.

You are witnesses, and God also, how devoutly and justly and blamelessly we behaved ourselves among you who believe; as you know how we exhorted [counseled], *and comforted* [a special reference to those who have lost a loved one or are seriously ill], *and charged every one of you, as a father does his own children, that you woud have a walk worthy of God who calls you into His own kingdom and glory* (I Thess. 2:10-12).

The first counsel is *"one called along side of"* to warn and challenge and motivate; to try to get people back on track. The second word is one of sympathy and love. These are two different things. Sometimes, we need to be "charged"; we need a kick in the pants, don't we?

Now, look at the last statement—*"as a father does his own children"*. The person who will counsel you best is someone with a father's heart. They will care about you as a child would be cared for by his own father. They will love you and understand you in a way that a father would understand.

Some people who have studied this matter tend to think that we should go to someone older than ourselves rather than someone the same age or younger. I'm not willing to say that younger people can't give you counsel. They certainly can! I've received a lot of counsel from younger people and sometimes, they have vision, excitement and understanding that older folks don't have. However, as a general rule, someone older is going to understand you better. In spite of what you think about people who are older than you are, they often understand you best.

At a rally where I spoke, one young man came up to me and said, "Wow! I had no idea you were such an old dude!" I wanted to clean him off the map! He looked pretty strong, however, so I decided not to take him on. I have learned a lot from younger people, but the best counsel I've ever received has come from older people. There is something wonderful about the wisdom God gives as we get older.

Remember that Rehoboam (the son of Solomon) made a great mistake in his life as he listened to the younger counselors instead of the older ones. That, in a sense, is a biblical warning to us to be very careful. It's like someone, who has never raised teenagers, telling you how you should raise yours! I've lived the fact that about the time you feel experienced as a parent, they are gone!

Sometimes as counselors, we want people to be aware that we know everything. We need to be careful. Counselors need to be people who have father's hearts who understand and care, and who are willing to tell you the truth.

HOW SHOULD COUNSEL BE GIVEN?

These simple things will help you when someone asks you for advice and counsel.

Always Use the Bible

It's amazing how we ignore the simplest thing! In Psalm 119:24 it says,

Your testimonies also are my delight And my counselors.

Now all these things happened to them as examples, and they were written for our [counsel] admonition, on whom the ends of the ages have come (I Cor. 10:11).

This has to do with the Children of Israel going "bonkers" at Mount Sinai and getting all kinds of idolatry, immorality and drunkenness in their lives while Moses was up on the Mount. The Bible says it was all written *"for our counseling"*.

Preach the word! Be ready in season and out of season. Convince, rebuke, exhort [counsel], *with all longsuffering and teaching* (II Tim. 4:2).

Speak these things, exhort [counsel], *and rebuke with all authority* (Titus 2:15).

What should you do when you get ready to counsel? Use the Bible! If you don't know where to find the answer, admit it and look it up. Find out what God says about the problem.

With Respect for Age and Sexual Differences

Do not rebuke an older man, but exhort him as a father, the younger men as brothers, the older women as mothers, the younger as sisters, with all purity (I Tim. 5:1-2).

You see clearly here that a younger person can counsel an older person. The number one reason that an older person does not receive the counsel given by a younger person is the attitude of the younger person. If the younger person is trying to put this older one down, or rebuke them, then forget it! That's why a lot of kids can't reach their parents-their attitude is wrong. God never intended for the younger person to rebuke the older person. You can give counsel, but not that way! Counsel him "as a father".

"The younger man as a brother" has to do with counseling someone in your peer group, but you're looking down on

them. It's possible to put people down even by the inflection of our voices. We act like we "know", and they don't—they have a problem, and we don't. That's not what the Bible says!

When we counsel, we are to be sensitive to each other and speak to each other as brothers. We can be friends and have an attitude that is biblical.

"The older women as mothers, the younger as sisters, with all purity," it says. The obvious point here is that if they are younger and you are young, the temptation is tremendous.

Some people have warned me about the things I have to say on this, and so I'm going to be careful. However, we must look at what the Word of God says. I don't find a specific command that forbids a man to counsel a woman or a woman counsel a man, but I do find an indirect implication that it is not wise. We find this in I Timothy 5:2 (above) and also in Titus 2:3-5:

> *... the older women likewise, that they be reverent in behavior, not slanderers, not given to much wine, teachers of good things-that they admonish* [there's our word, counsel again] *the young women to love their husbands, to love their children, to be discreet, chaste, homemakers, good, obedient to their own husbands, that the word of God may not be blasphemed.*

It is a sensitive subject, but somebody's got to talk about it. It belongs in our discussion of counseling. I don't say that we cannot counsel those of the opposite sex. I am going to say that it is very dangerous and, according to the Bible, there are several areas that we should not be dabbling in. Men should not be counseling young women about how to love their husbands and their children! That's what the Bible says.

Wait a minute! 80-85% of all known counseling is with women who are having marriage and family problems. Most of the counselors in America are men, so I am disturbed about this passage as it relates to present-day society.

This is not only true in the marketplace of secular society, it is also more true in the church! It is probably more serious in the church. I do not believe that God's Word teaches that the male pastor of a church has the responsibility of teaching the young women how to love their husbands and their families. That is not taught in the Bible!

To all the women, I say, don't get trapped into this because emotional dependency happens and you end up thinking the pastor walks on water! Let me tell you that I know from working with pastors, they don't! They're all ready to drown! Pastors are trying to do their job for the Lord, and counseling women presents a serious situation. I'm not referring to any sexual overtones, at all. What I'm saying is that the Bible teaches us that that is a danger!

When the counseling has to do with marriage and family problems, the Bible says it is the older women who should teach the young women. I like to say, "You can't fool those old turkeys!" Several things happen when we observe this order:

- The counseling sessions are shorter. You can't fool the older women!

- It's rather embarrassing, because they know exactly what you're talking about. You can fool a man. If you cry, they are ready to kill your husband, but not those old women! It doesn't work with them!

How on earth can we ever hope to get women to counsel when we call them "old women". No woman wants to be known as "the old woman who counsels." I'm going to clean that up for you—the "older woman" in the passage is one whose children are grown and gone. They are simply women whose children are grown and gone from home.

There is a counselor I know who has his Ph.D. and I would go to him anytime to talk to him. I've talked over these ideas with him and he said, "David, preach it. This is one of our greatest needs." There are a lot of people who have spent a lot of time and effort in order to be able to help others. They have to charge a fee, and we understand that. Most of them I know are very sensitive to people's needs and their financial conditions. They are more aware of these problems than most people. They know that we need to counsel others with respect to age and sexual differences. We need to be kind and we need to be careful.

There is a lot of trouble in the world. The occupation that has the most divorces in it are professional counselors, according to national statistics. This is a problem in our society. We're trying to live for the Lord and we go for professional counseling, but even the professionals tell me that more of God's people could do counseling, if they just thought about it. The problem is so immense that we need to realize that we don't need to say that only the person with training in counseling can help you. Sometimes that's necessary, but most of the time, if we were counseling each other all along, we wouldn't have such a big problem.

With Patience

No one is a good counselor who is impatient. We all need to learn to be patient with one another. We're not talking about patience toward circumstances-that's another Greek word. We're not talking about someone who gets ticked in a traffic jam or waiting in a long line. We're talking about the patience toward people. If you're going to be a good counselor, you've got to be patient toward people.

> *Now we exhort you, brethren, warn those who are unruly, comfort the fainthearted, uphold the weak, be patient with all* (I Thess. 5:14).

With Loving Confrontation

This is one of the most difficult areas of counseling—how do you confront? A lady came up to me in San Diego and she told me of a terrible situation in her home where she and her children are suffering abuse from her husband. She's trying to talk to him about it. She's trying to counsel him. I told her to stop—to give it up! My reason is that I have never found in all my ministry that it has ever done any good for a wife to try to confront an abusive husband. The way to do it is to get two godly men from the church and turn it over to them. Have them go and counsel that man! Men counseling men; men confronting men will do a lot more good than any wife trying to counsel her husband.

Some women are afraid of what their husbands will do if they even ask anyone to help them in that regard. It may be painfully embarrassing for a moment but we need to follow the Word of God and He will honor you and protect you. If you need to get out of the house, then get out of the house and go to your mother's or a Christian friend. Get counsel in a right way. Don't try to take it on yourself!

Loving confrontation is never easy because it is never counted as love. Most people in today's culture, want you to tolerate it and feel OK about it. They want to explain why the man has done these things instead of saying, "You're absolutely wrong!" It's embarrassing to be confronted.

> *If anyone does not obey our word in this epistle,
> note that person and do not keep company with him,*

that he may be ashamed. Yet do not count him as an enemy, but admonish him [counsel him] *as a brother* (II Thess. 3:14-15).

When a man is not obedient to the Lord, we have to confront him in loving confrontation.

With Emotional Identity

This is another of the sensitive areas of counseling. I want to be careful with it. Why do some people who seem to be well-equipped for counseling have no effect on the lives of the people they try to counsel? This is a common problem that I've observed for years. I think the problem may be "emotional identity."

"Therefore watch, and remember that for three years I did not cease to warn [counsel, admonish] *everyone night and day with tears"* (Acts 20:31).

Maybe the reason our counsel is ineffective is that there are no tears, no broken heart in the counselor. Just think about when the loss of a loved one occurs! The Bible says to *"comfort one another"* with words about the second coming of Christ (I Thess. 4:17-18). How do you comfort them? By referring to the second coming and the great resurrection of the dead. There will be a great reunion in the air when we are *"caught up together with them in the clouds to meet the Lord ... Therefore comfort* [counsel] *one another with these words."*

Blessed be the God and Father of our Lord Jesus Christ, the Father of mercies and God of all comfort [the same word—counsel] *who comforts us in all our tribulation, that we may be able to [counsel] those who are in any trouble, with the (counsel) with which we ourselves are (counseled) by God. For as the sufferings of Christ abound in us, so our (counseling) also abounds through Christ. Now if we are afflicted, it is for your (counsel) and salvation, which is effective for enduring the same sufferings which we also suffer. Or if we are (counseled), it is for your (counseling) and salvation. And our hope for you is steadfast, because we know that as you are partakers of the sufferings, so also you will partake of the (counsel)* (II Cor. 1:3-7).

This simple passage says that you will counsel best when you have experienced the counsel yourself in what you have suffered. Ezekiel said that he wept with those who wept. If someone has felt the burden and pain of life and they are a biblical counselor who loves the Lord, God is going to deepen their understanding and their emotional understanding when they counsel others. They've been through it.

Still, we are not always right in saying, "I want someone who has been through it," because it is better to have a believer than to talk to someone who has emotional identity but is not a believer. To be most effective, however, God teaches that there should be emotional identity in the counselor.

With Gentleness

> Brethren, if a man is overtaken in any trespass, you who are spiritual restore such a one in a spirit of gentleness, considering yourself lest you also be tempted. Bear one another's burdens, and so fulfill the law of Christ (Gal 6:1-2).

This is very important! Somebody has fallen, they've done wrong. They've "blown it." How do you counsel a person like that? Make sure, first of all, that your motive is always "to restore them". Some of us want them to feel bad for what they have done. You let the Lord handle that! This is up to the Lord; we are not to punish them.

Make sure that you are not trying to get revenge in any way shape or form. The Greek word for *"gentleness"* is an antonym for "revenge". Here we learn what a word is by what it is not! The opposite of *"meekness"* is "revenge". That was true in ancient Greek and it is still true today in modern Greek. God wants gentleness for that person, not revenge or retaliation. Don't try to bury the person to the point that they crawl in the dirt before you are willing to restore them. Our motive is to restore, and our attitude is gentleness.

Be very careful of accusing anybody of anything. The Bible says that we must consider ourselves *"lest you also be tempted."* When people become critical of a particular person's fault, they will fall into the exact, same problem. The Bible warns us of that in many different ways. Be very careful when you counsel someone. The best counselor is somebody who knows he could have done the same thing himself.

That kind of releases the tension because that kind of counselor says, "That could have been me! I understand that kind of temptation." Don't put people down when you counsel them. Let the Lord handle the repentance and shame. What you need to do is to try to restore them. Let them know that you could have had the same problem, were it not for the grace of God.

Speak to them as brothers and sisters in the Lord who are trying to help and encourage each other.